AN INTRODUCTION TO

AMERICA'S RIGGED DEMOCRATIC SYSTEM & SYSTEMIC RACISM

AFRICAN AMERICANS' EXTRAORDINARY PERSEVERANCE & PHENOMENAL RESILIENCY

Dr. Melvin Ray

Print ISBN: 978-1-09832-284-7

eBook ISBN: 978-1-09832-285-4

CONTENTS

ACKNOWLEDGEMENTS

This investigation or research project was truly a labor of love. It took a great deal of patience, perseverance, critical thinking, isolation, and nonrenewable time to complete. I feel compelled to first thank God for empowering me to overcome a series of unexpected challenges. My wife, Valerie Ray was a tremendous source of love, encouragement, and support. John and Missouri Ray, my deceased parents, were and continue to serve as bright and shining lights in my darkest of hours. Dr. Tommy Stevenson provided critical insights and constructive suggestions throughout the project. In addition, Akeem Ray, my son, provided invaluable technical and processing support. Among the host of others from whom I drew strength and inspiration were members of the Ray and Tate families, the historic Syrene M.B. Church, OktibbehaStarkville My Brother's Keeper Community Challenge (MBKC), and the Local Learning Community Foundation. A special appreciation goes to my editor, LaToya W. Bogard, for her professionalism and patience.

PREFACE

This book is intended to provide a preponderance of evidence to corroborate President Donald J. Trump's 2016 outreach to African Americans in which he proclaimed that the U.S. democratic system is rigged. His assertion was the impetus for a research project that was design to simulate a criminal investigation. A vast array of selected sources and quotes was included to help increase awareness and understanding of the complexity and robust nature of a rigged system that has been energized and perpetuated by systemic racism. The investigation produced evidence in the form of scholarly papers, newspaper articles, official government documents, and online material. Not all evidence reviewed during the investigation is presented. Sources included were strategically employed to provide context for topics covered and to serve as a starting point for additional study. Readers are enthusiastically encouraged to seek greater understanding of the material contained in this book prior to engaging in related open and frank conversations.

The results of the rigged system investigation identified interrelationships among several subsystems including political, economic, education, military, public health, and criminal justice. Laws, social policies, and patterns or practices in each of those subsystems were linked to systemic racism or racial inequality. In addition, the roles of religion/faith, mass communications, and sports/entertainment related to racial disparities were investigated.

Evidence uncovered during the investigation should open the eyes of Americans to the fact that black families and communities have a vast amount of underutilized human capital that has been stored away. Despite centuries of systemic racism, African Americans have and continue to contribute to the country's global economic competitiveness and national security. Ironically, during the war against COVID-19, blacks have been disproportionately designated "essential workers or front-line soldiers." African Americans' collective war against systemic discrimination should be a model for unwavering perseverance and extraordinary resiliency.

It is hoped that after reviewing and assessing the veracity of evidence contained in this book, most Americans will be more inclined to listen to and believe whistleblowers who disclose discriminatory laws, social policies, and/or patterns/practices. To date, black whistle blowers have not been afforded a chorus of "believe them" comparable to whistle blowers in the forefront of the credible and necessary "Me Too Movement."

SECTION I: INTRODUCTION TO RIGGED SYSTEMS AND SYSTEMIC RACISM

The Webster Dictionary defines system as "a regularly interacting or interdependent group of items forming a unified whole." In the U.S., there are several interrelated subsystems that work together to generate desired outcomes or to satisfy compelling government interests. Each subsystem has a specific function and is usually readily identifiable by its name including political, economic, education, healthcare, and criminal justice. Together, they form and guide what is commonly referred to as a democratic or capitalist system. At the very core of a democratic system is the promise and right of all members to have fair and untethered opportunities to vote and elect their representatives, own land, earn at least living wages, acquire relevant knowledge, skills, and credentials; accumulate wealth; and serve as decision-makers. When systems are designed to limit or deny some citizens fair or equal opportunities, it is often referred to as a "rigged" system and the implications for the disadvantaged are widespread and long-lasting.

CHAPTER 1

Rigged System Indictments

The impetus for the current investigation was the combination of what most Americans would define as bipartisan charges of a race-based rigged system in the U.S.

For centuries, rigged system assertions have been made by unlikely leaders and decision-makers. Initially, they were levied by early abolitionists, so-called liberal scholars or academicians, and later elected officials. Synopses of selected 20th and 21st century liberal and conservative thought leaders' rigged system proclamations are presented below.

An American Dilemma

A common practice in criminal and civil cases is to retain expert witnesses. In 2015, the Public Broadcasting System (PBS) aired a documentary about Swedish Economist Gunnar Myrdal's seminal work *An American Dilemma.* The hour-long documentary was entitled "American Denial." Myrdal was commissioned by the Carnegie Foundation to study race in America. Results of his groundbreaking research on race in America was revealed in his book that was published in 1944. A little-known fact is that some of his findings were cited as evidence in the landmark Brown v. Topeka, Kansas, Supreme Court case that found separate but equal accommodations, or Jim Crow practices, in public places to be unconstitutional.

The dilemma described by Myrdal was obvious. On the one hand, there was an American exceptionalism aspiration in the form of a true democracy in which all men are judged to be equal. Concurrently, African Americans were being bombarded by persistent and systematic discriminatory practices that limited or blocked their access to fair and unbiased competition for opportunities. For many, this dilemma still exists today.

Subsequently, President Lyndon B. Johnson and Senator Daniel Patrick Moynihan both addressed the dilemma America faced in dealing with its black citizens and their unique history and current existence. In his State of the Union speech in January 1965, President Johnson made some stunning revelations. First, he reasoned that enduring over three hundred years of severe inequality and cruel and unusual treatment had taken an enormous toll on black families, communities, and businesses. He explained the situation in terms of a lingering racist virus in the U.S. that was continuously, negatively impacting the descendants of African slaves or fellow U.S. citizens. Second, he estimated that blacks would be the victims of widespread individual and institutional discrimination for an additional twenty to thirty years or until about 1985-2005. Third, President Johnson stated that in the mid-1960s, blacks were lagging behind non-blacks as a group or race of people, but when given the opportunity, individual blacks excelled and exceeded all expectations. Finally, President Johnson stated that the plight of African Americans was getting worse, not better. As evidence, he focused attention on official statistics:

> "Indices of dollars of income, standards of living, and years of education deceive. The gap between the Negro and most other groups in American society is widening."[1]

Over five decades later in 2016, several leading white conservatives seem to have agreed with Gunnar Myrdal and President Lyndon B. Johnson's theses regarding the American Dilemma and its denial.

In the aftermath of widespread media coverage of police shootings of unarmed black men across the country, surprisingly, Newt Gingrich, a

---

1 https://www.theatlantic.com/politics/archive/2015/09/the-moynihan-report-an-annotated-edition/404632/.

staunch conservative, and former Speaker of the House, made a startling revelation in a:

> "It took me a long time, and a number of people talking to me through the years, to get a sense of this: If you are a normal white American, the truth is you don't understand being black in America and you instinctively under-estimate the level of discrimination and the level of additional risk." This text was gleaned from a July 8, 2016 Facebook live-streamed interview with Van Jones, a CNN Political commentator.

Shockingly, the primary impetus for this project came from observations made by a relatively newcomer to politics. During the 2016 presidential Republican primary, Donald J. Trump stated that his administration would address the "rigged system" that had perpetuated unfair and horrific treatment of blacks in the U.S. His words were broadcast by CNN on August 3, 2016:

> "You're living in poverty, your schools are no good, you have no jobs, fifty-eight percent of your youth are unemployed—What the hell do you have to lose?"

Gunnar Myrdal, President Johnson, speaker Newt Gingrich, and President Trump's rigged system indictments were insightful and thought-provoking for a short time. However, in each case, their revelations emphasized the obvious, but they failed to describe how the "rigging" took place. Moreover, they invariably failed to acknowledge the fact that the black response to the rigged system included several distinct behavioral adaptations that will be examined later.

CHAPTER 2

Anatomy of Rigged Systems

At least two concepts are invariably examined when rigged systems and race relations have been investigated. First, prejudice, or pre-judgements, reflect one's perceptions and attitudes toward a person, place, or thing. Prejudices or biases are usually reflected in terms of ethnocentrism, stigmatization, xenophobia, social distance, and stereotypes. It is important to note that all humans, regardless of race, sex, age, income, and country of origin, possess prejudices or biases.

Second, in the context of discussions regarding rigged systems and race relations, discrimination is the key concept. Discrimination refers to actions or behaviors that adversely impact out-group members; in addition, it infers the capacity to make decisions at different levels that have varying outcomes. Discrimination occurs on at least two levels, individual and institutional. Each type has one common feature and that is the existence of power or authority to make decisions that adversely impact the will and desires of others.

At the individual level, Americans have the right to make choices and decisions that are in their perceived best interest. However, if a homeowner refuses to sell to an individual because of their race, that would be an example of individual level racism.

Institutional discrimination refers to the intended or unintended outcomes of laws, policies, and practices that limit or block opportunities of specific groups of Americans. For example, hiring and promotion decisions are often based on previous related experience, educational attainment, and social networks without consideration of past discriminatory practices. There has been a host of court cases alleging that qualifications listed for certain jobs were irrelevant and disadvantaged blacks and women because they prioritize experiences that had been traditionally limited or blocked from those segments of the U.S. population. It is virtually impossible for people to demonstrate a proven record of effective leadership if they have not been given the opportunities to manage or lead projects. Institutional discrimination is often subtle and possibly unintentional.

Discriminatory Patterns or Practices

In the U.S., the Attorney General and the Justice Department investigate charges of civil rights violations that rise to the status of an "issue of general public importance." Often during prosecutions of defendants, they cite patterns or practices that resulted in unfair treatment. Specifically, according to the DoJ's publication "A Pattern or Practice of Discrimination,"

> "The courts have found a 'pattern or practice' when the evidence establishes that the discriminatory actions were the defendant's regular practice, rather than an isolated instance. This does not mean that the Department must prove that a defendant always discriminates or that many people have been affected. A 'pattern or practice' means that the defendant has a policy of discriminating, even if the policy is not always followed."

The latter point is extremely important because it affirms the belief prevalent in the current discourse that no American discriminates all the time, but a single instance can have profound, negative outcomes at both individual and group levels.

Racial discrimination and racism are highly charged concepts because when used, they cause defensive responses. In the U.S., given the unequal distribution of influence and decision-making authority, claims of discrimination have been frequently filed by people of color against leaders of businesses and institutions who were overwhelmingly white men. It is important to note here that all white men do not discriminate, but they have been the overwhelming majority of named defendants in discrimination cases. A possible explanation for their overrepresentation as alleged offenders is their seemingly near monopoly of decision-making positions. It warrants repeating that no reasonable claim has or will be made suggesting that all whites discriminate, but there should be little or no debate about their disproportionate capacity and opportunities to do so.

To test or assess the premise that blacks have been underrepresented as decision-makers, readers should engage in a non-participant observational research exercise. First, identify different decision-making bodies or positions at local, state, and federal levels. Second, review photographs of members of governing bodies and/or presidents/chairpersons. Third, count the members in each group and classify each person in terms of race/ethnicity. Finally, assess the distribution of influence or votes by race. A weakness of this exercise would be the underlying assumption that people vote along racial or party lines in most cases. Then, reflect on the plight of African slaves and their descendants as they have struggled to advance in the U.S. while having relatively no to little decision-making authority related to laws, social policies, and discriminatory patterns or practices.

CHAPTER 3

Typology of Decision-makers

In a 1949 book chapter entitled "Discrimination and the American Creed," Robert K. Merton offered a prejudice-discrimination typology that can help Americans create a real-world assessment of decision-makers related to their treatment of subordinates and/or members of other races. His four personality types were as follows: 1) Non-prejudice-Non-discriminatory (i.e., all- weather liberal); 2) non-prejudice-discriminatory (i.e., fair-weather liberal); 3) prejudice-nondiscriminatory (i.e., fair-weather bigot); and 4) prejudice-discriminatory (i.e., all-weather bigot).

Merton's race theory has received both acclaim and severe criticism. Proponents have argued that there is an indisputable intersection between attitudes and behaviors. They also believe the intersection between attitudes and associated behaviors is influenced by both social and structural factors. On the other hand, critics of Merton's prejudice-discriminatory personality types have accused the theory of being too deterministic. In addition, it failed to recognize that attitudes and behaviors are not set in concrete. Finally, his use of the terms "liberals" and "bigots" has caused his theory to be censored or ignored. The liberal label has been called partisan jargon, and the term bigot has been called highly offensive.

For the purpose of the current rigged system investigation, Merton's typology was revised. The revision accepted the existence of the intersection between attitudes and behaviors but allowed for a spectrum-like application of discriminatory actions by decision-makers. All Americans possess prejudicial attitudes, but their actions or decisions are not always guided by them. The resulting typology was as follows: 1) mostly fair; 2) conditionally fair; and 3) mostly unfair. It was assumed that African slaves and their descendants have had to negotiate or adapt to decision-makers whose patterns or practices corresponded with one of the revised personality types. Without question, the intersection of prejudices and capacity to discriminate is the primary culprit or foundation for President Trump's rigged system indictment of the U.S. related to the plight of African Americans.

CHAPTER 4

Black Modes of Adaptation

Throughout their history in the U.S., blacks have exhibited various responses or adaptations to the injustices that they have experienced. Yet, there is an undeniable propensity for elected leaders, decision-makers, and mass communication enterprises to suggest that an overwhelming majority are criminal offenders and their successes are limited to sports/entertainment. The current investigation attempted to obtain data and information regarding the disparate adaptations employed by blacks to cope with the stress/strain caused by persistent and overbearing racial injustices.

Asserting that members of oppressed groups respond differently to social and environmental conditions is not a novel idea, but that fact is often ignored when characterizing African Americans. Instead, racial stereotypes have been adopted to stigmatize all blacks.

A year prior to the release of Merton's prejudice-discriminatory typology of personality types, he published his groundbreaking Strain Theory in 1948. It was employed in the investigation to help identify distinct behavioral responses or adaptations among African slaves and their descendants while being confronted by systemic racial injustice and inequality.

As background, Merton's strain theory included at least four interrelated assumptions: 1) Among Americans, there is a near universal, cultural goal that is reflected in what is commonly referred to as the American Dream (e.g., freedom, fair competition, equality, status, homeownership, automobiles, small businesses, and wealth); 2) there are prescribed legal means (e.g., inheritance, jobs/careers, and educational attainment) by which the dream can be realized; 3) systems (e.g., political, economic, and educational) are put in place to limit or block some groups' access to legal or prescribed means, thereby generating stress/strain among members; and 4) stress/strain levels cause the emergence of distinct behavioral reactions or individual level modes of adaptation (i.e., conformers, innovators, ritualists, rebels, and retreatists).

Some critics of Merton's strain theory argued that it was too narrow in its focus on material assets. In 2001, Robert Agnew proposed to expand Merton's theory by shifting the focus from the single, utilitarian goal of money or material possessions. His expansion included a more "general" spectrum of values or goals such as family, educational attainment, entrepreneurship, and social status.

Drawing from assumptions inherent in Merton's original strain theory and Agnew's expansion, it was assumed that a majority of blacks have aspired to achieve aspects of the elusive American Dream. In addition, when they have been confronted by perceived or real systemic discriminatory patterns or practices in different sectors, they have historically adopted an array of behavioral responses or specific individual modes of adaptation. The latter are summarized below.

Figure 1: Individual Modes of Adaptation

	Conformers	Innovators	Ritualists	Rebels	Retreatists
Universal Value +	X	X			
Universal Value -			X	X	X
Legal Means +	X		X		
Legal Means -		X		X	X

+=Accept - =Reject

First, according to Merton's original formulation, African Americans who fully adopt and value the pursuit of the American Dream and attempt to employ traditionally prescribed means reflect the "conformer" adaptation. They represent a majority of blacks in the U.S. and should serve as models of extreme persistence and extraordinary resiliency.

Second, innovators are African Americans who fully embrace the American Dream but do not believe that they can achieve it through traditionally prescribed means (e.g., education and jobs/careers). Merton concluded from his research that young boys who could not obtain money, nice clothes, and other popular items because of poverty or relatively low annual household income would turn to illegal means to acquire those things. A clear extrapolation is that adults who aspire consistently with the Dream but perceive their access to legitimate means either limited or blocked will pursue success by any means available. It is important to note that the list of "prescribed or legitimate means" changes with the passage of time. Innovators can include individuals who earn GEDs, work two and three low wage jobs, gamble, or become entertainers or professional athletes. In comparison and true to Merton's original formulation, a relatively small fraction of strained individuals will turn to drug trafficking, burglary, robbery, and other crimes.

Third, groups of individuals who do not value the ideals of the American Dream or other status symbols but engage in legitimate means were called ritualists. They earn high school diplomas and have stable employment; however, they are not motivated by the ideals or material aspects of capitalism. This group might live from paycheck to paycheck, and the month is frequently longer than their money. They take pride in their work or careers but do not appear to have material aspirations.

Fourth, African Americans who experienced high levels of stress and strain might have sought emotional escapes or shields from the pressures of limited or blocked access to equal treatment and opportunities. According to Merton's taxonomy, this group's response reflects the "retreatists" adaptation because they are ambivalent about both the pursuit of the American Dream and prescribed means. Their social retreat is a coping strategy to avoid stressful or potentially painful interactions. They might also have mental and/or physical challenges. Retreatists are generally off official radars and exist in relative anonymity in a lot of cases.

Finally, according to strain theories, individuals and groups who are perpetually denied equal rights and dignity would naturally seek reforms or changes in norms and laws to afford them relief from the accompanying stress and strain. According to Merton, a percent of maligned individuals will adopt the "rebel" adaptation. It describes reactions of individuals who believe that cultural and economic changes are needed to decrease inequalities. Rebellion was offered as a type of social or political movement intended to bring about change.

Early abolitionists, President Abraham Lincoln, Dr. Martin L. King, Malcom X, and other civil rights leaders wanted to improve quality of life for all Americans. Their efforts to increase awareness of unfair treatment and practices leading to vast racial social and economic inequality were not aimed at destroying the country. Conversely, they wanted legal and social reforms to help all residents realize aspects of both the American Promise and Dream.

Drawing from both Merton and Agnew's[2] general strain theories, Americans can be more discerning of data and information related to racial comparisons. Public presentations of current official statistics comparing quality of life indicators by race/ethnicity without the benefit of historical trends is not only meaningless but mean. As stated previously, current racial comparisons do not tell the whole story. Failing to provide background information or context causes a lot of Americans to attribute racial inequality to merit, self-determination, and hard work. In terms of the plight of most blacks, there has been a seemingly intentional ignorance or disregard related to the effects of a "rigged democratic system."

Merton's modes of adaptation theory illuminated the fact that members of racial/ethnic groups respond differently to life situations and challenges. It should help Americans refrain from perpetuating racial stereotypes. While viewing or hearing statistics related to quality of life indicators (e.g., educational attainment, annual income etc.), it is imperative to analyze the number

---

2 Agnew, R. (2001). "Building on the foundation of general strain theory: Specifying the types of strain most likely to lead to crime and delinquency." *Journal of Research in Crime and Delinquency*, 38(4), 319-361.

and/or percent in different categories (i.e., dropout, GED, high school graduate, and some college) within a race/ethnic group.

SECTION II: RIGGED SYSTEM INVESTIGATION (RSI)

In criminal and civil cases, both sides aggressively and artfully seek and collect evidence to support their standing as either plaintiff (the accuser) or defendant (the accused). In criminal cases, prosecutors are charged with presenting evidence that proves their case beyond a shadow of a doubt in the minds of a jury. In comparison, in civil lawsuits, plaintiffs are tasked with presenting a preponderance of evidence indicating that the accused more likely than not was guilty or liable.

Let us pretend that President Trump decided to bring a civil lawsuit on behalf of blacks against the U.S. government based on his rigged system theory. The remainder of this book is intended to serve as a repository of both circumstantial and corroborating evidence to support his case. The investigation involved examinations of secondary sources containing copies or excerpts from official documents, relevant literature, quotes, documentaries, and codified laws and statutes.

While reviewing evidence contained in the remainder of this work, readers are also encouraged to seek greater understanding of the challenges, trials, and tribulations African slaves and their descendants have faced for centuries and the diversity of their modes of adaptation. In terms of the latter, a form of retrospective, empathic imagery is required. Essentially, readers must attempt to "role-take" or imagine themselves as African Americans in the theme of Eddie Murphy's hit movie *Trading Places*. Hopefully, readers will acquire a better understanding and appreciation of the perseverance and resiliency exhibited by a majority of blacks in the U.S.

CHAPTER 1

Measures of Racial Disparities

President Trump, along with most Americans, assess progress related to racial equality in the U.S. by viewing and analyzing official statistics. Therefore, a brief overview of standard statistics that policy analysts have employed to compare quality of life indicators among racial/ethnic groupings was warranted. Invariably, researchers begin by estimating the population at local, state, regional, and national levels. It is estimated that the U.S. total population is in excess of 320M. The population is then divided based on specific demographics (e.g., race/ethnicity, sex, age, and income). In 2016, it was reported that the three largest racial groupings in the U.S. were as follows: whites (61%); Hispanics (17%) and blacks (13%). Theoretically, from a social equity or parity perspective, assuming equal access to opportunities, one would expect blacks to occupy approximately thirteen percent of jobs and decision-making positions across political, educational, corporate, and employment sectors. Large deviations should prompt serious investigations.

Traditionally, policy analysts and researchers have used percentages, averages, and median scores to compare groups of citizens by race/ethnicity. Based on the racial composition of the U.S., should suspicions surround the fact that nearly 80% of mayors are white while a similar percentage of sanitation workers are people of color? Percentages can be misleading because they detract attention from raw numbers or headcounts. In a town of 10,000 residents with a racial breakdown of 6,000 (60%) white and 4,000 (40%) black, a newspaper report that 10% of both white and black residents received traffic violations would suggest that offending patterns were similar. However, upon further investigation, the reality would be that the total number of violations would be white (600) and black (400). Both percentages and raw numbers matter in a lot of cases.

Second, averages frequently appear in official reports. Averages or mean scores can be calculated easily but are often misleading because of either extreme low or high scores on a specific indicator. The average cost of five houses on a block is calculated as follows: $70K + $80K + $100k + $90K + $300K =$640K. The total divided by five (5) yields an average/mean property value of $128K. Imagine if those values were annual salaries. A local company advertising an average salary of $128K is likely to generate a lot more applicants than one that lists the actual salary for each job.

Finally, a median measure accounts for "outliers" by providing a midpoint statistic that divides a target population in two equal halves; whereby, fifty percent of the people score below it and fifty percent above it. A 2017 U.S. census report showed that the median household income in 2016 was approximately $60,000. That meant that fifty percent of American households earn less, and fifty percent earn more than that amount. When analysts and others attempt to compare one race to another, in terms of demographics (i.e., age, years of school completed, weekly income, home mortgages, debt, and wealth), median scores are favored over other measures.

Readers are encouraged to stay mindful of the distinctions between commonly used statistics contained in the following sections. Moreover, while assessing the veracity of President Trump's rigged system theory, it is imperative for readers to carefully examine evidence obtained from the 17th to the 21st century.

Based on the totality of evidence presented, readers are encouraged to render their verdicts. First, is there a preponderance of evidence indicating that it is more likely than not that federal and state laws and social norms have systematically limited or blocked blacks from fully achieving aspects of the American Dream? Furthermore, is there a preponderance of evidence indicating that it is more likely than not that blacks have and continue to exhibit extraordinary perseverance and phenomenal resiliency through their adoption of individual level modes of adaptation?

SECTION III : EMERGENCE OF THE RIGGED SYSTEM

This section includes uncovered evidence related to the emergence of what could be considered a fore-runner of the alleged rigged system in the U.S. It briefly documents several pivotal developments that led up to the formation of the United States of America and the ratification of the Constitution.

Information was sought to document actions and practices that created and have perpetuated racial disparities. A host of factors appear to have set the stage for racial injustices including religion, global trade, demand for "free" labor, and greed.

CHAPTER 1

European Explorers to West Africa

During the early to mid-1400s, Europeans were focused on finding a water route instead of the long and dangerous land route through the Middle East to reach Asia for its silk and spices. Portugal was a dominant force on the seas and its footprint was relatively large in the 15th and 16th centuries.[3]

Elmina Castle

Portugal lacked access to a coastline on the Mediterranean Sea, so they eventually settled on one in West Africa. Evidence was uncovered related to the scope and nature of early interactions between Europeans and West Africans where a majority of the first slaves were purchased. According to Howard La Fay, author of an article that appeared in *National Geographic* in October of 1965, early contacts between Africans and Europeans were cordial and eventually evolved into business to business transactions.[4]

In 1482, the Portuguese negotiated for a trading post that later became known as Elmina Castle on Africa's Western coast. The facility went through several renovations and eventually took on the function of a fortress-like castle with a dungeon in which slaves were kept in dark holding pens prior to their voyage to the Americas. The trading post was built approximately one hundred and thirty-seven years prior to the arrival of African slaves in the colonies.

---

3 http://factsanddetails.com/india/History/sub7_1c/entry-4120.html#chapter-0

4 https://www.u-s-history.com/pages/h436.html

Early trading partners did not use a common currency to purchase products. Instead, bartering or a system of exchanging goods of equal value was institutionalized.

As late as the 1700s, in West Africa, European trading ships contained cotton products from India and England that were symbols of status and prestige among African kings, tribal leaders, and elites. Tobacco, brandy, rum, guns, gun powder, brass, assorted cookware, and glass items were also included. Sparkling glass items were in high demand but were not made in West Africa. However, among African rulers, glass beads became important ornaments and jewelry. African tribes initially exchanged gold and ivory for European goods.

CHAPTER 2

Papal Bull of 1493

Missing from most history books is the role the Roman Catholic Church played in facilitating colonization and slavery in the new world. Roughly eleven years after Portugal built the Elmina trading post on West Africa's coastline, Pope Alexander VI issued the Papal Bull of 1493 that commanded Europeans to explore and claim new lands. Moreover, he ordered Europeans to enslave all non-Christians. To justify his decree, the Pope said it was a product of a revelation from God.

The Roman Catholic Church in a lot of ways facilitated so-called discovered lands around the world. The Pope's decree was the basis for what later became known as the "doctrine of discovery." It was later employed to justify the colonization of people and land in both South and North America (e.g., U.S.).

> "In 1494, shortly after Columbus' first voyage, the pope divided the newly discovered lands between Spain and Portugal — both Catholic nations, but fierce rivals. The line of demarcation crossed through the hump of South America. Spain was to have the lands to the west and Portugal those to the east (accounting for the use of the Portuguese language in Brazil today)."[5]

5 https://www.u-s-history.com/pages/h436.html

CHAPTER 3

Early Immigrants to America

The Virginia Company, LLC laid claim to the first English settlement and named it Jamestown, Virginia in honor of King James. Settlers arrived on three ships in 1607. A "black box" that contained the names of the seven leaders, including the governor and six councilmen, was stored in a secure place on the ships. The secrecy apparently was needed to prevent conflicts over power/authority during the voyage aboard the ships.[6]

Contacts between Native Americans and the new settlers transitioned from cordial neighbors to conflict. The settlers wanted their land and free or cheap labor. In terms of the latter, a combination of defiance and resistance by Native Americans and deadly diseases, including measles and smallpox, decimated indigenous populations and left the settlers in dire need of workers.

Originally, the Virginia Company's business plan for the settlement was to find and mine gold and silver, but those precious metals were short in supply, thereby making the venture unsustainable as a profit center. Alternatively, English settlers in Virginia began growing tobacco as a cash crop and needed a greater supply of labor. Times were tough for the first one hundred or so men and boys as they suffered from numerous diseases and a lack of food.

The shift from mining to agriculture in Virginia and other southern settlements called for a large, durable, trainable, and inexpensive labor force. Those conditions led to an insatiable demand for a prototypical laborer. Apparently, their selection or targeting system was similar to the Trump administration's

---

6 https://www.nps.gov/jame/learn/historyculture/a-short-history-of-jamestown.htm

proposed 2018 immigration policy intended to limit immigration to foreign workers who have desired skill sets to help boost the U.S.' global, economic competitiveness. At the time of the Jamestown settlement, Pope Alexander VI's Papal Bull of 1493 had been in effect for over one hundred and twenty-five years.

Melting Pot in Jamestown

Interestingly, three consequential developments occurred in 1619 in Jamestown that provided the foundation for racial inequality in the U.S. First, marriage and family became a top priority to populate the colony. Second, African slaves arrived to do the manual labor as chattel slaves and indentured servants. Finally, a general assembly was established to create and implement laws.[7] Virginia's assembly passed laws that were models for subsequent colonies. State assemblies, not a federal government, made and implemented all laws which led to the birth of the "states' rights" ideology that continues to fuel conflicts today.

Questions or debates have lingered about the source of the first African slaves who arrived in Jamestown, Virginia in August 1619. According to published sources, credit or blame is due to either the Dutch or Great Britain. Below is one account:

> "Arrival of '20 and odd' Africans in late August 1619, not aboard a Dutch ship as reported by John Rolfe, but an English warship, White Lion, sailing with a letter of marque issued to the English Captain Jope by the Protestant Dutch Prince Maurice, son of William of Orange. A letter of marque legally permitted the White Lion to sail as a privateer attacking any Spanish or Portuguese ships it encountered. The 20 and odd Africans were captives removed from the Portuguese slave ship, San Juan Bautista, following an

7 https://www.nps.gov/jame/learn/historyculture/african-americans-at-jamestown.htm

> encounter the ship had with the White Lion and her consort, the Treasurer, another English ship, while attempting to deliver its African prisoners to Mexico. Rolfe's reporting the White Lion as a Dutch warship was a clever ruse to transfer blame away from the English for piracy of the slave ship to the Dutch." [8]

Demand for African slaves grew stronger as additional settlements came online. Historical documents revealed that owners who bartered with African Kings were clear when giving instructions to ship captains regarding what they wanted. Based on one account, they only wanted able-bodied men and women, no children or elderly, and all the ivory they could acquire. [9]

Triangle Slave Route

The Atlantic slave-trade route, or voyage, resembled a triangle beginning in England, stopping in West Africa, proceeding to the Caribbean Islands and the colonies, and returning to Europe. African slaves were distributed widely in the Caribbean and Brazil, and a smaller percentage, numbering nearly four hundred thousand, came to the colonies.

The second leg of the slave trade from West Africa to the colonies was brutal and inhumane. Empathically, imagine being chained, starved, and dehydrated for months in quarters, estimated by some historians to equal about four square feet. Unlike modern day transport containers for pigs and chickens, early slave ships had little or no ventilation in the "cargo" area below deck where slaves were stored in the dark. There were no toilets, wash-pans, toilet paper, and soap/detergent. Slaves who became infected or died were immediately thrown overboard, and young girls and women suffered unmerciful verbal, physical, and sexual abuses. The second leg of the slave trade across the Atlantic became commonly known as the "middle passage." By some

---

8 https://www.nps.gov/jame/learn/historyculture/african-americans-at-jamestown.htm

9 http://www.discoveringbristol.org.uk/slavery/routes/bristol-to-africa/trade-goods/africa-cargo/

accounts, the scale of deaths on slave ships influenced the migratory paths of sharks as bodies were thrown overboard along the route. While millions survived the voyages, the death toll has been estimated in excess of 1.5M.

CHAPTER 4

War of Independence

The Revolutionary War was an unanticipated catalyst for change in terms of race relations in the colonies and eventually the union. Britain needed an additional revenue source to help pay for debt incurred during the French-Indian war. As usual, decision-makers employed taxes on goods to generate revenue. Historians point to a series of tariffs placed on items imported to the colonies that led to the phrase "taxation without representation" referring to the fact that the colonists paid taxes to Great Britain but had no representation in the British Parliament.

Several tax-related policies implemented by Great Britain warrant brief examination here. First, a year following the end of the French-Indian War, the Sugar Act of 1764 was passed requiring the settlers to pay taxes on sugar. Second, the Tea Act of 1773 led to the infamous Boston Tea Party during which crates of tea from Britain were dumped off ships into the Boston Harbor by settlers disguised as Indians. Third, to enforce tariffs and collect taxes, Britain established customs agents and empowered them to use intrusive tactics that also angered colonists. Finally, in 1774, a series of acts called the "intolerable laws" were passed that further inflamed opposition among the settlers to British rule and led to the start of the War of Independence in 1775. As a result, all of the colonies (i.e., free and slave) were united in the fight for their independence. Ironically, by that time, chattel slavery had existed for over one hundred and fifty years.

Early settlers' rebuke of Britain's control and perceived unfair taxation reflected a seemingly insatiable desire for freedom, independence, and self-reliance. These sentiments or ideals coexisted with slavery, especially in the South.

Decision-makers in the colonies either did not see how their treatment of blacks mirrored that of Great Britain towards them in a lot of areas, or they simply ignored the fact. They wanted freedom for themselves, while simultaneously denying freedom to African slaves.

During the Revolutionary War, it was estimated that twenty percent of the total population was African. [10] According to some historians, slaves accounted for over 50% of the populations of Virginia and Maryland. In 1976, Edgar A. Toppin in his book entitled *Blacks in the American Revolution* stated that according to the first U.S. Census of 1790, roughly eight (8%) of Africans were "free," and some fought in the war.

The colonies declared victory in the Revolutionary War in 1783 after about eight years of intense fighting. In the aftermath of the war, the colonies could have been characterized as a loosely aligned group of states without form or structure. Each state assembly passed laws to satisfy their unique economic, social, and political needs because there was no union or federal government.

10 http://www.history.org/almanack/people/african/aaintro.cfm

SECTION IV: BIRTH OF THE RIGGED DEMOCRATIC SYSTEM

Following the victory in the War of Independence, decision-makers from the colonies convened in 1787 to develop an agreed upon governing doctrine. A vivid description of the convention is contained in a 2005 book entitled *Constitutional Convention* derived from the notes of James Madison. Records of discussions and compromises negotiated during the convention were reviewed and cataloged as evidence in the rigged system investigation.

From a structural or macro-social level, it is more likely than not that the ratification of the U.S. Constitution is the centerpiece of President Trump's rigged system theory. His theory does not diminish the majestic democratic ideals included in the document. Instead, it is an example of how a system of ideals and laws can be enacted but not uniformly enforced, thereby disadvantaging one or more segments of the general population.

Framers of the Constitution were all white, men, and most owned slaves; as such, rights and privileges listed were applicable to only white men. Imagine that.

The ratification of the Constitution is often held out as the official starting-line for "equality" in the U.S. It was during that time that phrases alluding to equality among men and equal opportunities to pursue life, liberty, and wealth were being shouted from roof tops. But a huge fraud was being perpetrated because the system was rigged. Freedoms, rights, and privileges enumerated in the Constitution were not applicable to Native Americans, Africans, free and enslaved, and women.

Students of the Constitution agree that as a system of laws governing citizens' rights and privileges, it had two primary functions. First, it was designed to establish a system of "checks and balances" that would protect against autocratic rule or a dictatorship. Second, it provided a framework for how a central government would interface with states' rights. Individual rights were addressed later through amendments.

Even among a homogenous group of well-intentioned leaders, there was a recognition of man's insatiable appetite for power and authority. Among the framers, their greatest fears were for the new world to regress into an autocratic government with one individual or group having total control. Essentially, they did not trust one another. Moreover, issues or disagreements regarding slavery pitted southern states against northern states. The two sides were forced to endure spirited arguments and negotiations related to population counts, voting rights, number of seats in the U.S. Senate and House of Representatives, election of presidents, and appointments to the judiciary. Evidence uncovered during the investigation indicated that negotiated compromises related to those issues gave birth to an alleged "rigged system" of government that has denied African Americans both justice and equality.

SECTION V: POLITICAL SYSTEM

Framers of the Constitution debated the efficacy of different governing models. They chose to create three independent and equal branches of the federal government that would in a sense police one another. These three branches are the following: Legislative, Executive, and Judicial. Readers are encouraged to pay attention to how southern delegates negotiated stunning compromises to increase their capacity to influence federal laws.

CHAPTER 1

Legislative Branch

In terms of impact, the legislative branch designed and gave certain powers to the executive and judicial branches. The legislative branch of the federal government is divided between the Senate or upper chamber and the House of Representatives or lower chamber. Each state regardless of population has two senators who serve six-year terms.

Senate

As a body, the Senate is tasked with advising and consenting regarding presidential appointments including cabinet secretaries, defense and intelligence leadership, ambassadors, and both federal judges and Supreme Court justices. There are twenty-one senate committees, including judiciary, intelligence, armed services, and foreign relations, each having an odd number of members, a chair from the majority party, and a ranking member from the minority party.

According to the original Constitution, prior to and following the end of the Civil War, senators were appointed by all-white state assemblies or governors, and only a handful of blacks served. Nearly fifty years following the end of the Civil War, the 17th Amendment was ratified in 1913 mandating that senators be elected by the popular vote in states instead of being appointed by governors or state legislatures. Still, governors can appoint a replacement to complete an unfilled term of a sitting senator. It is worth noting that governors' appointing blacks to serve unexpired terms in the Senate has led to subsequent victories in some statewide elections.

Senators jockey for committee assignments and leadership roles to increase their ability to influence the work of the upper chamber. In a race-conscious Senate, a member of a relatively small racial/ethnic group is highly unlikely to serve as committee chairs, ranking members, or party leaders. As a result, the influence of black senators is limited in most cases.

House of Representatives

The House of Representatives and its members are tasked with being the voice and advocate for residents in districts drawn or revised following an official census. Moreover, the number of House members determines the weight of each state in terms of presidential elections.

The House is also responsible for originating revenue bills or federal budgets. It has twenty-two congressional committees including judiciary, ways and means, oversight and government reforms, and foreign affairs. Each state is required to have at least one representative, and each additional one is based on a ratio of seats to population counts. For instance, California has over fifty representatives compared to one for North Dakota. Congressional districts are redrawn every ten years based on census counts. This system of congressional apportionment poses both intended and possibly unintended challenges to blacks' democratic rights.

Three-Fifths Compromise

During the 1787 Constitutional Convention, southern house members pulled a gold rabbit out of the hat. Often misunderstood, the Three-Fifths (3/5) Compromise was a rather clever tool to unfairly increase the number of southern house members. Moreover, the scheme also gave them a larger share of the Electoral College. More details about this can be found in Article 1, Section 2, Clause 3 of the Constitution. To help preserve the Union, tensions had to be lowered between representatives of slave and free states, so compromises were made. Northern representatives wanted a federal tax and a national defense department but did not have the votes without help from some southern lawmakers. On the other hand, southerners wanted greater representation in Congress, so they proposed to include slaves in their states' census to increase their number of congressional districts. Initially, southerners lobbied to give slaves equal standing with whites only for the purpose of the census. Northern free states were forced to oppose the legislation because it would have shifted the balance of power in the House of Representatives to the South. As a compromise, James Madison proposed that slaves be counted as three-fifths of a white person in census counts, and the motion was passed. [11] What is even more astonishing is the fact that the Three-Fifths Compromise won out over other proportions including one-fourth, one half, and three-fourths. The Three-Fifths Compromise gave southerners the population counts to sustain a majority in the house between the mid to late 1700s to the half decade or so prior to the election of President Lincoln.

---

11 https://constitution.laws.com/three-fifths-compromise

CHAPTER 2

Executive Branch

The executive branch of the federal government includes the President, Vice President, and cabinet secretaries. Its responsibilities include enforcing laws passed by Congress, national security, foreign relations, and global economic competitiveness. Domestically, the executive branch provides leadership regarding economic policies and the appointment of federal judges including Supreme Court justices. An interesting note, however, is that the president can create laws through executive orders void of congressional consent.

Electoral College

Elections of presidents are not as simple and transparent as most Americans think. Through negotiations between southern and northern lawmakers, a separate structure was created to elect the president and, by default, nominations to federal and supreme courts.

The Electoral College has been in play since 1789, or about seventy-six years prior to the end of the Civil War, and has been described as a compromise between allowing Congress or the popular vote to elect the president at that time.[12] Southerners were at a numerical disadvantage if either Congress or the popular vote were used to elect presidents.

Their solution was to forge a compromise that would transfer the power to elect presidents to a relatively small number of politically connected individuals equaling the sum of the number of senators and house members.

---

12 https://www.archives.gov/federal-register/electoral-college/

Recall that the southern legislators had forged the Three-Fifths Compromise to increase their number of house members.

Surprisingly, in a model democracy, presidential candidates can fail to win the popular vote (i.e., one person, one vote) by literally millions but still become president if she/he gets a majority of the Electoral College votes.[13] In many ways, African Americans' votes or capacity to help determine winners of the presidency are virtually nullified by the Electoral College. Corroborating evidence can be found in the description of how its members are selected. The electorate is controlled by the two major parties. In each election year, the two parties at the state level either appoint or elect their electors equaling the total of two senators plus the number of U.S. Representatives. This means that the total number of electors can vary from one census to the next depending on the number of representatives in each state. There are five hundred and thirty-eight Electoral College members and it takes a majority of two hundred and seventy (270) to secure a majority and victory.

A challenge facing African Americans is the fact that state electors are people who have standing in one of the two major parties. They are invariably elected officials, party leaders, those having some association with the candidate, and of course big dollar contributors. According to the Constitution, electors only need to be "qualified voters." Recall that blacks were not allowed to vote when this clause was passed. Interestingly, most citizens do not know the identities of their state electorates because their names are generally not shown on ballots; however, in a minority of states, electorates' names are shown below presidential candidates'. It is assumed that a vote for one of the presidential candidates serves as affirmation of her/his party's electors.

Americans either knowingly or unknowingly cast their votes for the body of electors who then cast their votes to determine the winner of the presidency. Concerns have been voiced regarding the extent to which electors can arbitrarily cast their votes for a candidate irrespective of the popular vote in their

13 https://www.pbs.org/newshour/nation/the-racial-history-of-the-electoral-college-and-why-efforts-to-change-it-have-stalled/

states. According to the U.S. Supreme Court, electors are bound by either their state's popular vote or their party's candidate. [14]

14 https://www.archives.gov/federal-register/electoral-college/electors.html#qualifications/

CHAPTER 3

Judicial Branch

The third co-equal branch of the federal government is the U.S. Supreme Court, or judiciary, which was designed to function like an umpire or referee in terms of assessing the constitutionality of laws, presidential executive orders, and alleged discriminatory patterns or practices.

The Judiciary Act of 1789 established the U.S. Supreme Court. Appointments to the court are for life, and compensation for justices is not determined or influenced by results of presidential or congressional elections.

Initially, only six justices were seated; however, following the Civil War Congress settled on nine justices, which includes one chief justice and eight associates.

For a long time, Supreme Court justices were nominated and appointed by presidents who were selected by the Electoral College and U.S. senators appointed by either state legislatures or governors. Blacks had virtually no involvement in the nominations and confirmations of federal judges. Keep in mind that the framers of the Constitution did not foresee "tribal politics" or red, purple, and blue states. That fact alone has serious implications regarding the ideological makeup of the court. The senate's confirmation process for Supreme Court nominees has been standardized. First, the president nominates someone, usually a lower court judge, to fill a vacancy on the high court. Second, nominees are then subjected to a thorough background check by the Federal Bureau of Investigations (FBI) and senate staff. Third, background information is shared with the senate's judiciary committee that interviews the nominee. Fourth, after hearings, the chair of the senate judiciary committee decides if and when to recommend that the nominee be submitted for a vote in the full Senate. Finally, only a simple majority is required to confirm the nominee.

Surely, tribal politics have influenced the make-up of the federal courts. Controversy erupted in 2016 when the Republican-led senate failed to hold a vote on then President Obama's nomination of Judge Merrick Garland to fill a vacancy on the court. That seemingly partisan act illuminated a key reality regarding who had the power to control the confirmation of nominees for the Supreme Court. The make-up of both the senate judiciary committee and the full Senate is critically important. Recall, blacks have been severely under-represented in the Senate.

During the nearly two hundred and thirty years of its existence, there have only been two African Americans nominated by a president and confirmed by the U.S. Senate. President Lyndon B. Johnson nominated Thurgood Marshall, a lawyer, who served from 1967-1991. Upon Marshall's retirement, President George W. Bush nominated Justice Clarence Thomas who joined the court in 1991. With all things considered, is it reasonable to believe that only two African Americans have been "fit" to serve on the high court?"

Judicial Reviews (Strict Scrutiny)

As a member of the highest court in the land, justices are assumed to be fair and unbiased in their judicial reviews. That assumption is in stark contrast to Merton's race theory or personality types. Surely, justices possess biases and therefore, in most cases, their votes can be accurately predicted regarding cultural issues.[15] Rulings are the results of a majority vote generally five to four along party lines.

In 2018, public attention and interests were directed to President Trump's nominees to lower federal courts and the U.S. Supreme Court. Some pundits have suggested that more conservative appointments to the courts might lead

15 https://www.scholastic.com/teachers/articles/teaching-content/role-supreme-court/

to reviews of case laws related to reproduction rights, voting rights, affirmative action, and Obamacare. Particular attention was given to the fact that nearly ninety percent of Trump's nominees were relatively young, conservative white men. Of course, there is nothing inherently wrong with those nominees, but concerns about a lack of diversity/inclusion of thoughts and beliefs were warranted.

Federal and state courts employ three types of tests having varying levels of rigor to assess the constitutionality of laws and/or public policies. The three levels in descending order of rigor are strict, intermediate; and rational. [16] In each case the burden of proof is on the government to prove that its treatment of a protected class is essential or serve a compelling interest. The fact that the government can and does treat people differently based on specific characteristics is news to a lot of Americans.

Suspect Classifications or Protected Classes

Today, Americans can be classified by the government and addressed specifically in laws and regulations. Groups are labeled as discrete, insular, suspect, or protected classes. According to published sources, Supreme Court classifications of groups were based on the following criteria:

- Be definable as a group, based on 'obvious, immutable, or distinguishing characteristics'
- Have experienced a history of discrimination
- Be a minority, or be 'politically powerless'
- Have little relationship to the government's proposed legislative or policy goals.[17]

---

16 https://blogs.findlaw.com/law_and_life/2014/01/challenging-laws-3-levels-of-scrutiny-explained.htm

17 https://legaldictionary.net/strict-scrutiny/

Regarding the plight of African Americans and laws, the Supreme Court has routinely reviewed laws and rendered decisions that impacted blacks in terms of citizenship, access to public accommodations, educational and employment opportunities, and political representation. A strict scrutiny judicial review is reserved for the following types of laws: 1) laws passed by legislatures that on their face appear discriminatory; 2) laws that allegedly violate a fundamental constitutional right; and 3) laws that intentionally or unintentionally adversely impact suspect categories or classifications (e.g., race, lineage, religion, or country of origin). The concept of strict scrutiny is strongly associated with alleged violations related to racial equality or equal protection. It should be reiterated that laws impacting protected groups to satisfy a compelling interest must be narrowly tailored to achieve desired outcomes. [18]

Based on the strict scrutiny criteria, descendants of African slaves who are now U.S. citizens can be treated differently than members of other groups if lawmakers can successfully argue that the law or policy satisfies a compelling government interest. Keep in mind that the U.S. Constitution was and is the law of the land and it was initially for whites only. Moreover, in terms of the plight of blacks, decisions regarding whether a law or practice is deemed a compelling government interest is determined by folks who do not have comparable experiences, do not look like them, and do not reside in their neighborhoods.

Stare Decisis

The journey from slavery to citizenship and equal protection involved changing laws and patterns and practices related to the rights and treatment of African Americans. Those changes were in stark contrast to existing laws and social norms. Stare Decisis is a Latin phrase meaning to stand by things already decided. It is often raised in higher courts' decisions or discussions and is a cornerstone of legal reasoning and persuasive arguments. Lawyers

---

18 https://www.law.cornell.edu/wex/strict_scrutiny#

invariably look to case law or precedent to find previous court rulings that support their arguments. By doing so, they claim that previous rulings or decisions regarding similar cases have already been rendered and those decisions ought to be upheld. Recently, during Supreme Court nominees' hearings in 2018, senators often quizzed them about their beliefs regarding what is commonly called "settled law." For instance, reproduction rights or choice as contained in the 1973 Roe v Wade ruling is thought to be settled law, but a change in the composition of the Court could facilitate another review and ruling. Generally, justices seldom reject previous case law.

For over two hundred and fifty years, the judicial branch has played pivotal roles in African American's trials, tribulations, and triumphs. Their rulings both gave hope at one time and crushed aspirations and racial equality at other times. Examples of this pattern of judicial review will be shared throughout the remainder of this book.

CHAPTER 4

Overarching Structural and Cultural Factors

This chapter was designed to highlight overarching structural and cultural factors that existed prior to and following the ratification of the Constitution that provided the foundation for slavery and institutional discrimination. Data and information that focused on geographical determinants, tax policies, North-South compromises, constitutional amendments, technological advancements, and Supreme Court rulings were reviewed.

Regional Economies

Distinct economies emerged in the colonies, influencing demands for cheap labor. Settlers took advantage of locations, climates, and natural resources in different regions to produce goods or services for both domestic and foreign markets.

Northeast or New England

The economies of Massachusetts, Connecticut, Rhode Island, New Hampshire, and other northeastern coastal ports included shipbuilding for England, fishing, and ironworks. For the most part, demand for labor was not nearly as intense as it was in the more southern colonies.

Mid-Atlantic

According to official geological maps, what is now defined as Mid-Atlantic states are the following: Maryland, Delaware, Pennsylvania, Virginia, and portions of New Jersey, New York, and North Carolina. Among mid-Atlantic colonies, cereal crops, including corn, wheat, barley, and oats, proliferated for both domestic and export. Forestry and small manufacturing also emerged as profitable sectors.

Southeast Atlantic Colonies

The southern states that formed the Confederacy had soils and climate perfect for growing different agricultural products detailed as follows: Virginia and Maryland (tobacco); North Carolina (forestry/pine); and South Carolina and Georgia (rice and indigo). The former requires large tracts of cleared land and a huge and reliable supply of water. Growing and harvesting rice was labor-intensive; incidentally, some African slaves had mastered rice production including elaborate irrigation systems back in their homelands. However, there was not a huge demand for rice globally and transporting the perishable product posed insurmountable challenges at the time.

An examination of regional economies prior to the ratification of the U.S. Constitution provided some additional context for conflicts between northern and southern lawmakers. Agricultural enterprises well suited for southern climates and soils required an enormous pool of free or extremely cheap labor to quickly acquire profits and wealth. In comparison, northeastern economies were composed of primarily small industries and agricultural enterprises.

Slaves as Real Estate Property

To fully understand and appreciate the negative impact of the U.S. Constitution on the plight of African slaves and their descendants, Americans must first examine the status afforded them prior to and following the ratification. A PBS series entitled *Africans in America* chronicled the institutionalization of chattel slavery in the colonies. The Virginia General Assembly in 1705 was credited with passing the model legislation:

> "All servants imported and brought into the Country... who were not Christians in their native Country...shall be accounted and be slaves. All Negro, mulatto and Indian slaves within this dominion...shall be held to be real estate."[19]

The framers of the U.S. Constitution did not address state laws governing chattel slavery. So, by default, slavery was deemed as a constitutional right of southern plantation owners.

Federal Budget and Slavery

The newly formed federal government was challenged to generate revenue to fund its operations. Several taxation schemes were proposed including the following:

> "(1) in proportion to population, (2) according to land value, and (3) according to the value of all property. A motion to apportion state obligations based on all property except household goods and apparel failed. Finally, it was agreed that states' obligations would be based on the estimated value of lands and improvements. In reality, each state was responsible for a fraction of the federal budget, and they had the freedom to decide how the funds were generated." [20]

Subsequent tax codes varied by state and regions. Some levied taxes on real estate and personal property. In the South, taxes were levied on African slaves. The newly formed Union was desperate for revenue and southerners wanted states' rights to enslave Africans. Clearly, the need for tax dollars can help

19 https://www.pbs.org/wgbh/aia/part1/1p268.html

20 https://taxfoundation.org/how-failed-tax-policy-led-constitutional-convention/

explain how such a powerful and majestic social contract could turn a blind eye to literally millions of enslaved Africans.

Familial Wealth and Slavery

A fact that is often evaded or ignored related to motivations of slave owners was that slaves generated more than profit or monetary wealth. Evidence uncovered during the investigation suggested that slaves helped to boost the social status of residents. In the South, familial status, prestige, and wealth were measured in terms of number and quality of slaves owned instead of size of plantations. Ownership of slaves was a status symbol. During the time frame in question if cotton was "white gold," then slaves were "black gold."

Legacy of Slave-Based Taxation

An article entitled "A Permanent Wound: How the Slave Tax Warped Alabama's Finances" described how slave taxes were assessed. In Alabama and Louisiana, taxes were assessed for each slave by age. Those below ten were assessed at twenty-five cents and those older were assessed at one dollar; additionally, in Louisiana their schedule on slaves included age and sex. In comparison, Georgia assessed taxes on slaves equal to the value of one hundred acres of land. [21]

The slave tax had both intended and unanticipated consequences. Tax revenues generated by slaves were used to satisfy federal government support obligations and to fund states' operating budgets. Without slave-based tax revenue, southern states could not adequately fund their militaries.

Fugitive Slave Act of 1793

Clearly, the U.S. government supported and aided chattel slavery in the South. The first Fugitive Slave Act, which made running away or escapes by

21 https://www.montgomeryadvertiser.com/story/news/politics/southunionstreet/2017/02/05/permanent-wound-how-slave-tax-warped-alabama-finances/97447706/

slaves a criminal offense, was passed by the U.S. Congress in 1793. The law gave slave owners the right to hunt and recapture run-away slaves. Moreover, it made slavery a life sentence in the U.S.

Cotton Processing Technology

Initially, cotton was not the preferred cash-crop in the South because it required enormous manual labor to complete a host of jobs: clearing and cultivating the land; planting seeds; weeding, chopping, picking and cleaning the cotton; removing seeds; storing and shipping bales; and spinning and weaving finished products. Cotton became "king" only after innovations came online including the spinning jenny and water and steam powered processing technologies that made textiles of higher quality at a lower cost. Arguably, those technologies fueled the surge in the global demand for cotton and the importation of slaves to southern states. This was the first time in U.S. history in which the introduction of technology increased the demand for African slaves and their descendants.

Eli Whitney was credited with the design and fabrication of the first mechanical cotton gin in 1794. His invention made processing cotton, which included separating the seeds from the fiber, less labor intensive and time consuming thus increasing its net value exponentially. Historians estimated that a pound of clean cotton (seedless fiber) took about ten hours to process by hand. In comparison, the gin was able to boost production to roughly a thousand pounds of cotton per day.

Southern plantation owners saw the demand for raw and cleaned cotton abroad, which is the equivalent to the global demand for smart phones today. They were willing to do whatever was necessary to meet the seemingly insatiable demand for cotton. The thirst for wealth and riches blinded white southerners' awareness of them becoming grossly outnumbered by their slaves. Like staffing at overcrowded county jails, at times, the ratio of free white to African slaves was 1 to 50.

Being drastically outnumbered could have facilitated fears and stress/strain among plantation owners and staff. As a result, one possible mode of adaptation was to employ cruel and unusual treatment to increase productivity, deter escapes, and thwart potential slave revolts.

Vertical Integration and Cotton

Slave labor made a lot of folks rich. The range of benefactors was vast, but a majority of the focus has invariably been directed towards plantation owners. Business and economic analysts often provide a graphic showing the vertical integration or sequential development stages in the life of a finished product. In terms of cotton, farmers produced the raw fiber that generated income at each successive stage until products were sold at retail centers.

The cotton industry had a variety of stakeholders. As such, a lot of people's fortunes were dependent on cotton grown and harvested by slaves. Benefactors or investors resided in both the North and South, free states, and slave states.

Locally, cotton gin equipment suppliers and gin owners supported cotton farmers. Of course, banks flourished as they made loans to farmers and related businesses. Bales of cotton had to be first stored and then transported by barges, rails, and roadways to shipping ports. Like the third leg of the slave triangle route, cotton bales were then shipped to England's textile mills.

Estimated Value of Slaves

In a PBS documentary, Steven Deyle reported that between the 1830s and 1860s when cotton was king, the value of the slave population was described as follows:

> "In 1860, the value of the slaves was 'roughly three times greater than the total amount invested in banks,' and it was 'equal to about seven times the total value of all currency in circulation in the country, three times the value of the entire livestock population, twelve times the value of the entire

> U.S. cotton crop and forty-eight times the total expenditure of the federal government that year.'"[22]

It is reasonable to assume that the value of slaves was equal to or greater than the U.S. gross domestic product (GDP) in that year. A basic definition of GDP follows:

> "Gross Domestic Product (GDP) is the broadest quantitative measure of a nation's total economic activity. More specifically, GDP represents the monetary value of all goods and services produced within a nation's geographic borders over a specified period of time." Imagine that.

It is fair to conclude that the cotton gin helped to increase both the demand for and value of slaves.

Amistad Rebellion (1841)

About twenty years prior to the start of the Civil War, a surprising Supreme Court ruling gave temporary hope to African slaves. The infamous slave revolt aboard the Spanish slave ship the Amistad, which was later depicted on the big screen, centered around fifty-three African slaves captured in March and April of 1839 in Sierra Leone. They were subsequently shipped to Cuba, which was then a Spanish colony. While in Cuba, they were again put on auction blocks and sold to work in sugar cane fields. According to historical accounts, there were forty-nine adults and four children boarded on the Amistad23 where conditions mirrored those of other slave ships. At some point, the slaves hailing from nearly ten different ethnic groups in Africa banded together and used their creativity and mechanical prowess to free themselves from the chains and locks. They found sugar cane knives in containers and used them to take control of the ship. Because their captors

---

22 http://www.pbs.org/wnet/african-americans-many-rivers-to-cross/history/why-was-cotton-king/

23 https://www.history.com/news/the-amistad-slave-rebellion-175-years-ago

had guns, the slaves' revolt or escape strategy centered on the elements of surprise and low expectations. Fortunately, the crew and slave owners did not have time to use their guns strategically. Some of the crew were killed and some jumped overboard. According to sources, the leader of the revolt, a man named Cinque, was a previous ricer farmer in Africa. They ordered the new crew to turn the ship around and set out for Sierra Leone. They were directed by the sunrise in the east, but during the night the crew turned away. They ended up near Long Island where they were apprehended by the U.S. Navy and jailed in Connecticut. After being arrested and jailed, President Van Buren ordered that they be shipped back to Cuba, but white abolitionists retained legal counsel for the slaves and began seeking their freedom through the courts. Eventually, they retained the services of former President John Quincy Adams who successfully argued their case before the U.S. Supreme Court. In a 7 to 1 decision, on March 1841, the Supreme Court ruled that the former slaves had a right to fight for their freedom and were released.[24] This ruling is covered more extensively in United States v. Schooner Amistad, 40 U.S. (15 Pet.) 518 (1841); however, by then southern slave owners had mastered the art of the deal.

1850 Compromise

Following the Schooner Amistad ruling in 1841 and the Mexican American War in 1846 there was aggressive expansion to the West. Southern lawmakers had to ensure that their "right" to enslave was not taken away by Congress. Negotiations were hard and heated but eventually culminated in the 1850 Compromise, in which northern or free states relinquished their outright opposition to slavery in the South in exchange for southern states' support and commitment to the Union. [25] The compromise resulted in specific agreements: 1) California was admitted as a free state, thereby giving that group a slight majority in both houses; 2) the 1793 Fugitive Slave Law was enhanced;

---

24 https://www.history.com/news/the-amistad-slave-rebellion-175-years-ago

25 http://time.com/4039140/fugitive-slace-act-165/

3) Utah's form of government was ratified; 4) slavery was outlawed in the areas captured in the American -Mexican War; 5) slavery was abolished in the District of Columbia; and 6) a resolution regarding a financial bail-out for Texas was passed.

Fugitive Slave Act 2.0

A top priority of slave states in the 1850 congressional negotiations was a section that strengthened the 1793 Fugitive Slave Act. The key provision stated that slaves could not obtain their freedom by escaping to a free state. In the 1850 Compromise, additional restrictions made it illegal for northerners and abolitionists to aid or conceal runaway slaves, and rewards were paid for the slaves' return. Like the current Immigration and Customs Enforcement (ICE) agency, federal slave deportation squads were authorized to search private property for runaways in both free and slave states, often employing blood hounds to track them. Enforcement of the law was shockingly invasive, brutal, and inhumane, even some ambivalent abolitionists became energized.

By most accounts, the number of run-away slaves, about one thousand out of three to four million slaves at that time, was relatively low. Southern lawmakers were threatened by the rising popularity of both black and white abolitionists and run-away slaves including but not limited to Frederick Douglas, Henry Highland Garnet, Harriet Beecher Stowe, Sojourner Truth, and Harriet Tubman.

The 1850 Compromise is an example of individuals possessing racial biases and the authority to make life-altering decisions. So, in terms of Merton's revised typology, how would northern congressmen who voted for the Compromise be characterized—mostly fair, conditionally fair, or mostly unfair?

Dread Scott v Sanford

Both northern and southern free blacks faced a devastating setback by one Supreme Court ruling. In the late 1850s Dread Scott, a former slave who resided in a "free state" and sued for his and his family's freedom on that basis, lost several lower court appeals, but eventually his case was argued before the Supreme Court. His basic argument was that his former "master" had given him to a relative who lived in a free state, and after residing in that state, he was eligible for U.S. citizenship. However, surprising to many, the U.S. Supreme Court ruled in 1857 that anyone of African descent was not eligible for citizenship in the North or South.

While the Schooner Amistad ruling and statehood granted to new territories were victories for northern states and abolitionists, the 1850 Compromise and the Dread Scott v Sanford Supreme Court ruling were temporary victories for slave states.

Election of President Abraham Lincoln

Mounting pressures for an expanded and strong central government and ideological differences regarding chattel slavery provided the conditions for a civil war. On one side were mainly southern plantation owners and their stakeholders, and on the other were supporters of the Union, northern industrialists, and abolitionists. The election of Abraham Lincoln in 1860 was perceived as a real threat to southerners' way of life and their dependency on slave labor. To calm tensions, President Lincoln stated that he was against the expansion of slavery in new territories but would not interfere with its existence in current slave states.

President Lincoln gave the southern states the opportunity to commit to the Union or face war. His trump card was a threat to free their slaves. Southern landowners and decision-makers had a difficult decision to make. From an economic perspective, their income or wealth had come on the backs of slaves, and to maintain or grow their wealth, they had to ensure that slavery was perpetuated by any means necessary. From their perspectives, Lincoln's ultimatum would have given too much authority to the federal government and potentially created a "free-state" majority in both houses indefinitely. So, the southern states failed to capitulate.

For varying reasons, states had threatened to secede from the Union prior to the Civil War. The South Carolina general assembly had previously threatened to secede from the Union in the 1830s because of a tariff that allegedly benefitted northern industries but drove up the cost of southern imports. In the wake of permanent injunctions against the expansion of slavery, which resulted in a severely diminished slave-state federal footprint, South Carolina persuaded six other states (Alabama, Mississippi, Texas, Florida, Louisiana, and Georgia) to secede and form a new confederacy. The general assemblies in those seven states voted to tear up their contracts with the U.S. federal government.

Once the deadline for southern states to commit to the Union passed, Lincoln declared war and showed that the Union army was somewhat formidable by driving the Confederate army out of Maryland by some accounts. His victory sent a message around the world that the Union was strong and likely to be victorious.

Emancipation Proclamation

At the start of the Civil War, historians maintain that the slave population numbered between 4 and 4.5 million. A little-known fact is that in some southern counties there were more slaves than whites, and no form of gerrymandering could have given whites the majority in some congressional districts. Ponder on that fact for a moment.

Lincoln and his advisors must have reasoned that freeing slaves would have dismantled the southern economy, thereby rendering the South incapable of funding and waging a successful defense. In addition, a sizeable portion of freed slaves joined the Union army.

On January 1, 1863, roughly two years into the Civil War, Abraham Lincoln made one of the most consequential political and moral decisions ever executed in the U.S. He freed slaves. Because there was virtually no way for him to get a constitutional amendment ratified through Congress to free slaves,

Lincoln was forced to issue an executive order, known as the Emancipation Proclamation, to initially achieve his objective.

The Emancipation Proclamation was clearly a strategy by President Lincoln to strengthen and preserve the "Union," which consisted of all the states with a central government and department of defense. The war ended on May 9, 1865.

SECTION VI: BIRTH OF A NATION 2.0

If the ratification of the U.S. Constitution in 1787 represented the official birth of the U.S., then the end of the Civil War and Reconstruction signaled a second birth containing nearly five million new black citizens. The new political reality was that millions of former slaves were theoretically given the right to register and vote in local, statewide, and federal elections. As mentioned earlier, blacks outnumbered whites in many congressional districts and about two states at the time. That fact alone was a major threat to southern culture. Readers are encouraged to pay attention to both northern and southern lawmakers' "give-and-take" that directly or indirectly suppressed black progress or advancements.

CHAPTER 1

Constitutional Amendments and Race

As stated earlier, constitutional amendments are corrective actions which take bipartisan support to be passed and ratified. This chapter chronicled the passage and implementation of both the 13th and 14th amendments which were arguably the most overarching and consequential.

Thirteenth Amendment

The Thirteenth Amendment, which abolished slavery, was passed by both the Senate and House in 1865 and was then ratified by three-fourths (75%) of the states; however, this amendment must be read carefully. Most Americans are unaware that slavery was not totally abolished. Interestingly, language included in this amendment states that individuals convicted and sentenced to prison are slaves, thus slavery is still perpetuated.

1866 Civil Rights Bill

A little-known fact is that following President Lincoln's assassination, a Republican-led Congress submitted the first Civil Rights Bill to his successor, President Andrew Johnson, who quickly vetoed its passage.[26]

---

26 https://history.house.gov/HistoricalHighlight/Detail/36863?ret=True

According to the Minneapolis Federal Reserve Bank,

["the proposed 1866 Civil Rights Act that was vetoed stated that every citizen of the United States, including former slaves, had the same right to inherit, purchase, lease, sell, hold, or convey property, both real and personal. The definition of citizen, however, excluded women and Native Americans."] [27]

There is an unmistakable similarity between the proposed 1866 Civil Rights Act and the suite of civil rights laws passed in the mid-1960s.

27 https://www.minneapolisfed.org/community/cra-resources/history-of-the-cra-new

CHAPTER 2

Affirmative Reconstruction

The time period between 1865 and 1896 was characterized by enormous ambivalence related to the futures of "southern culture" and newly freed slaves. President Lincoln and the Republican Party had to design a plan to stabilize and grow the once thriving southern economy without the advantages derived from slave labor. Moreover, the latter were expected to miraculously become self-sufficient.

Confederate Reunification

The first order of business was to bring the defeated confederate states back into the Union. A contractual agreement that contained criteria for reunification had to be signed. To be recognized as a member state, Lincoln's executive order called for at least ten percent (10%) of the eligible voters in each of the former slave states to pledge their allegiance to the Union and to rebuke slavery. [28] So, ninety percent (90%) of the eligible electorate could have remained supporters of the Confederacy. Moreover, pardons were to be awarded to everyone except military officers and high government officials; however, among many in Lincoln's party, his remedy was far too lenient.

Freedmen's Bureau

To some freed slaves, their plight was analogous to Maya Angelou's caged bird. For centuries, they had been totally dependent on plantation owners for food, water, shelter, clothing, and even security. Now that the chains were off and the doors to cages were opened, they were forced to secure those things

28 http://guides.lib.jjay.cuny.edu/c.php?g=288398&p=1922435

on their own, which led to unimaginable stress/strain levels among some of them. Some things had changed, but discriminatory patterns or practices in some areas were energized.

President Lincoln and Congress were challenged to either provide public assistance to over four million freed slaves and poor whites in the former Confederate states or give them the means to support themselves. For example, a plan had to be developed to empower approximately forty thousand refugees and slaves who had been detained on the Sea Islands on the Atlantic coast since the beginning of the war in 1861.

40 Acres and a Mule

General William T. Sherman led the southern military campaign and allegedly went on a scorched earth rampage from Atlanta to Savannah, Georgia's coast prior to heading to South Carolina. He left abandoned lands, burned-out production plants, and hundreds of thousands of freed slaves in his wake. President Lincoln authorized General Sherman to develop and implement a plan to redistribute confiscated coastal rice plantations in Georgia, Florida, and South Carolina. To that end, General Sherman issued Special Field Order 15 on Jan 15, 1865. The order promised freed slaves with families forty acres of land. It has been reported that the promise of a much needed mule was added to the restitution package in a subsequent field order.

Reconstruction did not solely focus on restoring infrastructures and the southern economy. A huge challenge was the acceptance and socialization of more than four million former slaves. Cultural change had to occur in order for them to realize full citizenship rights and freedoms.

Priority one was to provide freedmen places to live, grow food, and row crops to sell. Moreover, the Union needed to collect taxes from the former Confederacy. The forty acres and a mule field order was the proposed solution. However, managing and coordinating transfers of land titles or deeds to former slaves was not easy. In addition, the proposed new black settlements had to become self-sufficient. President Lincoln and a Republican-led Congress authorized the creation of the Bureau of Refugees, Freedmen, and Abandoned Lands on March 3, 1865, and it was charged with implementing the proposed land redistribution order.

Unfortunately, President Lincoln was assassinated on April 15, 1865 and the "forty acres and a mule" promise disappeared. His successor President Andrew Johnson rescinded the "promise" and gave the land back to plantation owners.

New Opportunities for Blacks

It is noteworthy that in the South, against grave odds including threats and viciously violent attacks, the Bureau, with help from northern abolitionists, the American Missionary Association, and other white oriented organizations, empowered some blacks to acquire land, build homes, and start small businesses. Moreover, public elementary, secondary, and postsecondary educational institutions specifically for blacks were established. The latter included Fisk, Hampton, and Howard universities.

The Bureau was disbanded in 1872 under severe pressure from southern whites and then President Andrew Johnson. Even during its peak, it was under funded and under minded by some elected leaders.

Birth of the Klan

Reconstruction arguably gave birth to the Ku Klux Klan (KKK). According to some historians, General Nathan Bedford Forrest founded the Ku Klux Klan in Tennessee in 1866, one year following the end of the Civil War. It began as a social group but quickly morphed into a network of white supremacists and terrorists in local communities throughout the South. Referred to by some as the "Invisible Empire of the South," their costumes allegedly symbolized the ghost of deceased confederate soldiers. The Klan was credited with thousands of violent assaults, rapes, castrations, cross-burnings, murders, and lynching of blacks in efforts to thwart their progress. By some accounts, membership in the Klan included elected officials, bankers, business owners, doctors, lawyers, teachers, clergy, and law enforcement officers. As such, the organization was powerful and far-reaching.

Members of the Klan had enough influence to deter or block wholesalers from buying black farmers' crops causing them to become in debt and/or to lose their land. They burned schools and churches. In the political realm, they threatened or attacked Republican and black candidates and newly freed blacks who dared to register to vote. Without a doubt, the Klan was partially responsible for the emergence and perpetuation of Jim Crow patterns and practices that were prominent until the 1960s.

Fourteenth Amendment

The Klan was a formidable foe to racial equality and sternly enforced racial segregation in all aspects of social life. Despite being "free," blacks had no or little legal standing in the eyes of the justice system.

The Republican-led U.S. Congress passed the Fourteenth Amendment that was ratified in 1868. It was designed to prevent state legislatures from denying due process rights to blacks. The primary text was as follows:

> "No State shall make or enforce any law which shall abridge the privileges or immunities of citizens of the United States; nor shall any State deprive any person of life, liberty, or property, without due process of law; nor deny to any person within its jurisdiction the equal protection of the laws."[29]

Prior to the ratification of the 14th Amendment, a lot of blacks were essentially suspended in time and place, having nowhere to go and no means to protect themselves and whatever personal property they possessed. Suddenly, the

---

29 https://en.m.wikipedia.org/.../Fourteenth Amendment to the United States Constitution

14th Amendment supposedly transformed over two centuries of culture and assured the newly freed slaves equal protection by the laws and due process.

However, the amendment did not include any accountability or checks and balances to ensure that decision-makers did not discriminate against former slaves. There was no punishment or repercussions for individual and institutionalized racial discrimination in many jurisdictions. Passage of related landmark civil rights legislation that addressed these issues will be discussed later.

Even after the passage of the 14th amendment, blacks were often systematically denied rights including the following: equal employment opportunities; education; housing; voting rights; unlawful search and seizures of persons and property; self-incrimination safeguards; legal counsel; speedy trials; jury of peers; right to cross examine witnesses; and fair and impartial judges. In fact, many of the same decision-makers who had supported and benefitted from slavery remained in positions of authority during and following Reconstruction in the South or the old Confederacy.

1876 Reconstruction Compromise

The 1876 presidential election between Democratic candidate Samuel Tilden and Republican Rutherford B. Hayes was highly contested. In some ways, it was a forerunner of the 2000Bush v Gore contested election. Debates surrounded the counting of electoral votes from about three southern states. A deal or compromise was reached to award the contested electoral votes to Hayes in return for a couple of devastating agreements or quid pro quos. First, Hayes and the Republican-controlled Congress agreed to end the final Union military occupation of Louisiana and South Carolina, thereby completely ending military occupation in the South. Void of military rule, southern lawmakers regained power and authority.

The second compromise allowed southern lawmakers to enact a form of "home rule" or "states' rights" as it related to blacks. Essentially, the Republican Congress ended Reconstruction and sent a clear message to southern governors and legislatures that they were free to continue both implicit and explicit discriminatory practices used in the former confederacy.

Plessey v Ferguson (1896)

Approximately twenty years following the 1876 Compromise, a Supreme Court ruling was handed down that clearly supported discriminatory patterns and practices. Plessey, a black man residing in Louisiana during the Jim Crow era, mustarded up the courage to take a seat in the front of a streetcar reserved for whites. He refused to move to the rear and was arrested and jailed. After his court appearance, Judge Ferguson ruled against Plessey in a New Orleans court. As usual, some white sympathizers funded Plessey's appeals and finally the Supreme Court agreed to hear his case. In 1896, the court ruled that forcing Plessey to sit only in the rear of the public streetcar did not violate his constitutional right under the Fourteenth Amendment. There could be separate, publicly funded accommodations for the races, thereby strengthening Jim Crow segregation norms and harsh punishments by law enforcement and/or the Klan for violations.

The Plessy ruling had widespread and long-lasting negative consequences for blacks. Keep in mind that the ruling was rendered nearly four decades following the ratifications of the 13th, 14th, and 15th Amendments.

NOTES

SECTION VII: PERSEVERANCE, RESILIENCY AND RACE

The previous sections presented evidence of what could be called "over-arching" cultural and structural determinants of racial inequality in the U.S. They were over-arching or cross-cutting forces and their impacts on blacks were assessed broadly or on an extremely high level. In comparison, the following sections contain results of investigations related to alleged institutional discrimination in specific areas or aspects of social life.

Recall that a complex system is invariably composed of a number of interdependent subsystems. The U.S. constitution created the framework and guidance for the creation and functionality of a host of subsystems. The list of subsystems investigated were as follows: 1) politics/voting; 2) economy; 3) education; 4) criminal justice; and 5) national security/defense.

In addition, a second group of non-governmental or private subsystems was investigated to identify their possible contributions to lingering racial disparities. While they are not government entities, they have either influenced public policies and/or benefitted from them. The list of non-governmental subsystems and institutions included in the investigation were as follows: 1) religion/faith; 2) communications; 3) familial or marriage and family; 4) health and wellness; and 5) sports/entertainment.

Each subsystem was investigated to obtain and disclose relevant data and information regarding its history and to chronicle major developments. To be transparent, each subsystem was treated like a crime scene, and the federal government was the alleged offender.

In addition to evidence of systematic or institutional discrimination in the various subsystems, the results of the investigation illuminated behavioral differentiation among blacks in terms of their responses or reactions to inequalities. Readers are encouraged to pay close attention to in-group comparisons or distributions before examining racial comparisons when possible.

Readers should keep in mind that racial disparities have been identified and measured by reviewing and analyzing official data. In most cases, those data cover a relatively narrow time frame. It has been reported that systematic collection of quality of life measures by race/ethnicity began less than a century ago. As a result, statistics related to racial comparisons prior to the 1950s were not readily accessible. Subsequent or more recent racial comparisons must be viewed with caution. In general, they show progress made following the 1960s Civil Rights Movement but do not reflect advancements made by blacks prior to that time which can be attributed to their extraordinary perseverance and phenomenal resiliency.

Challenge to Readers

While reading or immediately following completion of a section, readers are encouraged to compile exculpatory evidence to either exonerate or decrease the government's potential liability. Recall that the goal of the investigations was to produce a preponderance of evidence that would convince the average American that it is more likely than not that laws and public policies were at least partially to blame for observed racial disparities.

SECTION VIII: VOTING AND ELECTION SYSTEMS

Passage of the 13th and 14th Amendments did little to ensure blacks their right to register and vote for candidates void of threats or intimidation. In addition, apparently there were discriminatory practices that were employed to suppress the participation of blacks in the elections of decision-makers at local, state, and federal levels. This section contains the results of an investigation into decisions made by the U.S. Congress, Supreme Court, and state legislatures that have influenced African Americans participation in political systems as voters and elected officials.

CHAPTER 1

Voting Rights and Race

For nearly two hundred and fifty years, African slaves and their descendants were denied the right to participate in elections in the U.S. They were not allowed to vote for mayors, supervisors, district attorneys, judges, state legislators, U.S. representatives, senators, and presidents. On paper that rigged system was re-engineered following the end of the Civil War. Ratified on February 3, 1870, the 15th Amendment to the U.S. Constitution was intended to give former slaves and their descendants the right to register and vote. It is summarized as follows:

> "Section 1. The right of citizens of the United States to vote shall not be denied or abridged by the United States or by any state on account of race, color, or previous condition of servitude."

The 15th Amendment facilitated change while major challenges to the one-person, one-vote ideology remained in place. Most importantly, it abolished the Three-Fifths Compromise that only allowed African slaves to be counted in the census to increase the number of southern congressional districts and members in the House of Representatives.

However, the 15th amendment did not address the function and make-up of the Electoral College. Recall that its members elect the president, and the number of Electoral College votes equals the number of U.S. house members plus the number (100) of U.S. senators.

Black participation in elections became a definite reality following the passage of the 15th Amendment. What remained the same, however, was that they were blocked from membership in the Electoral College or participation in the elections of presidents.

Surprisingly, more blacks served in the U.S. Congress during and immediately following Reconstruction than almost any other time. At local and state levels, former slaves had to overcome fears, threats, beatings, and lynching to register and cast votes; as a result, racial gerrymandering was not necessary. However, side-bar compromises were made in some cases to allow blacks to serve in state and federal legislative bodies during Reconstruction.

Ironically, during Reconstruction, blacks appeared to have benefitted from the role state legislatures played in the appointment of U.S. congressmen. In some former Confederate states, legislatures appointed U.S. senators, so blacks did not have to obtain votes from whites in general elections.

The first black U.S. senator hailed from the state of Mississippi. Hiram Revels, a Republican, served from 1870 to 1871. Then, Blanche Kelso Bruce, another Republican from Mississippi, was the first black to serve a full term in the U.S. Senate from 1875 to 1881.

The Revels story requires or demands a little context. Revels claimed that he was never a slave and had known nothing but freedom.[30] He was the son of a preacher and his mother allegedly was of Scottish descent. Both smart and articulate, Revels earned higher education credits and graduated from seminary schools. He spent most of his adult life in the North but came south just prior to the start of the Civil War and served as the chaplain for at least two black Union regiments. In about 1866 he settled in Natchez, Mississippi and soon was elected to its board of aldermen. He then ran for the state legislature as a Republican, which was the majority party, and won. Keep in mind that Mississippi had not been reinstated to the Union at that time, and its two U.S. Senate seats had been vacated when the state seceded.

---

30 http://history.house.gov/People/Listing/R/REVELS,-Hiram-Rhodes-(R000166)/

Mississippi Fix

The white majority Republican legislature proposed to send a black member to complete a two-year senate term, with the understanding that a white member would be seated to fill the next full term. Records suggest that Revels' moving prayer on the floor showcased his extraordinary presence and communication skills which sealed his U.S. Senate confirmation. Reportedly, Democrats, who were in the minority, went along hoping that the decision would be the downfall of the state's Republican controlled legislature. [31]

Voter Disenfranchisement

A review of historical records and public accounts revealed evidence of widespread disenfranchisement techniques that proliferated primarily in former Confederate states between 1865 and the 1950s. They included violence, fraud, poll taxes, literacy tests, restrictive registration practices, and all white primaries.[32]

Arguing for states' rights, southern state legislatures were notorious for passing laws that directly and blatantly violated blacks' voting rights. Neither Congress nor the U.S. Supreme Court intervened in most cases. Without question, the courts were responsible for assessing the constitutionality of alleged voter suppression laws and practices.

It has been alleged that all three branches of the federal government were complicit in the suppression of the black vote following the passage of the 15th Amendment. The situation was described as follows:

> "The history of black disenfranchisement demonstrates that it was a product not simply of the actions of Southern states and individuals, but of a failure to uphold and exercise federal power. Congress failed to fully exercise its powers

---

31 http://history.house.gov/People/Listing/R/REVELS,-Hiram-Rhodes-(R000166)/

32 http://umich.edu/~lawrace/disenfranchise1.htm

under the 14th Amendment (for example, it never reduced Southern states' congressional representation in proportion to its illegal disenfranchisement, as it was authorized to do). The Supreme Court actively undermined federal executive powers to protect black voting rights, refused to acknowledge racial discrimination even when it was obvious, and acquiesced in blatant constitutional violations by resorting to specious reasoning. Although it slowly came around in some cases…."

1965 Voting Rights Act

Nearly a century after the 15th Amendment presumably gave blacks the right to register and cast votes, Congress for an assortment of reasons felt compelled to pass the 1965 Voting Rights Act:

> "Be it enacted by the Senate and House of Representatives of the United States of America in Congress assembled, that this Act shall be known as the 'Voting Rights Act of 1965.' SEC. 2. No voting qualification or prerequisite to voting, or standard, practice, or procedure shall be imposed or applied by any State or political subdivision to deny or abridge the right of any citizen of the United States to vote on account of race or color."[33]

The 1965 Voting Rights Act reaffirmed the rights of blacks that were articulated in the 15th Amendment. Americans must question why another voting rights law was required.

33 https://www.ourdocuments.gov/doc.php?flash=false&doc=100&page=transcript

CHAPTER 2

Residential Patterns and Voting

According to U.S. Census Quick Facts, the racial composition of the U.S. population in 2016 was as follows: black (13.3%); white (61.3%); American Indian or Alaska Native (1.3%); Asian (5.7%); Native Hawaiian (0.2%); two or more races (2.6%); and Hispanic or Latino (17.8%). [34]

African Americans must contend with the fact that their capacity to influence elections, and thereby laws and social policies, is a function of where they live and their percent of the target area. Since the 2000 census, the percentage of the black alone-or-in-combination population increased in the South, stayed about the same in the West, and decreased in the Northeast and the Midwest. Of all respondents who self-identified as black in 2010, 55 percent lived in the South, 18 percent in the Midwest, 17 percent in the Northeast and 10 percent in the West.

In a color-blind, society race has little to do with the outcomes of elections; however, in the U.S. race matters. Theoretically, there ought to be a positive relationship between the percent of the black population and their elections to local, state, and federal offices. In other words, jurisdictions with larger black population counts should have a greater probability of electing African American candidates. According to U.S. census counts, there are approximately seventeen states in which the black population ranged from about fifteen to thirty-seven percent. At the top of the list is the District of Columbia having roughly fifty percent African Americans followed by Mississippi (37%), Louisiana (32%), Georgia (31%), Maryland (30%), South Carolina

---

34 www.census.gov/quickfacts/fact/table/US/PST045216

(28%), Alabama (26%), North Carolina (22%), Delaware (21%), Virginia (20%), Tennessee (17%), Florida (16%), Arkansas (16%) New York (15%), Illinois (15%), New Jersey (14%), and Michigan (14%). Based on black population counts, the probability of them being victorious in statewide elections is highest in the Southeast. But records show only a hand-full of statewide, black elected lawmakers hailing from the region.

Residential Patterns and Election Results

An often-ignored fact is that where blacks live determines their potential capacity to influence election outcomes ranging from planning and zoning committees to general elections. Reports showed that there were approximately 3,140 counties in the U.S. The percent black in counties was summarized below:

> "The black alone-or-in-combination population comprised 50 percent or more of the total population in 106 counties. All these counties were in the South except for the city of St. Louis, which is considered a county equivalent. In contrast, 62 percent of all counties had less than 5 percent of the population identified as black."[35]

Prior to the 2018 mid-term elections, much was made about voting patterns in coastal, flyover, and suburban areas. In comparison, little, if any, attention was given to urban dwellers. According to 2010 census counts, outside the South, concentration of blacks was primarily located in urban areas or inner cities. In addition, among the more than three hundred counties with a black population between twenty-five and forty-nine percent, only seventeen were not in the South, and only two of these were not urban centers.

Cracking v Packing Gerrymandering

---

35 https://www.census.gov/newsroom/releases/archives/2010_census/cb11-cn185.html

Public policies often have good intentions but are accompanied by unanticipated and undesired consequences. Historically, redistricting was thought necessary to ensure that minority voters could have a realistic chance of electing a representative of their choosing because it was assumed that white voters fall somewhere along the revised Merton prejudice-discrimination spectrum (i.e., mostly fair, conditionally fair, or mostly unfair) and only a few would vote for a black candidate. Likewise, given their experiences at the hands of white elected officials and segregated neighborhoods, blacks in most cases would vote for a black candidate.

Allegedly, when drawing voting districts at local and state levels, decision-makers of both major parties have employed two procedures "cracking" and "packing" to either dilute black voting strength or to load certain districts with preferred potential voters. Cracking is characterized by lines that split black neighborhoods into two or more wards or districts. In comparison, packing refers to oddly shaped districts drawn to include as many blacks as possible.

The naked truth is that residential segregation has demanded affirmative measures to increase the likelihood of blacks being elected. As long as the race of candidates matters, elected officials will likely mirror the race of the majority of residents in a ward/district at all levels. There have and will be "exceptions" to the rule, however.

At city and county levels, intentional race-based drawing of voting districts has produced one or two black elected officials out of five or seven seats. As a result, appointments to boards and committees generally reflect the racial makeup of the governing bodies; therefore, the racial composition of a wide range of decision-making bodies including planning and zoning, public housing, and school boards can be traced back to the number of majority-minority districts/wards.

U.S. Supreme Court and Redistricting

Surprisingly, in 2018, it was both common and constitutional to consider "race" in specific situations. For example, race has been used narrowly to advance a "compelling government interest" if it passes the test of "strict scrutiny." In December 2016, the U.S. Supreme Court heard a case involving "racial predominance" in legislative redistricting in Alabama and Virginia. The case was filed after observations of a pattern of Republican-controlled state legislatures using 2010 census data counts to draw congressional districts. Questions arose concerning the weight given to the racial make-up of areas on final boundary markers. Plaintiffs argued that race was the predominant determinant of lines drawn reflecting racial gerrymandering. Defendants countered by arguing that other factors or variables were taken into consideration. Litigants on both sides agreed that race played a role; however, disagreement surrounded the extent to which "race" was a key determinant.

Recently, racial gerrymandering dumbfounded a college educated African American who believed he was somewhat politically astute:

> A special election was held in late 2017 to replace a long-time state representative in a deep southern state. Candidates for the unexpected vacant seat campaigned aggressively. The seat had been held by a black democrat for decades. So, there was no doubt that a black democrat would be elected. On Election Day, many black voters went to the polls to cast their votes only to find that they were not eligible because of their physical address. The affected voting district had been packed to include a critical mass of blacks from several contiguous counties. So, blacks who resided in relatively higher income neighborhoods found themselves ineligible to vote in the election and realized that they lacked the number of votes in their residential area to meaningfully impact the outcome of local and congressional elections. It can be said that they had been "cracked out."

Shelby County v. Holder

Following the landslide election of President Barak Obama in 2008 and re-election in 2012, Republican-led state legislatures were zealous in their efforts to dismantle or severely weaken provisions of the Voting Rights Acts that had ensured blacks unrestricted opportunities to register and cast votes. The Supreme Court reentered the fray when it agreed to hear the Shelby County v Holder case. At issue was whether states who had entered consent decrees had a right to implement laws that seemed to be contrary to the voting rights act without clearance from the Department of Justice.

In 2013, the U.S. Supreme Court, in a 5 to 4 vote, ruled that discriminatory patterns or practices that were evident prior to the 1965 law had been practically eliminated; therefore, states that had been found in violation and entered decrees should be cleared to invoke state laws consistent with the times and progress made in race relations. The key point in the ruling was that pre-clearance by the Justice Department was no longer required.[36]

The Shelby County ruling has led to the implementation of a new round of voter suppression methods and tactics that have either decreased or eliminated the following: online registration; early voting; "Souls to the Polls" Sunday voting; same-day registration; and pre-registration for seventeen-year-olds preparing to vote. State legislatures have passed voter ID laws and secretaries of state have arbitrarily purged voters from registration rolls in some states.

An example of passing laws to rig elections emerged in 2018. Several breaking news segments highlighted the fact that in North Dakota, a Republican-led legislature passed a bill requiring voters to have an ID that contained a street address. Here is the catch. Nearly ten thousand Native Americans, who have primarily voted for Democrats in the past, are legal citizens in that state and live in jurisdictions that do not have street addresses. Imagine that. Limiting

---

36 https://www.brennancenter.org/blog/qa-voting-rights-five-years-after-supreme-courts-shelby-county-decision

or blocking their votes due to the lack of a street address could have influence the outcomes of local and statewide elections.

Rucho v. Common Cause

State legislatures have been accused of rigging congressional redistricting efforts or partisan gerrymandering. In Rucho v. Common Cause, plaintiffs in North Carolina and Maryland filed suits in lower courts alleging that new districts were being drawn to advantage either democratic or republican candidates. Partisan gerrymandering theoretically avoids the issue of race. In late June of 2019, the U.S. Supreme Court, in a 5 to 4 vote ruled that partisan gerrymandering was not a matter that should be resolved by the court. It was reasoned that the framers of the Constitution were aware and approved the partisan nature of congressional redistricting. State legislatures were given the green light to use party affiliation to "pack" or "crack" congressional districts following the 2020 census.

Criminal History Records and Voting

Felony disenfranchisement laws have also diluted or decreased the number of eligible black voters. According to some historians, southern states passed laws that stripped felons of their voting rights while simultaneously assigning harsh penalties to what most would define as petty crimes. Generally, offenses that rise to the felony level have fines in excess of one thousand dollars and/or at least a one-year prison term. Those laws were challenged in the 1974 case of Richardson v. Ramirez in which the Supreme Court ruled that states could deny felons the right to vote. In about half of the states, felons cannot vote while imprisoned and on parole/probation, but their voting rights are restored when their sentences are fulfilled. Policy analysts have estimated that as many as 5.5 million ex-felons have been disenfranchised, accounting for roughly 2.5% to 3% of all eligible voters. Fortunately, reforms have been implemented and a growing number of ex-felons' voting rights have been restored.

Elections Results and Race

At the state level, blacks remain literally shut out of executive offices. Records showed that there was not a black governor in 2019, and there have only been two (2) since Reconstruction. Readers are also encouraged to research the racial composition of the nation's lieutenant governors, secretaries of state, and attorney generals.

Diversity in the Lower Chamber

According to a 2017 PEW Research Center report, the 115th Congress was the most diverse in the history of this country composed of non-whites who identified as black, Asian, Native American, and Hispanic. Specifically, ninety-five of the four hundred and thirty-five (22%) U.S. representatives were non-white.

Following gains achieved in 2017, mid-term elections in 2018 produced another record in terms of diversity. The new class was characterized by a record number of women; an increase in race/ethnicity; and religious diversity.

In terms of the election of U.S. senators, recall that in 1913 the 17th Amendment was ratified. It required senators to be elected by the popular vote instead of being appointed by governors or state legislatures. In the history of the U.S. Senate, there have not been more than a few blacks serving concurrent terms. In 2013, there were two. In comparison, by 2017, there were three: Cory Booker (NJ), Tim Scott (SC), and Kamala Harris (CA). Since 1913, blacks have accounted for only 2% or 3% of sitting senators.

Blacks have found limited success on the national level or in terms of presidential elections. Presidents are not elected by the popular vote. Recall that they are elected by a relatively small group of electors that make up the Electoral College. With the two major parties controlling both their party's nominee and appointments to the Electoral College, the system could be susceptible to institutional discriminatory patterns or practices. There have been forty-five men elected president in these United States since 1789. The first and only black president was Barak Obama (44th) who was elected in 2008 and re-elected in 2012.

At local, state, and federal levels, proven cases of black disenfranchisement and voter suppression tactics should have meaningful consequences. Congressional apportionment is theoretically based on the census count in each state. To encourage voter registration and voting, the percent of the eligible voting population that cast votes in general elections should be included in some federal funding allocation guidelines. In general, governors and state legislatures would be incentivized to recruit as many citizens to vote regardless of race, sex, income, and/or zip codes.

For more than four hundred years, blacks have resided in what is now fondly called the United States of America, the model democracy that shines like a light on a hill for the rest of the civilized world to observe and emulate. At its core are the ideals of equality, rights, and privileges to cast votes for candidates at local, state, and federal levels. The naked truth for blacks is that in most cases, Americans still vote along racial lines. Consequently, black candidates need other races to either vote for them or not vote at all; otherwise, their numerical minority status spells defeat in most cases. In the face of voter suppression tactics, their numerical minority status, and racial biases, a relatively large fraction of eligible blacks have still continued to navigate unnecessary barriers to register and cast their votes.

Ironically, there is a surprising but indisputable truth related to the power of the black vote. While not in the majority as electorates, blacks often can be the critical swing or tipping voting block that determines winners and losers. They find a way to matter.

NOTES

SECTION IX: PATRIOTISM, MILITARY SERVICE, AND RACE

This section contains evidence gleaned from the RSI related to laws, policies, and patterns or practices within national security or the military. Attention was given to the treatment of blacks in terms of recruitment, duty details, deaths, awards and recognition, the draft, enrollment in service academies, and receipt of veteran benefits.

CHAPTER 1

Fight for Freedom and U.S. Expansion

A small contingent of black indentured servants and "free" blacks in the colonies lived in the colonies; however, early on, settlers were uneasy about blacks possessing firearms. Prior to the War of Independence, some colonies passed laws forbidding blacks from participating in militias, thereby banning their possession of firearms.[37]

Prior to the Civil War, colonists or settlers waged at least three wars: American Revolution (1775-1783); War of 1812-1814, and Mexican War (1846-1848). In all three conflicts, free and enslaved Africans lost blood, limbs, and lives.

It is extremely important for Americans to know that blacks fought for others' freedom, citizenship, and representative governments despite their own enslavement. Having no choice in the matter, historical records indicated that blacks fought for both Great Britain and the Colonial military during the War of Independence.[38] [39]

The fact of the matter was that blacks contributed to the war that won America's independence in 1783. Roughly five years later in 1788 the Constitution was ratified that perpetuated chattel slavery.

Civil War

37 https://www.history.org/history/teaching/slavelaw.cfm

38 http://www.history.com/topics/american-civil-war/black-civil-war-soldiers

39 https://www.army.mil/africanamericans/timeline.html

Approximately seventy-three years following the ratification of the Constitution, slavery emerged again as a major source of conflict between free and slave states. Historical records indicate that African slaves fought on both sides of the Civil War; however, documents suggest that they encountered similar treatment in both militaries. Discrimination was rampant in both the Union and Confederate armies. Blacks were assigned to an array of non-combat tasks including cooking, construction, burial details, and moving supplies.

Slaves who fought for the Confederate faced a dilemma. At the beginning of the war, they were wholly owned and controlled by large plantation owners who employed cruel and harsh punishments for even minor, so-called disrespectful words and/or gestures. In fact, Virginia law made it legal for slave owners and other whites to kill runaways or to take blacks who did not have proper paperwork into custody. And, in most cases, black men could not escape with their entire familial units. Moreover, there was no guarantee that the North would win.

Union military decision-makers did not wholly embrace black recruits. Segregation was maintained by the very people who were allegedly fighting to "free" slaves. In 1863, the U.S. War Department issued General Orders No. 143, establishing the United States Colored Troop (USCT) that numbered in excess of 200,000 with about 40,000 or 1 of 5 being killed fighting for freedom and equality.[40] By some estimates, by the end of the war the troop accounted for about 1 out of 10 Union soldiers.

Buffalo Soldiers

Even settlements of the West must be attributed in part to the extraordinary role black soldiers played in protecting would be settlers from Native Americans who were trying to stop encroachment on their lands. Around 1866 at Fort Leavenworth, Kansas, the 10th Army Cavalry was formed, along

40 https://www.civilwar.org/learn/collections/united-states-colored-troops

with a black regiment that would later be called "Buffalo Soldiers," and was revered for its hunting, tracking, and tactical skills in protecting white settlers. Some sources reported that about fourteen Buffalo Soldiers earned the Medal of Honor for their bravery and service between 1870 and 1890. In addition, the 9th and 10th cavalries earned distinctions for their service. Decision makers in the U.S. have established a pattern of employing creative and courageous black soldiers to serve and protect critical human and military assets under difficult circumstances.

CHAPTER 2

Foreign Wars

By the early 20th century, blacks had proven their commitment to the U.S. by bleeding and dying to secure and protect its freedoms and democratic ideals. What is missing from this discourse is the fact that their service was unofficial and on a voluntary basis. At no time prior to the 20th century had blacks been officially required to serve in the military.

Ironically, blacks have been instrumental in helping to obtain freedom and create democracies all around the world while being deprived of the same back in the U.S.

The two world wars created opportunities for the beginning of racial desegregation at the federal level. As stated previously, most major decisions have both intended and unintended consequences.

WWI and Race

WWI began in 1914 and ended in 1918. Conflicts arose between Germany and the central powers and allied forces including France, Great Britain, Italy, the U.S., and the former Soviet Union. On April 6, 1917 after Germany's increasing aggression in the Atlantic Ocean, President Woodrow Wilson joined the war as a tool for preserving democracy and self-determination globally.

The war coincided with the mass migration of southern blacks to northern urban centers including Chicago, Cleveland, New York, Pittsburgh, and Detroit. It has been estimated that between 1914 and 1920 almost a million blacks migrated north in hopes of securing living wage jobs and voting rights.

During the same time frame, southern cotton crops were devastated by boll weevils causing severe economic strain and massive unemployment which further contributed to the mass exodus of blacks to the North.

Abroad, thousands of African Americans served in the military during WWI. At least one black division, the 369th Infantry Regiment, commonly referred to as the Harlem Hell fighters, was assigned to the French military. A New York National Guard unit, the 369th reportedly spent the most time in combat and received more casualties than any other U.S. regiment. They performed exceedingly well and gained the respect of their French counterparts. When asked to fight, black soldiers exceeded expectations, and some were eventually awarded the Distinguished Service Cross. However, few, though deserving, were awarded the coveted Medal of Honor, the highest military recognition for bravery, courage, and service above self. It is reserved for soldiers who often placed themselves in eminent danger to protect or defend others and whose battlefield actions were defined as "going beyond the call of duty." Alleged discriminatory patterns related to awarding the medal has been the focus of an on-going investigation.

Similar to patterns or practices reported during the Civil War, among U.S. foreign forces black units were assigned almost exclusively to support functions (e.g., kitchen, latrine details, burial teams, transportation, and loading and unloading supplies). Their restricted assignments helped to thwart their opportunities to display leadership, courage, and survival skills on the battlefields. Those decisions helped to limit or block their opportunities to earn medals and public recognition back in the U.S.

A plantation-like mentality was extant in the armed services. All black units were led by white officers, which had become traditional practice. However, black leaders voiced concerns about the lack of black officers, and in 1917 under the auspices of Howard University, a commissioned officer training academy was established in Des Moines, Iowa. Over six hundred commissioned black officers were produced.

Unwelcome Veterans

At the end of WWI in 1918, returning black soldiers erroneously expected greater equality and access to educational and employment opportunities. Instead, most encountered even stiffer and harsher treatment even while adorning their military uniforms.

The cold reception afforded returning black soldiers was mystifying to some of them. After being cordially accepted by the French citizenry, they had hopes of being welcomed back to the U.S. by both blacks and whites. Unfortunately, that was not the case. The influx of returning soldiers, black and white, wreaked havoc on employment sectors in the North. It was extremely difficult to absorb returning soldiers into a workforce that had been filled by women and southern blacks. Those conditions fueled what some have referred to as the "Red Hot Summer of 1919." In that year, there was an explosion of racial violence including a surge in lynching of black men. Shockingly, a disproportionate fraction of the victims were black veterans.

WWII and Race

WWII lasted from 1939 to 1945, nearly twenty years following WWI. On the one side was so-called Axis powers—Germany, Italy, and Japan. On the other side, the Allies were formed by France, Great Britain, the U.S., and the then Soviet Union, with China playing a minor role. [41] The war called for the mobilization of many soldiers.

Selective Training and Service Act of 1940 (21-45)

In 1940, President Franklin D. Roosevelt instituted the first draft in U.S. history. The draft was an "equal opportunity" endeavor. Going forward, black men had to commit to fight on behalf of the U.S. government if their numbers were called. They had to enlist and possibly die despite having political or religious objections. An estimated one million soldiers were needed, and to

---

41 https://www.britannica.com/event/World-War-II

a lot of blacks, President Roosevelt's draft proclamation was enticing because they hoped it signaled a commitment to equality in the U.S. Vigorous debates among blacks on both sides of the war issue ensued, some wanting to fight on foreign soils for freedom and democracy. On the other hand, some wanted to first secure racial equality and civil rights in the U.S. before going abroad.

During WWII, blacks could expand their roles in the fight for freedom and democracy abroad. However, their overall treatment was remarkably similar to that faced by their WWI predecessors. Racial segregation was enforced vigorously as enlisted black men and women could only receive training on bases that had separate accommodations for the races. Their numbers were estimated at around 1.5M.

Tuskegee Airmen

Black units again exceeded expectations even among airmen. During WWII, for the first time they could become fighter pilots. Stationed at Tuskegee, the 99th Pursuit Squadron was created, trained, and deployed. They quickly earned a reputation for their flying acumen and combat dexterity. White bombing crews and the Germans praised the tenacity of the 99th and their red tail Mustang planes. Still, they were not treated fairly and equally by the military, but they did not let the harsh and bitter treatment they received diminish their love of country and zeal for keeping all white bomber crews safe. It has been reported that they were initially denied access to the more advanced planes. Imagine what black airmen could have accomplished if they had been given access to the more technologically advanced planes initially.

As in other sectors of society, black achievements in aviation have been either concealed or ignored. The 99th Pursuit squadron has received most recognition as heralded escorts for U.S. bombers. In comparison, the success of the 332nd Fighter Group remains hidden. It was recently revealed that members of the 332nd squadron competed in the annual U. S. Continental Gunnery Meet held in Las Vegas, Nevada. This competition involved shooting aerial and ground targets and accurately bombing targets for which the crew received a perfect score; however, for decades the winner of the 1949 competition was listed as "unknown."

By some accounts, Tuskegee produced nearly one thousand black pilots and over sixteen thousand ground support personnel. Veteran black airmen often recount the discrimination they faced from U.S. airlines by not being hired as captains and co-captains. According to Lieutenant Colonel Harry T. Stewart, a Tuskegee airmen and author of *Soaring to Glory*, airlines did not question their qualifications but blamed persistent racial prejudices. He stated that during one job interview with an airline, the hiring executive justified his discriminatory practice by saying that if a white female passenger saw a black flight crew, she might become fearful and refuse to fly.[42] Similar justifications might have been employed to explain limited or blocked hiring of black mechanics, technicians, ground crews, and even cabin hostesses.

Racial Desegregation in the Military

Racial desegregation in the U.S. was fueled by a presidential executive order that allowed black and white servicemen to fight, survive, and die side-by-side. Like President Lincoln's executive order that freed slaves, in 1948 President Harry S. Truman issued Executive Order 9981 that desegregated all branches of the military. By some accounts, President Truman was shaken by revelations related to an outbreak of violent crimes against returning black war veterans, especially in the Deep South. Newspapers contained stories of black soldiers being brutally beaten and killed in their hometowns by local mobs for violating Jim Crow norms. Presidential historians maintain that Truman believed that respect for black soldiers would increase if they could train and fight alongside their white counterparts; however, he faced push-back from some military leaders. According to numerous sources, the Air Force and Navy had desegregated by 1950, but the Army held out for a short time. Below is an account worth reviewing:

---

42 https://www.c-span.org/video/?461484-1/soaring-glory

> "In October 1951, the all-black 24th Infantry Regiment, a unit established in 1869, which had served during the Spanish-American War, World War I, World War II and the beginning of the Korean War, was disbanded, essentially ending segregation in the U.S. Army." [43]

Historical records indicate that some Army officers either resigned or were forced out because they rebuked the executive order to desegregate. The cold, hard fact is that black soldiers have only been allowed to train, fight, and die alongside fellow Americans for less than seventy (70) years.

Korean and Vietnam Wars

The Korean War in many ways mirrored the Civil War in the U.S. It was a war between what is now North Korea and South Korea and was waged from 1950 to 1953. At the start of the Korean War, about one hundred thousand blacks were in the U. S. armed forces; however, by the close of the war, more than a half million blacks had served, composing roughly eight percent of the U.S. military at that time.

During the Korean War, African Americans were given greater opportunities to acquire training and technical skills to command regiments and serve in specialized units. They also acquired skills that were transferable to civilian life. As in the past, when given opportunities to serve, African Americans earned a host of medals of valor and honor for amazing heroic acts of courage, bravery, and tactical fidelity during combat.

The Vietnam War (1961-1973) brought about full racial integration in the armed forces when President John F. Kennedy addressed institutional racial discrimination in the armed forces by commissioning a panel to identify

43 https://www.nj.gov/military/korea/factsheets/afroamer.html

patterns or practices that suppressed black enlistments. An aggressive campaign to lure blacks into the military was waged prior to and during the Vietnam War.

Military Draft Loopholes

By most accounts, the draft was a porous pipeline for certain Americans who managed to avoid it at higher rates than blacks. Loopholes to avoid the Selective Service were readily available to categories of individuals who possessed credentials or access to "influential people." Deferments were granted based on several factors including college students, so-called essential professional/workers in certain sectors, and questionable medical diagnoses. The late Senator John McCain (Rep.) publicly proclaimed that the draft was rigged. Contributing to racially skewed deferment patterns was the fact that by some accounts, blacks represented less than one percent of members on Selective Service boards and there were none in at least a half dozen states. Members of those boards were responsible for calling and screening prospective draftees. So, the draft cornered a disproportionate number of the poor and blacks who did not have access to available deferments enjoyed by some of their white counterparts.

Racial parity seemed achievable in the military. Prior to the Vietnam War, blacks were about thirteen percent of the general population and roughly nine percent of the military. However, during the Vietnam War, the black death rate was significantly greater than their counterparts. The situation was described as follows:

> "African Americans often did supply a disproportionate number of combat troops, a high percentage of whom had voluntarily enlisted. Although they made up less than 10 percent of American men in arms and about 13 percent of the U.S. population between 1961 and 1966, they accounted for almost 20 percent of all combat-related deaths in Vietnam during that period. In 1965 alone, African

> Americans represented almost one-fourth of deaths. In 1968 African Americans, who made up roughly 12 percent of Army and Marine total strengths, frequently contributed half the men in front-line combat units, especially in rifle squads and fire teams."[44]

Being assigned to rifle and fire squads caused blacks to be overrepresented in kill zones. Reports suggest that, as a result, military leaders made some adjustments by 1966 to lower the black death toll. Imagine how many black lives would have been spared if corrective actions had been implemented by decision-makers earlier.

The draft ended in 1973; however, young men must still register with the Selective Service upon their eighteenth birthday. Since 1973, the U.S. has waged military operations with a largely volunteer military abroad in Grenada, Panama, Afghanistan, Iraq, and Syria. By some estimates, there is an excess of one hundred thousand armed servicepersons stationed around the globe despite the draft being inactive.

---

44 www.http://www.english.illinois.edu/maps/poets/s_z/stevens/africanamer.htmf

CHAPTER 3

Armed Forces by Race

The composition of the different branches of the military varies primarily by race and age. Data obtained from Census.gov (2016) provided the breakdown. Among veterans age 18-34, the distribution was as follows: whites (65%); blacks (15%), Hispanics (14%), and other (10%). Among older veterans ages 35 to 54, the breakdown was the following: whites (71%), blacks (18%), Hispanics (8%), and other (6%). African Americans surpassed their percent of the general population (13%) in both cohorts. Unfortunately, African Americans' overrepresentation among veterans is invariably ignored by elected officials and media. Based on this knowledge, what causes a disproportionate percent of young African Americans to initially choose the armed forces over the civilian workforce, postsecondary education, public assistance, or unemployment?

Recently, the Department of Defense (DOD) undertook a visioning update entitled "The Future Force" which looked at the new demands placed on all service branches related to recruitment, retention, and compensation/benefits. The concept of talent management was at the forefront of the discussion. Only about thirteen percent of the U.S. population is eligible to be inducted into one of the branches. Once enlisted, they are struck by relatively low compensation packages. As a result of numerous deployments and relatively low pay, many are failing to reenlist, signaling a potential shortage in the now volunteer armed forces.

Increasingly, 21st century degrees and skill sets are required to operate and maintain highly automated and sophisticated weapon systems. As stated elsewhere, those skills are in high demand in the civilian labor market; as a result, competition for highly skilled service personnel has become fierce. Eventually, the DoD will be forced to compete in the open labor market for talent. These changes will impact the number of slots available to many individuals who in the past saw the military as an alternative to traditional educational pathways and employment opportunities.

Volunteer Soldiers

To fully appreciate the unselfishness and bravery of enlistees, keep in mind that since 1975 serving in the military has been on a volunteer basis. Persons eighteen to forty-four are considered eligible to be active duty in the military. In 2015, blacks made up seventeen percent of active enlisted DoD personnel, surpassing their representation of thirteen percent in the general population.[45]

The size of each branch of the military is rarely examined. In 2015, the Army accounted for 36% of the enlisted, followed by Air Force and Navy at twenty-five percent each, and Marines at about 14%. [46]

Even in the armed forces, career advancements appear to vary by race. Data regarding a breakdown of the military by branch and race of both officers and enlisted personnel are presented below:

The 2016 Defense Manpower Data Center's website contained data regarding military personnel by race. Among officers the breakdowns by service were as follows: 1) Army (black 12.9%); white (74.3%); Hispanic (5.7%); Asian (4.5%); American Indian/Alaskan Native (0.5%); 2) Navy (black 7.9%, white (81.6%); Hispanic (13.6%); Asian (3.9%); American Indian /Alaskan Native (0.6%); mixed (1.8%), and Pacific Islander (0.3%); 3) Marines (black (5.1%); white (82.4%); Asian (2.5%); American Indian/ Alaskan Native (0.7%); mixed (1.2%); and Pacific Islanders (0.4%); and 4) Air Force (black (5.8%); white (80.7%); Asian (3.2%); American Indian/

45 http://www.pewresearch.org/fact-tank/2017/04/13/6-facts-about-the-u-s-military-and-its-changing-demographics/

46 http://www.pewresearch.org/fact-tank/2017/04/13/6-facts-about-the-u-s-military-and-its-changing-demographics/

Alaskan Native (0.4%); mixed (1.2%); and Pacific Islanders (0.3%). Only in the Army was the percent of black officers approximately equal to their presence in the general population. In comparison, black officers accounted for only about 5% in other branches of the military.

Service Academies

The recruitment and training of prospective military officers was investigated to identify patterns or practices that could intentionally or unintentionally suppress the number and percent of black commissioned officers. The two primary military postsecondary options are the Reserve Officer Training Corporation (ROTC) and elite military service academies. The latter was the focus of this investigation.

Prior to the end of the Civil War, the U.S. has had military service academies that offered postsecondary degrees and commissions as officers. Histories of service academies lack details regarding the admissions and treatment of descendants of African slaves. Given the culture of the times, it is reasonable to assume that the academies were for whites only for decades if not a century. Even in the wake of the Civil War, Brown v Topeka, Kansas, and1960's Civil Rights legislation, African Americans remained underrepresented in military academies, despite their impressive military service records.

The underrepresentation of African Americans in elite military service academies has helped to limit or block their career advancements and wealth accumulation. Graduates of elite military academies are "fast-tracked" for promotions and leadership assignments that often lead to post-service honors and recognition. Many of those graduates have secured political appointments, lucrative executive jobs, corporate board memberships, and a host of consulting and/or paid speaking opportunities.

Currently, there are five recognized service academies: 1) Military Academy (USMA) in West Point, New York, founded in 1802; 2) Naval Academy (USNA) at Annapolis, founded in 1845; 3) Coast Guard Academy (USCGA) in New London, Connecticut, founded in 1876; 4) Merchant Marine Academy (USMMA) in Kings Point, New York, founded in 1943; and 5) Air Force Academy (USAFA) at Colorado Springs, founded in 1954.

Each year, total admissions to military academies range from about 1,100 to 1,300. Admissions to service academies is akin to a full-ride fellowship to an elite Ivy-league college, and some of the perks include tuition and room and board for at least four years. In addition, upon graduation, cadets/midshipmen are afforded opportunities to become commissioned officers for a minimum of five years.

During President Obama's administration, concerns regarding the lack of diversity in military academies among cadets/midshipman prompted the U.S. Congress to request the Secretary of Defense to conduct or out-source an investigation into several areas: recruitment, admissions, first year survival rates, graduation rates, and initial service obligation outcomes. The Rand Corporation was commissioned to analyze related data gleaned from U.S. service academies. Results of the investigation were presented in a 2010 research brief prepared by the RAND National Defense Research Institute entitled "Diversity of Service Academy Entrants and Graduates." Unfortunately, only data covering 1992 to 2009 were available for analysis.

Between 2007 and 2009, diversity increased across all service academies. In terms of admissions, the percent of women and blacks was 22% and 6%, respectively. The woefully low percent of blacks enrolled in service academies was alarming. Further investigation revealed a potentially potent contributing factor. Applicants to all service academies, except for the Coast Guard, are encouraged to seek a nomination from a member of the House of Representatives, vice president, or the president. Each member of Congress can have a maximum of five (5) cadets enrolled concurrently and can submit up to ten applicants to fill a vacancy. For centuries, there was only a handful of black Congress members, so the requirement in a race-based culture placed prospective African Americans at a disadvantage in most states.

Furthermore, just as postsecondary educators place a high priority on the first-year college experience, the same sentiment exists at military academies. Overall, first year completion rates average between 85% and 90%. Data were not provided by sex and race. In terms of graduation rates, the average was between 77% and 80% with no significant difference between men and women. It was noted that the black graduation rate had increased to about seventy-two percent, but their baseline rate was not disclosed.

Graduates of service academies are obliged to commit to five years of active duty. Rates of initial service obligation success saw a significant decline across the service academies during the time frame in question. Among women and people of color, ISO completion rates dropped from about 90% to approximately 77%.[47]

It warrants repeating that many graduates of military academies are immediately thrust into leadership roles at home and abroad. They help develop military or defense plans and strategies. The underrepresentation of blacks among graduates of military academies unavoidably leads to their underrepresentation among officers who help make life and death decisions in all branches of the military.

Enlisted Personnel

In 2016, the bulk of military personnel was enlisted soldiers. Enlisted personnel by service and race was as follows: 1) Army (black (21.5%); white (68.9%); Asian (3.6%); unknown (1.5%); 2) Navy (black (20.2%); white (59.2%); Asian (5.9%); mixed (5.8%); Pacific Islanders (1.2%); and unknown (2.4%); 3) Marines (black (10.8%); white (78%); Asian (2.2%); American Indian/Alaskan Native (1.1%); mixed (0.9%); Pacific Islander (1%); and unknown (6%); and 4) Air Force (black (16.7%); white (71.6%); Asian (2.5%); American Indian/Alaskan Native (0.7%); mixed (2.5%); Pacific Islanders (1.2%); and unknown (4.8%).

47 https://www.rand.org/pubs/research_briefs/RB9496/index1.html

As noted, in at least three branches of the military, blacks are overrepresented. They account for at least sixteen percent of enlistments in the Army, Navy, and Air Force, but their overrepresentation in the military is often ignored by the media.

CHAPTER 4

GI Bill and Race

This chapter contains evidence of widespread discriminatory patterns and practices perpetrated by the Veterans Administration that limited or blocked black veterans' access to the same benefits afforded their counterparts. The investigation focused primarily on data and information related to funding for education and job training, employment opportunities, and home mortgages.

Nearly seventy years ago, it was deemed important to honor and assist servicemen who risked their limbs, mental health, and lives to protect and preserve the greatest democracy in the world. Assistance to veterans was first provided through the Servicemen's Readjustment Act of 1944, which was later revamped and is now commonly referred to as the "Montgomery GI Bill." The GI Bill included support for healthcare, postsecondary education, job training, and homeownership.

Congress enthusiastically passed the GI Bill and it did not include discriminatory practices. However, instead of federal control, a group of legislators voted to allow each state to manage their veteran affairs programs. This meant that decision-makers, who in some cases supported discriminatory practices and segregation, oversaw approving or refusing GI benefits to black veterans.

A relatively large body of published works related to black veterans' pursuit of equal benefits under the GI Bill exists. However, a majority of evidence included in this chapter was obtained from the notable works of Ira Katznelson's 2005 and 2008 publications. His 2005 riveting and thought-provoking book *When Affirmative Action was White: An Untold History of Racial Inequality in Twentieth-Century America* provided data and information to corroborate a rigged system claim related to the distribution of a host of federal programs. In addition, his 2008 article "On Race and Policy History: Dialogue about the GI Bill" co-authored with Suzanne Metler presented data related to racial disparities in awarding GI Bill benefits.

Postsecondary Education

Under the GI Bill, educational support for blacks was hampered by strong coalitions including the U.S. VA, American Legion, and Veterans of Foreign Wars (VFW). They were all-white organizations that controlled or influenced the allocation of benefits to veterans.

Nevertheless, the GI Bill was instrumental in helping to dismantle racial segregation at the postsecondary level. Initially, black veterans' education benefits were restricted ensuring that they could only attend vocational schools or Historically Black Colleges and Universities (HBCUs), but the potential, additional revenue stream quickly caught the attention of northern Historically White Colleges and Universities (HWCUs), and things began to change. In comparison, though viewed as inferior, colleges in the South still denied admissions to black students. It has been estimated that around 1946 about 28% of white and only 12% of black veterans were approved for college scholarships. Even HBCUs, due to capacity limitations, had to deny over 20,000 black veterans' admissions.

Home Mortgages

Black veterans were systematically denied loan guarantees to purchase homes in the suburbs or other areas where property appreciated in value faster.

It was reported that of the first 67,000 mortgages funded via the GI Bill, less than one hundred were obtained by people of color. Reports indicate that in the summer of 1947, approximately 3,000 VA home loans were approved in Mississippi but only two went to blacks. Based on national home loan rates by race between the 1940s and 1950s, discriminatory practices in Mississippi were the norm, not an outlier.

Employment

Through both vocational training and postsecondary credits and degree attainment, black veterans were able to make some advancements in the workplace. However, some disturbing employment patterns were uncovered.

Recall that racial tensions were escalating, and segregationists were publicly issuing a clarion call. In general, African Americans were not in decision-making positions related to the hiring and firing of employees. Accounts indicate that even when black veterans received thorough training, they still were overlooked or bypassed for jobs/careers that matched their skill sets. According to published reports, it was estimated that during the time frame in question nearly ["90% of skilled, professional, and semiskilled jobs went to white veterans. On the other hand, over 90% of low-wage, nonskilled and service positions went to black vets."][48]

An excerpt from a 2006 article by Edward Humes published in the *Journal of Blacks in Higher Education* detailed the disadvantages blacks have faced related to VA benefits:

> "Black veterans and their families were denied their fair share of the multigenerational, enriching impact of home ownership and economic security that the G.I. Bill conferred on a majority of white veterans, their children, and their grandchildren." Such an imbalance went against Roosevelt's intentions, as he had purposefully created the first social legislation that did not discriminate based on race."[49]

---

48 Humes, Edward (2006). "How the GI Bill Shunted Blacks into Vocational Training." *The Journal of Blacks in Higher Education*, 53, 92-104.

49 https://daily.jstor.org/the-inequality-hidden-within-the-race-neutral-g-i-bill/

Beginning with their official arrival in 1619, African slaves and now their descendants have been counted on to fight to secure freedom and democratic rule in the U.S. and on foreign soils. Still, they are confronted by the realization that those in decision-making positions in general do not look like them, and they might harbor racial prejudices that could influence the scope and nature of their assignments on and off the battlefields. Similar fears have existed upon their honorable discharges and entrance into the civilian labor force. Despite evidence of systemic discriminatory patterns or practices in the military, blacks continue to be overrepresented in most of the armed services.

SECTION X: ECONOMIC SYSTEM AND RACE

President Trump was quick to point out the staggering unemployment rate among blacks during the 2016 campaign, while presumably courting their votes. Their unemployment rates were linked to his rigged system theory. This section contains summaries of federal laws and patterns or practices in both public and private sectors that limited or blocked blacks from jobs/ careers, income, land, homes, and wealth accumulation.

It is important to point out the difference between income and wealth. Income refers to compensation for work performed. If a person does not work, they do not get paid. That income stream would no longer exist. In comparison, wealth is generally defined as assets or valuables (e.g., land, homes, rental property, livestock, mineral rights, small businesses, and stocks and bonds) that can be handed down to heirs or subsequent generations.

CHAPTER 1

Employment, Unemployment and Race

Black unemployment was unheard of between 1619 and 1865. In both the North and South, blacks could not eat if they did not work. In addition, failure to work often resulted in cruel and unusual punishment.

Following the Civil War, blacks were essentially on their own in terms of trying to compete for industrial/manufacturing jobs (e.g., manufacturing, ship building, stockyards, meat packing etc.) and professional positions (e.g., managers, directors, supervisors etc.). Of course, the available job market in the South remained heavily concentrated in agriculture. Be reminded that separate "but" equal laws and Jim Crow patterns or practices were ferociously enforced, especially in the South. And, between 1865 and the late 1950s, hiring decisions were in the hands of primarily men who possessed racial biases and the authority to hire and fire applicants or employees "without cause." In addition, freed blacks faced strong opposition in the workplace from organized labor unions.

Labor Unions and Race

In 1997, an article included in *Prologue Magazine* entitled "African Americans and the American Labor Movement" by James Gilbert Cassedy chronicled black participation in unions and labor movements spanning the 19th and 20th centuries. The article presented a treasure trove of reference material including minutes and records from a host of government agencies. [50]

---

50 Federal Records and African American History (1997). 29(2).

Records show that even prior to the Civil War, blacks fought for better work conditions. In 1835, black caulkers went on strike at the Washington Naval Shipyard. Their collective actions were powerful because imperfect caulking generated non-seaworthy ships.

Post-Civil War collective bargaining strategies emerged in different industries. Trade unions proliferated during Reconstruction, but most excluded blacks.

Only four years following the end of the Civil War, in December 1869 over two hundred black delegates attended the Colored National Labor Union Convention in Washington, DC that was established to offset the actions of the white National Labor Union. Specifically, the union unsuccessfully lobbied Congress two times (1869 and 1871) to alleviate the unfair work conditions of black workers in the rural South. Their proposal would have divided public lands into forty-acre plots to be owned and farmed by blacks and supported by low interest government loans.

In 1873, black dock workers in Pensacola, Florida went on strike in the face of an influx of white Canadian dock workers who were brought in to take their jobs. On the other hand, it was a common practice for companies to temporarily employ desperate blacks as "strike-breakers" to force white workers to cave in. Of course, that strategy only heightened conflicts between black and white laborers.

The "Common Rights of Working Men" coalition culminated in what is commonly referred to as the Great Strike of 1877 which brought together both black and white laborers to protest in St. Louis, Louisville, and other cities. The push for integrated labor unions was short-lived, however. According to archival records, in about 1894 Eugene Debs, leader of the American Railway Union, was unsuccessful in persuading his white co-workers to allow blacks to gain membership. His plan would have decreased the probability of blacks becoming "strike-breakers" for the Pullman Company. Rejections by white unions expanded to Chicago-area stockyards and meat packing companies whose workers supported the white rail unions. Blacks wanted and needed jobs as either members of the brotherhood or "strike-breakers." As usual, they were not going to just give up and sit on the sidelines.

Later in a related effort, in 1925 A. Phillip Randolph aggressively mobilized efforts to persuade the American Federation of Labor (AFL) to certify and recognize the Brotherhood of Sleeping Car Porters employed by the Pullman Company. It took over twelve years to succeed, but Randolph became a nationwide labor union advocate. He reportedly persuaded President Franklin D. Roosevelt to give federal relief and equal employment opportunities to African Americans.[51]

During the two world wars, blacks were welcomed in industrial and manufacturing sectors. Significant employment gains were realized in several sectors (e.g., steel, automotive, shipbuilding, and meatpacking). It has been estimated that in a single decade (i.e., 1910-1920), black employment in industry doubled, surging from about a half million to nearly one million workers.

Tenant Farmers and Sharecroppers

At the end of the Civil War and passage of the 13th and 14th amendments, particularly in the South, there were two complimentary needs. First, freed slaves had no way to provide for themselves and their immediate families. On the other hand, former slave owners had massive agricultural farmland but no free labor to work it. As a result, two types of labor agreements emerged, contract laborers and sharecroppers.

Some former slaves became contract laborers or tenant farmers who transitioned from no pay to low pay. This group of workers earned wages and often were provided housing or paid rent. Of course, there were no wage guidelines, health and safety assurances, overtime pay, health insurance, retirement, vacation time, or sick leave. It should be noted that some plantation owners were honest and showed some compassion; however, it is thought that the majority took advantage of the enormous illiterate labor pool to keep wages and

51 https://www.archives.gov/publications/prologue/1997/summer/american-labor-movement.html

other overhead costs extremely low. Those practices ensured greater profits for the landowners.

A second type of labor contract was called sharecropping, essentially a land lease or rent agreement between the landowner and a tenant farmer. Keep in mind that the newly freed slaves had little to no collateral or "credit" to purchase essential products and equipment to farm; however, they had acquired the "know-how" and skill sets to be successful. As such, it is important for Americans to give credit to some former slaves for successfully managing small businesses or agricultural enterprises.

Sharecropping was a type of outsourcing, and contracts generally included provisions for the renter to get advances to purchase seeds and equipment to produce crops to sell. In most cases, the landowner used projected income from the crops as collateral for the loans. The rent for the land each year ranged from one fifth (1/5) to one fourth (1/4) of the gross sales or profit. With the balance, black sharecroppers had to reimburse landowners for supplies, food, and clothing advances. Strapped for money to cover farming operations, the cycle repeated itself annually in a lot of cases.

It should not be surprising to learn that most sharecroppers compiled untold debt and died owing their landlords, and credit came with questionable accounting and predatory interest rates. Still, some former slaves had the wherewithal to save enough money to rent and/or buy land to farm on their own. The point here is that black men and their families could not afford to be lazy and financially illiterate. They either worked or did not eat. As hired laborers or sharecroppers, their goal was to provide for their families.

Southern Labor Unions

In the South, agriculture was king, and unions were unwelcome. So, farm workers had no collective bargaining or union representation. These conditions surely had negative implications for most black agricultural workers.

According to published sources, the Social Security Act, the National Labor Relations Act, and the Fair Labor Standards Act of the 1930s were not applicable to agricultural workers; however, most African Americans residing in the South were employed in agriculture.

Under Roosevelt's New Deal a host of federal programs were implemented to help increase employment and consumerism to fire-up the economy. In the rural South, however, federal policies had negative effects on black tenant farmers and sharecroppers.

Agricultural Adjustment Act of 1933

The Agricultural Adjustment Act (AAA) of 1933 set black tenant farmers and sharecroppers back economically. Provisions of the Act paid large plantation owners to take some of their production land out of service. Plantation owners, working with local AAA boards, defrauded black farmers out of government payments and changed some tenant and sharecroppers' status to laborers to make them ineligible for payments.

In the aftermath of fraudulent practices by large landowners, several agricultural labor unions sprung up sporadically. Most faced violent opposition from landowners and local law enforcement. In addition, union fees were prohibitive in a lot of cases, and unlike industrial workers, black agricultural laborers had personal relationships with their "business partners" or plantation owners. The fact of the matter was that most of the tenant farmers and sharecroppers had few available options to secure food and shelter for their families.

The Southern Tenant Farmers Union (STFU) was established in 1934, one year following the passage of the AAA. It was an interracial union but had all black and all white chapters. Its membership exploded in the mid-1930s to over thirty thousand across seven states. With support from other racial justice type organizations and strategic strikes, the STFU was instrumental in helping to improve deplorable living conditions and unfair employment practices that confronted poor and black agricultural workers in the Deep South.

Executive Order 8802.29

On July 25, 1941, President Franklin D. Roosevelt issued Executive Order 8802.29 which was the first anti-discrimination order issued in the U.S. Initially, the EO was somewhat restricted to the Department of Defense, but ultimately led to the creation of the Fair Employment Practice Committee. Between 1941 and 1946, the FEPC received over fourteen thousand discrimination complaints and over eighty percent were filed by blacks. Apparently, the committee had some authority as the percent of blacks employed in the defense industry increased from 3% to 8%.

Katznelson's 2005 seminal work, "When Affirmative Action Was White," provided compelling evidence of a rigged public assistance system. Data and information included in this work suggested that provisions in Franklin Roosevelt's New Deal and Harry Truman's Fair Deal in the 1930s and 1940s were implemented on a racially separate and "unequal" basis. Katznelson concluded that whether intended or unintended, unequal distribution of tax funded public assistance by race helped to perpetuate and widen gaps in educational attainment, employment opportunities, home ownership, and wealth.

Executive Order (10925) Affirmative Action

Apparently, to President John F. Kennedy, high unemployment rates among blacks in the U.S. had to be the result of centuries of a combination of individual and institutional discriminatory patterns or practices. To compensate blacks for past discriminatory hiring and promotion decisions, approximately one hundred years following the end of slavery and the Reconstruction Era, President Kennedy issued Executive Order (10925) on March 6, 1961. It was named Affirmative Action (AA) because it stipulated that entities receiving federal funds should actively seek to increase the representation of blacks and other underrepresented groups in their programs, staffing/hiring, and awarding both prime and subcontracts.

There are at least three indisputable truths regarding affirmative action in the U.S. First, it signaled the realization that institutional barriers had limited and blocked African Americans from obtaining "living-wage" jobs and professional careers. Second, affirmative action strategies were limited to the government sector. Finally, based on official statistics, AA has not led to racial parity in terms of decision-making positions and higher-wage jobs.

Acceptable Affirmative Action Models

Recently, some high-profile decision-makers revealed their astute observations of patterns or practices that limited underrepresented group members' inclusion in prestigious, high income, and career-advancing jobs. Summaries provided here is evidence of the role decision-makers can play in promoting diversity/inclusion across employment sectors. Moreover, they give readers a view of what many African Americans see every day.

In early September 2018, Supreme Court nominee Brett Kavanaugh indirectly provided an example of a pattern or practice that had limited the number of women who had been selected as clerks throughout the federal courts. Their underrepresentation among clerks decreased their chances of subsequent appointments to an appellate and/or the Supreme Court. According to Kavanaugh, he observed a dearth of women clerks and wondered why they were noticeably underrepresented. He recalled reviewing the application and screening process and found possible inherent barriers to outstanding women being included in applicant pools. He identified the following barriers: 1) tradition or norm of only securing recommendations from professors at mainly elite law schools who were overwhelmingly white men; 2) practices of overlooking women in classroom discussions and exercises that depressed their academic self-efficacy; and 3) exclusion of women from research teams that produced an array of publications. Those patterns or practices helped to create institutional hurdles for women in their quest to build competitive resumes. Should his accounts be believed?

As a decision-maker, Kavanaugh said that he intentionally sought ways to identify and recruit high performing women lawyers to clerk for him. At one time, all of his clerks were women. After his Supreme Court confirmation in early September 2018, it was revealed that for the first time in the history of the Court, he was the first Justice to have all women clerks. Imagine if Kavanaugh had had the same epiphany regarding the underrepresentation of African Americans among judicial clerks. To what extent did his being the father of two intelligent daughters influence his employment patterns or practices?

The second example involves Jon Stewart, an internationally acclaimed political satirist, who was interviewed by Charlie Rose on PBS in November 2016. He talked about unintentional patterns or practices that limited or blocked employment opportunities of women and people of color in the production of the heralded "Daily Show. According to Stewart, for a long time, he was oblivious or unaware of the racial make-up of his writers. While sitting in a staff meeting, he took a mental "power" photo. The picture revealed an all-white cast of well-compensated employees. While there is nothing inherently wrong with white men earning high salaries, there should be a concurrent realization that women and people of color could perform those jobs equally as well. Confronted with that indisputable truth, Stewart investigated the show's personnel recruitment and hiring system. He found that when a position opened, they would call known talent agencies to obtain applicants. Their pools of applicants were disproportionately white males. So, the Daily Show had to be intentional about requiring a diverse pool of qualified applicants; otherwise, if left alone, systems tend to perpetuate themselves.

During the segment, Stewart did not explicitly address the show's ratings after intentionally increasing diversity among staff; however, his continued popularity and elevation on the surface suggest that diversity did not lower meaningful standards or quality of the workforce, a common criticism of diversity initiatives.

Both associate Supreme Court Justice Brett Kavanaugh and nationally acclaimed thought leader Jon Stewart observed what they believed to be discriminatory patterns or practices in their employment systems. Both concluded that their systems unnecessarily disadvantaged people of color and women. As decision-makers, they called for "affirmative action" which led to increases in diversity and were not accused of "reverse discrimination." The overall workforce and median incomes might be more diverse if other decision-makers followed their examples.

Equal Employment Opportunity Commission (EEOC)

For nearly one hundred years following the end of the Civil War, blacks faced stiff and constant opposition across most employment sectors, except in agriculture and other labor intensive and low-waged fields. During that time period, they had no rights in terms of minimum wage, health and safety of work conditions, and due process related to employment decisions. Accounts indicate that black workers frequently were subjected to racial epithets, unfavorable work assignments, and what has come to be known as "hostile work environments." Their responses to unfair employment practices included: endure and remain employed, submit a complaint and get fired, or quit.

In 1965, the Equal Employment Opportunity Commission (EEOC), a federal agency, was established and charged with protecting the civil rights of workers by investigating claims of discriminatory infractions filed by a worker or a class of employees (e.g., blacks, women, etc.).

Unfortunately, the EEOC report card does not engender hope in employees who file discrimination charges against employers. Watchdog groups have examined EEOC annual performance reports and found that a ridiculously small number of cases were filed by the EEOC on behalf of workers:

> "...in its 2014 Performance Report, the EEOC reported that it filed only 133 'merit' suits; that is, lawsuits in which the EEOC found cause and decided to sue on behalf of an individual or group of employees. There were 88,778 charges filed with the EEOC by employees. That means that the odds of the EEOC filing suit on your behalf are about one in 1000, or 1% (133/88778=.001). So, the statistic continues to hold true for another year."[52]

Geo-Manufacturing and Race

Over the past three or so decades, the number of jobs that traditionally funded middle-class lifestyles but were largely unattainable by blacks have been on the decline. Economists and political leaders credit a host of factors for the job losses including trade agreements, federal regulations, higher corporate tax rates, advances in artificial intelligence and manufacturing technology, and cheap foreign labor.

When tracing the migration of so-called high-tech or skill jobs in the U.S. from one region to another, racial stereotypes appeared to have either directly or indirectly influenced decisions. Invariably, states involved in competitions for plants or jobs focused on educational attainment rates as a proxy for quality of the available workforce. For decades, states with relatively large poor and black populations were stereotyped as incapable of providing a labor force with the capacity to build airplanes and automobiles. Still, to lower personnel and often operating costs, some major corporations moved to the alleged "illiterate" Deep South and remain there today. African Americans are helping to build airplanes, helicopters, drones, ships, and automobiles

---

52 https://calltherightattorney.com/2015/06/23/should-i-file-with-the-eeoc-or-should-i-get-a-lawyer-best-employment-discrimination-law-reply/

in Mississippi, Alabama, South Carolina, Kentucky, Tennessee, and Georgia. Chasing even greater profits, some American corporations shifted production to other countries, primarily to decrease labor costs. Business decisions have left hundreds of thousands of former "middle/working class" individuals unemployed or underemployed. Unfortunately for many blacks, they were the last hired and thereby the first fired or laid off when production is decreased or eliminated.

Unemployment among Generation Z (18-25)

Among a lot of older blacks, hope is rested in increasing equality among the next generations. Based on results of federal laws and favorable work histories, racial gaps in unemployment among younger Americans might be expected to decrease. According to the Bureau of Labor Statistics, in 2014-15 unemployment among late teens and young adults by race and gender revealed some interesting trends. Data for the fourth quarter of 2015 suggest that total unemployment for all workers age sixteen to nineteen was 4.8%. Unemployment rates by race were as follows: white (4.1%); black (8.8%); Asian (3.8%); and Hispanics (6.2%). Also, unemployment rates among men was 5% compared to 4.7% among women.

When data were analyzed by race and gender, differences in unemployment by race and gender (female/male) were as follows: white (4%/4.3%); black (8.1%/9.5%); Asian (3.6%/4%); and Hispanic (6.7%/5.8%). Among teens and young adults, women had relatively lower unemployment rates except among Hispanics. See Table 1.

Table 1. Unemployment by Race/Gender

	Female	Male
White	4%	4.3%
Black	8.1%	9.5%

Asian	3.6%	4%
Hispanic	6.7%	5.8%

Source: Bureau of Labor Statistics.gov (2015)

Despite a myriad of undeniable barriers to their pursuit of living wage jobs, a majority of eligible blacks seek employment and go to work each day with the knowledge that their opportunities for raises, professional development, and career advancements are generally less likely than their counterparts. According to official reports, in the first quarter of 2018, black unemployment hit the lowest mark since related statistics were first publicized and tracked. Still their unemployment rate was at least two times that of their white counterparts. In addition, employment by race across different job/career sectors is seldom publicized in favor of overall measures. Upon closer inspection, it becomes clear that black unemployment and underemployment have been relatively high in sectors that paid competitive salaries and fringe benefits but were overrepresented in low-wage, labor intensive, and service jobs. A leader or executive with the service trade union reported that in 2019 there were roughly two million nursing home workers, two million home-help workers, and fifty million food service workers. Data related to the racial composition of the service workforce was not disclosed; however, based on daily observations, it appears that people of color are overrepresented.

CHAPTER 2

Income Inequality and Race

Being employed is usually a prerequisite for generating income in a capitalist system for an overwhelming majority of citizens. This chapter contains the results of an investigation of laws and/or patterns or practices that limited or blocked blacks from either earning income or receiving equal pay for comparable work.

Income inequality and racial disparities have existed since the arrival of the first African slaves in the colonies. A review of literature regarding average annual earnings in the mid-1860s revealed a plausible baseline measure for white settlers. It was reported that the average annual income among early settlers ranged from about $490.00 to $500.00. In comparison, African slaves had virtually no income and no land in most cases. It should be noted that there were black indentured servants and free Africans who did fare better in terms of income but were clearly exceptions, not the norm. As stated previously, to obtain a greater appreciation for black persistence and resiliency, Americans must examine their personal or median household incomes over time.

For the purpose of this discourse, it is assumed that paid employment opportunities for freed blacks began to become available more readily after the end of the Civil War and passage of the 13th Amendment in 1865. Granted, blacks had secured paid employment in northern states prior to the Civil War. Little is known about racial disparities in terms of weekly and annual household median incomes; however, by all accounts the gaps were off the charts. Those gaps disadvantaged blacks in terms of their capacity to buy land/property, materials and equipment, and homes/rental property, thereby thwarting their wealth accumulation that could have been transferred to their heirs.

Post-Civil War work conditions for freed slaves left a lot to be desired. Void of labor laws, employers paid former slaves whatever they wanted, and it was up to the applicant to accept or reject it. There were no safety and health protocols to protect workers from hazards, harm, and/or death. Without historical validation, it is conceivable that blacks earned only five cents ($.05) to every twenty-five cents ($.25) paid to their white counterparts in 1938.

Unionization and Income Inequality

Federal laws were passed following the Civil War to manage labor relations between interstate rail companies and their employees who joined unions. The Erdman Act of 1898 helped to increase employment opportunities and decrease pay inequities among rail workers prior to the 1900s.

Pay differentials were revealed in archived records related to labor unions. Apparently, it was common practice early on for blacks to be systematically paid less than their counterparts. Corroborating evidence of pay differentials was contained in the following excerpt:

["In 1909 white employees of the Georgia Railroad, represented by the Brotherhood of Locomotive Firemen and Enginemen, walked off their jobs, demanding that lower-paid black firemen be replaced by higher-paid whites. A Federal Board of Arbitration, appointed under the provisions of the Erdman Act of 1898, ruled two to one against the Brotherhood, stating that blacks had to be paid equal pay for equal work, thereby eliminating the financial advantage of hiring blacks."][53]

Interestingly, opposition to employing blacks was not based on their alleged inability to do the jobs. Instead, they were perceived as formidable competitors for better paying jobs and work environments. Business and industry stoked tensions between black and white laborers by paying the former less for the same work.

---

53 Erdman docket file 20, the Georgia Railroad Co. v. The Brotherhood of Locomotive Firemen and Enginemen, Records of the National Mediation Board (RG 13).

Fair Labor Standards Act (1938)

Employers were notorious for keeping hourly wages extremely low but the lowest paid were invariably blacks. According to the U.S. Department of Labor (DoL), under the Fair Labor Standards Act of 1938, there have been a series of minimum wage increases. The Act also addressed overtime pay and child labor concerns. According to data contained in a table on the DoL website, the minimum wage by selected years was as follows: a) 1938 ($.25); b) 1956 ($1.00); c) 1970 ($1.45); d) 1980 ($3.10); e) 1990 ($3.80); f) 1997 ($5.15); and g) 2009 ($7.25). [54]

The table had a column for both "farm" and "non-farming" minimum wages but farm wage cells were empty. Possibly, farm workers were somewhat exempt from the minimum wage requirement. If so, southern black agricultural workers were paid less than the federal minimum wage in a lot of cases.

A little over sixty years following Reconstruction, the federal minimum wage was less than $0.40 per hour, totaling less than fourteen hundred dollars ($1,400) annually.

National War Labor Board

In the early 1940s, the U.S. was somewhat desperate for industrial workers. To help lure or recruit more blacks, the federal government ordered an end to pay differentials by race. According to a 1943 opinion issued by Frank P. Graham of the National War Labor Board, Case No. 771 (2898-CS-D), America desperately needed blacks to maintain its wartime manufacturing output. Graham went so far as to state that the country needed blacks to win the war. To guard against work slowdowns or strikes by black workers, pay differentials by race had to be eliminated.

1963 Equal Pay Act

---

54 https://www.dol.gov/whd/minwage/chart.htm

While black workers were deemed essential in terms of gross domestic production and the war efforts, it was no secret that African Americans were systematically denied equal pay. That discriminatory practice, however, was not publicly debated or directly addressed by the federal government.

President John F. Kennedy, in the wake of his Affirmative Action executive order, signed into law the Equal Pay Act of 1963. Curiously, the Act solely addressed unequal pay between men and women. Surely, an abundance of evidence revealed mind-boggling pay differentials between blacks and non-blacks during the same time period.

Median Weekly Income and Race

Today, investigating pay inequities calls for examination of official wage or income data. With the passage of time, racial disparities in median income should have dissipated. The youngest segment of the workforce is expected to contain smaller racial disparities. However, a casual review of the Bureau of Labor Statistics data for the fourth quarter of 2015 regarding median weekly income for workers sixteen to nineteen revealed significant differences by race and sex. The total number of workers in the target age range was 109,000 and the median weekly income was $825.00. There were 48K females with a median weekly income of $729.00 compared to 61K men with incomes of $907.00. Even among young workers, median income disparities existed between females and their male counterparts. The total number of workers by race and median income was as follows: whites (86.1K/$847); blacks (13.7K/$643); Asian (6.7K/$1,091); and Hispanics (18.3K/$624). Median weekly income varied by race, with Asians outpacing all other groups. Blacks and Hispanics earned the lowest weekly median incomes. There was a four-hundred-dollar difference in the median income between Asians and both blacks and Hispanics and roughly a two-hundred-dollar difference between the latter and whites. Despite lower earnings, young people of color appeared willing and committed to working.

Traditionally, males have been socialized and expected to be the primary wage-earner in a marriage or household. Their inability to do so for whatever reasons often results in stress and adoption of different modes of adaptation. Data were gleaned and analyzed to see if there were untraditional earning patterns between young men and women. Median weekly income by race and gender was identified as follows (i.e., female vs male): whites ($745 v $931); blacks ($621 v $674); Asian ($943 v $1,178); and Hispanics ($570 v $679). Income inequality was highest among Asians, followed by whites, Hispanics, and blacks. It should be noted that median weekly income for black females and black males was almost identical. This phenomenon in the black community undoubtedly affects gender role expectations. See Table 2.

Table 2: Median Weekly Income by Race/Gender

Race	Female	Male
White	$745	$931
Black	$621	$674
Asian	$943	$1,178
Hispanic	$570	$679

Source: Bureau of Labor Statistics.gov (2015)

Income Inequality Trends

Researchers have been at a loss in explaining the persistent black versus white wage disparities in the U.S. On September 5, 2017, the Federal Reserve Bank of San Francisco released the results of a study designed to help measure the relative effects of several factors to account for black-white wage differentials. The structural regression model included type of job sector, educational attainment, age, state, and other potential contributors. Between 1979 and 2016, researchers found that the black-white wage gap increased significantly.

Among men, the gap in income between blacks and whites has been steadily increasing. In 1980, black men earned about 80 % of their white counterparts' hourly wage (i.e., $15 v $19). The report stated that by 2016, black men were only earning about seventy percent 70% of what their counterparts were paid. The gap among women was even more drastic. In the early 1980s, black women earned an average of ninety-five (95%) of what white women earned, but by 2016 the wage gap had widened, and black women were paid only eighty-two (82%) of the average income of their white counterparts.

To account for some variance in wages, the researchers pointed to differences in participation in job sectors (e.g., drilling/mining vs. retail), educational attainment, age, and state of residence. Still, much of the gaps in wages could not be explained by forces that can be measured by official data. Invariably, economic gaps cannot be completely explained away by educational attainment and job sectors. The point here is that researchers face challenges when trying to empirically measure the effects of race and discriminatory patterns or practices on income inequality. Current measures or indicators are not convincingly amenable to the rigor of scientific research. In plain talk, it is widely believed that prejudicial attitudes and racial stereotypes exist, and some people in decision-making positions discriminate, but that belief is almost impossible to empirically verify beyond a shadow of a doubt.

Education and Income

Regardless of employment sector, a relatively small number of decision-makers decide what each of their employees will earn in a year. For decades, African Americans have been told that racial disparities in income and wealth accumulation were primarily a result of their relatively lower academic attainment. However, evidence revealed recently indicated that even blacks with comparable education face discriminatory practices in an array of life-changing situations. In 2016, Tavis Smiley stunned many Americans when he stated that educational attainment in the U.S. is not a "racial equalizer" nor does it level the "playing fields" on which blacks compete for job/careers, competitive interest rates, start-up loans for small businesses, and home mortgages. In other words, with all things being equal, race or being black is a stronger predictor of a person's annual income, zip code, school district, and overall quality of life than educational attainment or anything else.

In a fair and just society, educational attainment should eliminate wage gaps, controlling for tenure and experience which are usually advantages for whites due to past discriminatory practices in hiring and promotions. Persons with comparable education and experience should receive similar compensation packages in most cases. Moreover, one would assume that as educational attainment increases, pay inequities would decrease.

Results of a September 5, 2017 report by the San Francisco Federal Reserve Bank were both shocking and mind-boggling. According to the report, African Americans possessing college degrees earn less equitable compensation than those having high school diplomas. Below is a summary of the full report:

> "Among men, the black-white earnings gap is now slightly higher for those with a college degree or more than it is for high school graduates. This marks a change from earlier in the sample, when male high school graduates fared worse than male college graduates. For women, the gaps in earnings remain larger for high school graduates than for college graduates, but they have been growing for both levels of educational attainment."[55]

Realizing that earning good grades and obtaining college degrees do not level the playing field generates strain/stress among some African Americans. But, from most accounts, a majority appear to be "conformers" who go to work knowing that they are not being compensated fairly. Many remain on jobs

---

55 Federal Reserve Bank-San Francisco FRBSF, September 5, 2017

until retirement or death with that fact in mind. Their perseverance and resiliency are nothing short of amazing.

Working Poor

Intuitively, one would think that people who work forty or more hours per week would earn enough to cover reasonable household expenditures with a little discretionary reserve; among many blacks, merely being employed does not necessarily increase one's access to the American Dream. C-Span's Book TV aired an interview December 30, 2017 during which Kathryn Edin discussed her book entitled "$2 a Day." In the book, she described the plight of a growing population of what she called "the working poor." According to the researcher, these workers work only to retain their "poor" status. The most striking revelation was that there are people across America who survive on approximately $2 in cash per day which is less than $800 in cash per year. It should be noted that most of the subjects also received non-cash public assistance. A longitudinal research design was employed to track participants in different geographies over time.

Edin observed that a common narrative regarding the poor is that they are responsible themselves for their low socioeconomic position, and all they need to do is get a job. That philosophy is etched in public policy in that statutes have been passed requiring some of the poor to work in order to receive public assistance.

To date, little is known about the characteristics of the working poor except for those who must report their employment status in order to receive public assistance. Most of them happen to be primarily women, people of color, and single heads of households. Debates surround possible unanticipated consequences associated with "forced" labor rules related to receiving or maintaining public assistance. When both employers and employees know that "employment status" is the key to receiving public assistance (e.g., food, shelter, and healthcare), there is a grave imbalance of power. The working poor's employment is generally characterized by the following attributes: minimum number of hours per week; minimum wage; little to no overtime pay, no fringe benefits, erratic schedules, and absence of mutual respect.

Non-participant observations and anecdotal accounts suggest that a lot of black men work under similar conditions but are underreported. Their plight is what many Black Boys and Young Men of Color (BYMOC) see every day, men going to work but earning barely enough to feed and clothe themselves. Critics will point to their lack of education and job skills, while ignoring the fact that their employers remain profitable because of low wages and no benefit expenses. Some employers also cut overhead by paying in cash, thus alleviating payroll preparation costs and their payroll tax liabilities while at the same time limiting their workers' options related to filing for unemployment, federal and state income tax returns, and their contributions to social security. The advent of COVID-19 has shed light on the productivity and compensation related to what has been defined as the "gig economy." In black communities, those jobs have been called "hustles."

Median Household Income and Race

The U.S. census reported that the 2015 median household income was a little more than $57,000. To break this down further, the estimated 2015 median household income by race/ethnicity was as follows: Asian ($81,000); white ($61,000); Hawaiian and Pacific Islander ($57,000); Hispanics/Latino (($47,000); Native Americans and Alaskans ($40,000); and blacks ($37,000). Recall that the median represents the dollar amount at which half of the group earns more or less than that amount in terms of annual household income.

Historically, median income for blacks is a relatively new concept. Prior to the Civil War, black median household income on average, particularly in the South, was literally at or close to zero dollars, only a little more than one hundred and fifty years ago.

CHAPTER 3

Wealth and Race

This chapter contains results of an investigation into laws and practices that have and continue to limit or block African Americans' wealth accumulation and inheritance. Many Americans have benefitted from wealth transfers that were directly or indirectly generated by institutionalized racism. To corroborate the existence of a rigged system related to wealth accumulation, evidence must be revealed that shows how laws and social norms impeded or blocked blacks from acquiring land, homes, livestock, and businesses.

Headright System (Land Acquisition)

Governing bodies in the colonies developed marketing and recruiting strategies to satisfy labor force demands. The Virginia Company, LLC, which owned and operated the Jamestown settlement, initially deployed workers to look for gold and silver, but there was no profit realized. To keep from going belly-up, the investors turned to tobacco as a cash crop which was a labor-intensive enterprise. In 1618, to attract and recruit new immigrant labor, land was used as the primary incentive. Here is how it worked. First, existing settlers were given two headrights (100 acres). Second, each new settler or immigrant was given one headright (50 acres). It was advantageous for whole families to relocate at fifty acres per eligible member. Finally, folks with money could pay the passage of an immigrant and receive five to seven years of labor and a headright for each eligible person including some slaves. [56] [57]

---

56 https://www.u-s-history.com/pages/h1153.html

57 https://study.com/academy/lesson/headright-system-definition-lesson-quiz.html

The headright system was one of the first examples of blacks being systematically excluded from competition of land ownership in the U.S., and it created huge racial disparities in terms of land ownership that persist today. European immigrants received vast tracts of land and underground mineral rights that have been passed down from one generation to the next.

In addition, there were other restrictions placed on people of African descent in the colonies.

The Virginia general assembly made it illegal for slaves to own horses, cattle, and pigs in about 1692.[58] This act not only stunted slaves' accumulation of assets, but it also restricted their consumption of lean meats and influenced dietary practices which might have inadvertently affected their health.

African slaves and their descendants were often barred from accepting and owning assets given to them by sympathetic whites. Even "free" blacks or "emancipated" blacks faced an array of challenges in the courts. Their "free" status was often challenged in courts related to wills and the transfer of familial wealth. Interestingly, many of the cases involved widows of plantation owners who freed and, in some instances, deeded land or other assets to former slaves. That practice was frequently opposed by heir-apparent or her children. The latter fought to keep land and slaves to work the land.

An indisputable truth is that land is not a manufactural product or asset. There is an infinite number of acres that can be purchased and owned. Imagine how many acres blacks could have owned and transferred to their heirs if they had been eligible for headrights.

Johnson v McIntosh

Prior to signing the U.S. Constitution, European settlers competed with one another to purchase or take Indian lands. To avoid conflicts between different ethnic settlements over discovery rules, a federal remedy had to be

58 https://www.history.org/history/teaching/slavelaw.cfm

forged. In 1823, the U.S. Supreme Court ruled in Johnson v McIntosh that it was constitutional for the federal government to colonize and sell tribal lands. Chief Justice John Marshall authored the Court's decision. The basic premise of the ruling was that the precedent for colonial powers to claim land belonging to foreign sovereign nations was essentially settled law. Native American land could be either purchased or taken by the federal government. Titles and deeds to lands obtained from Indian tribes prior to the end of the Revolutionary War were not recognized by the U.S. government. Unlike the original Roman Catholic doctrine of discovery, religion was not implicitly or explicitly mentioned in the Johnson v McIntosh decision. The ruling, however, did not give blacks rights to purchase land from the federal government.

According to sources, Johnson v. McIntosh was a landmark case. It is often the first case that law school students review related to property or real estate. The key take- away is that titles or deeds issued by government entities take precedent over those issued by tribes or private entities.

Homestead Acts

Nearly forty years following the Johnson v. McIntosh ruling, the federal government took the lead in making land available to eligible citizens. President Abraham Lincoln, in an effort to accelerate westward settlements, signed into law the Homestead Act of 1862. The Act literally gave primarily non-blacks one hundred and sixty (160) acres of land to farm or develop in other ways. To receive clear titles to the property, homesteaders were required to reside on the land for a minimum of five (5) years. After about ten percent or two hundred and seventy million acres of public lands had been claimed, the law was repealed in 1976.

Southern Homestead Act of 1866

In the old Confederacy, Reconstruction was a source of hope among newly freed slaves in terms of potential acquisitions of farmlands. During President Andrew Johnson's administration with a Republican-dominated Congress, the Southern Homestead Act of 1866 was signed into law. It has been estimated that the legislation put up approximately 46M acres in lots of eighty (80) and later one hundred and sixty (160) for sale to both blacks and loyal whites in Alabama, Arkansas, Florida, Louisiana, and Mississippi. Of course, southern lawmakers and decision-makers opposed the Act and engaged in practices to delay and deny blacks access to the lands. Prior to the Act being repealed ten years later in 1876, the vast majority of the lands was purchased by non-blacks. By some estimates, of the more than six thousand applications submitted by blacks, only about one thousand were approved.

Challenges to Black Landownership

Surprisingly and counterintuitively, black land ownership peaked during the half century or so following the end of the Civil War. Since that time, their percent of land owned in the U.S. has been on a steady decline. Several factors were identified that can help explain the gradual erosion of black landownership.

In about 1920, blacks owned over 925,000 farms representing or accounting for about 14% of all farms in the U.S. However, by 1975, it was estimated that only about 45,000 black farms remained.

Of the more than one billion acres of family owned land in the U.S. today, blacks own about one million acres that can be transferred to heirs. In essence, blacks account for only one percent of landowners and about two percent of farmers.

Abandoned Lands and Tax Forfeitures

Between 1916 and 1970, an estimate of more than 6M blacks migrated from the South leaving behind acres of land. The Klan, tax assessors, business owners, and large farmers employed tax codes and terrorist methods to acquire land from blacks. First, accounts indicate that many left land and other assets out of fear due to cross-burnings, house and church arsons, rapes, and lynching. Land abandoned by fleeing blacks or murdered landowners was subsequently deemed abandoned and/or acquired through payment of delinquent property taxes.

Real estate laws in the Deep South have also contributed to decreases in black land ownership. Below the Mason Dixon Line, heir land or real estate is equally owned by all living heirs, often exceeding seventy-five to one hundred members and ranging in age from literally three months to ninety-five. In most cases, a single family member is not assigned as the primary owner and executor, meaning that all matters must be approved by "all" of the heirs in writing. Today, corporations and developers aggressively employ "family-busting" tactics to acquire black owned land. They purchase selected family members' portions of heir-property, thereby becoming heirs themselves. Then, they can file a petition in the courts to force an auction of the property that is often not approved by other heirs. Partition sales have been the prime method of acquiring formerly black owned real estate:

> "A 2001 report from the US Agricultural Census estimated that about 80 percent of black-owned farmland had disappeared in the South since 1969. Approximately half of that land was lost through partition sales."[59]

Not having a designated principal owner of heir-property limits or makes the property ineligible for most government assistance. Because there is no "clear title" to the property, it is ineligible for federal and state financial assistance

59 https://www.thenation.com/article/african-americans-have-lost-acres/

even after natural disasters. Imagine the hardships experienced by a lot of black landowners in the wake of hurricanes, tornadoes, and massive floods. They had to cover most costs to replace family homes, barns, livestock, and farm equipment. The situation was summarized as follows:

["Without a clear title, heirs'-property owners are limited in what they can do with their land. They cannot get mortgages or do extensive repairs on their homes, as a consequence, some live in trailers. They aren't eligible to apply for state or federal housing aid (such as funds provided by the Federal Emergency Management Agency) or for nearly any of the programs administered by the Department of Agriculture, including the crucial loans and conservation funding that keep many rural landowners afloat."] [60]

During the last century, rural gentrification has slowly helped to decrease black land ownership. Gentrification involving new commercial and retail developments drive up property values and of course assessed property taxes. The latter can force some poor property owners into selling their land instead of putting all of their income and savings into paying taxes.

The Sea Islands in South Carolina were once predominantly black owned and deemed low in value. But developers gradually started eyeing and purchasing or acquiring those lands. Hilton Head Island, an upscale resort area in South Carolina, was once predominantly owned by African Americans. As hotels, homes, and golf courses were built, property taxes skyrocketed forcing many black landowners to either sell or abandon their property.

Black Farmers' Lawsuit

The United States Department of Agriculture (USDA) was established to design laws and regulations to promote and strengthen agricultural-based enterprises or businesses. It is managed by the Secretary of Agriculture who is nominated by the president and confirmed by the U.S. Senate.

---

60 https://www.thenation.com/article/african-americans-have-lost-acres/

After years of allegations of racial discrimination in awarding financial assistance to black farmers, a preponderance of evidence was eventually revealed, but the damage had been done. For decades, black farmers' requests for subsidies, loans, and financing for equipment and other farming operations had been systematically delayed and/or denied causing a lot of them to lose their land and farming enterprises.

The public saga of black farmers was brought to light successfully by two plaintiffs, Timothy Pigford and Cecil Brewington both of North Carolina. Their persistence and resiliency led to a 1998 class action lawsuit against the USDA on behalf of thousands of black farmers. The plaintiffs accused the agency of blatant discriminatory patterns or practices between 1981 and 1996. The case was heard and adjudicated by U.S. District Judge Paul Friedman. In most corners, the suit is commonly referred to as Pigford vs Glickman or the Black Farmers' Lawsuit. In April of 1999, the USDA agreed to a consent decree and created two options for black farmers to be made "whole" or compensated for losses. Option A awarded a fifty-thousand-dollar payout, loan forgiveness, and priority for future loans. Option B required more corroborating evidence of past discrimination that was often unattainable, but successful plaintiffs received significantly larger awards, loan forgiveness, and other punitive damages. According to a story found in Black Enterprise Magazine, the plaintiffs were awarded a total of $1.5 billion. [61]

There were upwards of eighteen thousand claims approved and approximately five thousand were estate claims.

The Pigford vs Glickman case was adjudicated based on a preponderance of evidence, meaning that it was more likely than not that the USDA loan denials and late posting of available funds were practices that adversely impacted black farmers as a group. Whether it was a rigged system or individual decision-makers at fault, black losses were enormous and stripped families of tangible assets, collateral, and transferable wealth.

---

61 https://www.blackenterprise.com/black-farmers-to-receive-payouts-in-1-2-billion-from-federal-lawsuit-settlement/

Older black farmers are facing another related challenge. USDA discriminatory practices limited or blocked their accumulation of savings or greater returns on their investments to cover retirement and/or elder care expenses. Published sources indicate that the average farmer is about fifty-five, and most are resident farmers. If they require nursing home accommodations at some point, those corporations can place liens on the farms to ensure payment.

CHAPTER 4

Small Businesses, Entrepreneurship and Race

A portion of familial wealth is often associated with equity or shares of businesses that create and/or sell products and services. Some family-owned enterprises have operated for centuries.

This chapter discloses the results of an investigation into laws and Jim Crow norms that limited or blocked blacks from starting small businesses, especially those that would compete with their white counterparts. Successful black businesses, like all businesses, had to provide products and/or services that were in demand. In addition, they often needed start-up loans, retail or office space near critical masses of patrons who had the wherewithal to make regular purchases, and access to government and private sector contracts.

As stated earlier, West African slaves who were imported to the colonies brought valuable skills that could have been the source of revenue. They were artisans, textile workers, builders, and farmers.

Evidence indicated that upon their arrival in the colonies, slaves employed principles of Bandura's Social Cognitive Theory (SCT) of learning new behaviors as they began observing different roles and occupations extant in both the North and southern areas. Essentially, some slaves participated in unpaid and unintended apprenticeships in education, medicine, veterinary science, law, mechanics, and manufacturing. The skills and knowledge they acquired allowed plantation and other business owners to live leisurely while generating enormous profits.

Unfortunately, prior to the Civil War and passage of constitutional amendments awarding blacks citizenship, their business aspirations were subject to the approval of decision-makers. They were restricted in terms of the types of businesses that they could own and where they could be located. In many cases, social norms placed restrictions on who could publicly patronize their businesses. Moreover, non-blacks could request black owned products and services at sale prices or no cost. Prior to the ratification of the 14th Amendment, black business owners had virtually no legal recourse when their products/ services were damaged or taken by force or threats of violence.

Post-Civil War conditions facilitated the need for black professionals to serve freed slaves. Black entrepreneurship could have been an unanticipated outcome of efforts to perpetuate racial segregation. Among the first black professional class were funeral directors, educators, healthcare providers, and lawyers. And of course, blacks operated food service enterprises, beauty salons, shoeshine parlors, hotels, and night clubs.

Black Inventors and Patents

Creators of intellectual property have been honored and rewarded handsomely in the U.S. Individuals who either invent new or substantively enhance existing products apply for patents to protect others from copying their designs and specification so they can either create a production line and/or license the invention to one or more manufacturers. Motivated by a need for more efficient means of completing tasks or providing services, several black inventors have been recognized over the years, especially during Black History month. Their names and inventions are highlighted on numerous websites. [62]

However, a list of some the more notable black inventors often includes Frederick McKinley James, George Washington Carver, Elijah McCoy, Benjamin Banneker, Madam C. J. Walker, Otis Boykin, Granville Woods,

---

62 http://www.black-inventor.com/

Lewis Howard Latimer, and Garret Morgan. Their inventions were dated between the late 1700s and early twentieth century.

Again, blacks faced stern opposition in business and industrial sectors. To file for patent protection, they had to submit all their intellectual property or trade secrets to decision-makers who did not look like them. If they tried to mass produce their inventions, they faced credit and start-up funding barriers. License agreements would only have had to be nominally enforced because black inventors had no real standing in the courts. In sum, black inventors have not earned millions from their innovations which helped bolster the U.S.' exceptionalism and global economic competitiveness.

Small Business Administration and Race

By the end of WWI and the start of WWII, black owned businesses were paying taxes and some even had several employees. But decision-makers and Jim Crow norms limited or blocked them from breaking into larger markets and earning government contracts.

The federal government involvement in assisting small businesses began under President Franklin D. Roosevelt in 1942 when contracts were awarded to firms to support the war effort. In 1953, President Dwight Eisenhower established the Small Business Administration (SBA) that was charged with ensuring that small businesses got a portion of federal contracts and purchases of surplus government property.

During President Dwight D. Eisenhower's administration, the Investment Company Act created the Small Business Investment Company (SBIC). It was coupled with the passage of the Small Business Investment Act of 1958. SBICs were private venture capital organizations commissioned by the government to invest in start-up companies that showed promise of flourishing. They invested both private funds and low interest government funds to stimulate small business development in local areas. SBICs traditionally were associated with venture capitalists, banks, and insurance companies. Because of eligibility thresholds, poor people with little or no collateral were excluded from receiving SBA assistance.

1964 Equal Opportunity Loan (EOL) Program

Supported by President Lyndon B. Johnson, the 1964 Equal Opportunity Loan (EOL) Program was implemented to stimulate small business development among lower income segments of the population. It relaxed some of the credit history and collateral requirements. [63]

To address past discriminatory practices, the Minority Small Business and Capital Ownership Development Program or 8(a) Program was implemented to help increase the number of successful minority-owned businesses. [64]

During President Richard Nixon's administration, in 1972 regulations were implemented to specifically assist socially and poor groups including blacks, Latino, Native Americans, and Alaskans/Pacific Islanders. All federal agencies participate in the SBA program and the target protected groups are now defined as follows: small businesses, small businesses owned by women, small disadvantaged businesses, service-disabled veteran-owned small businesses, and small businesses located in Historically Underutilized Business Zones. [65]

The program has two primary initiatives intended to address past discriminatory practices. First, set asides were designed to give minority owned businesses start-up contracts, or a "foot in the door," to prove their competencies. Second, sole-source contracts have been issued to a single 8(a) firm in a non-competitive program for specific products and/or services.

The SBA defines eligible 8(a) firms as being at least fifty-one percent (51%) owned and managed by a socially disadvantaged group member. In addition, the member must be a U.S. citizen with "good" character, have a net worth

---

63 https://www.sba.gov/about-sba/what-we-do/history

64 https://www.everycrsreport.com/reports/R44844.html

65 https://www.sba.gov/about-sba/sba-newsroom/press-releases-media-advisories/federal-government-achieves-small-business-contracting-goal-sixth-consecutive-year-record-breaking

less than $250,000, excluding equity in their primary residence, and is associated with the firm. With an expected increase in business, the net worth ceiling goes up to $750,000. Firms must have at least two years of operating experience prior to becoming 8(a) certified.

According to a recent report, women and minority owned businesses with 8(a) certifications were awarded billions in government contracts. In FY2017, over 3,400 certified 8(a) firms received over $27.1B with set-asides and sole source contracts totaling $8.0B and $8.4B, respectively. [66] Those dollar totals, though impressive, must be compared to the more than $500B in unclassified contracts awarded in the same fiscal year. When viewed from that perspective, 8(a) firms received less than five percent (5%) of the total contractual expenditures of the entirety of the U.S. government.

Congress has supported 8(a) programs, but the Supreme Court's rulings have been mixed. The Court has upheld federal government procurement programs but have ruled against similar state and local 8(a) initiatives. In a recent decision, the high court approved government set-asides only for verifiable and documented past discriminatory practices that are almost impossible to prove beyond a shadow of a doubt or with a preponderance of evidence. Recall that the program was established because minority and women owned companies were severely underrepresented among recipients of government contracts.

Tens of thousands of African Americans with business aspirations have overcome a myriad of challenges to compete domestically and globally. Some amazing success stories, though not covered here, reflect extraordinary resolve. In 2016, *Black Enterprise Magazine* listed its top one hundred (100) black owned companies in the U.S. Their analysis included total amount of revenue generated from products and/or services and the number of employees. At least one CEO, John A. James, founder and CEO of James Group International, had to go all the way to the U.S. Supreme Court to be allowed to start and grow his interstate transportation and logistics company. Despite

66 https://www.everycrsreport.com/reports/R44844.html

his astonishing grit, persistence, and resiliency, his story is unfortunately the norm instead of an outlier. Business schools should include successful black businesses as case studies in classes and be intentional and creative in efforts to engage those chief executive officers (CEOs) to obtain first-hand accounts and "best practices."

Controlling for quality of products/services, prices, and responsiveness, black businesses face patterns or practices that place them at a disadvantage in a lot of cases. Even with government assistance in terms of promoting minority-owned vendors, most institutions and corporations have long established social networks that bleed over into their contractual relationships. Business-to-business relationships have endured for centuries. Many of those relationships were started and flourished during racial segregation and the Jim Crow era. Those business relationships generally exclude out-group members who are intentionally or unintentionally excluded from country club meetings, golf outings, poker games, church groups, alumni networks, and dinner parties. The situation described here is an example of a rigged system that is perpetuated by decision-makers like those rebuffed by Justice Kavanaugh and satirist John Stewart. Recall that they observed disparities in their organizations or institutions, and being decision-makers, they took intentional and corrective actions.

Results of data analyzed from a 2014 U.S. census survey of businesses revealed that minorities own two percent (2%) of all registered businesses, and among the more than five million with one or more paid employees, they own less than one million. By race/ethnicity, the report showed that African Americans accounted for about one hundred and nine thousand seemingly profitable companies, and Asians and Hispanics accounted for roughly 500K and 300K, respectively. [67]

Furthermore, a recent study conducted by the Aspen Institute of small business owners in the U.S. found that Asians and whites have about one-third

---

67 https://www.inc.com/helena-ball/new-entrepreneurship-us-census-survey-black-owned-businesses-increased-lag-remains.html

of their wealth in business assets compared to Hispanics and blacks at fifteen and eight percent, respectively. [68] In addition, survey results showed that black businesses tend to be smaller, and the percent of white, Hispanic, and black businesses that reported profits in 2014 was 63%, 58%, and 45%, respectively.

Historically, black-owned businesses were concentrated in service and retail, but in the last decade or so there has been an uptick in construction and business services sectors.

Black business owners in the U.S. have faced unique challenges. Unlike a lot of their counterparts, to realize their dreams of owning businesses, they have not been aided by inheritance, life insurance payouts, familial assets, and social networks to secure needed upfront capital. Even successful black entrepreneurs often are saddled with greater collateral demands and higher interest rates. Still, nearly fifty percent reported making a profit in a recent DoJ survey.[69]

---

68 https://www.aspeninstitute.org/blog-posts/racial-gap-business-ownership-explained-four-charts/.

69 https://www.justice.gov/crt/equal-credit-opportunity-act-3

CHAPTER 5

Financial Institutions and Race

Upon settlers' off-boarding into the new world, individuals and eventually corporations provided both personal and business loans to those not having the money to make desired purchases and investments. During colonial times, loans were consummated with a verbal covenant and a handshake. Loans were given based on mutual respect, trust, and hope for a "collective" good. To test the validity of the rigged system theory, this chapter contains evidence regarding laws and patterns and practices among financial institutions that limited or blocked African slaves and their descendants from acquiring assets.

Financial institutions have played critical roles in helping citizens achieve aspects of the American dream. Specifically, through loans and investments, financial institutions helped launch and boost U.S. companies into global competitors. These institutions were, and still are, the primary source of money that has helped Americans finance an array of major purchases including real estate, homes, businesses, automobiles, and costs of attending college.

To be clear, from 1619 to the late 1860s, especially in the South, most blacks could only dream about being able to apply for or receive bank loans.

Following the War of Independence, U.S. businesses and agricultural enterprises depended on financial institutions for startup and gap funding. Regional economies demanded different types of credit or capital. Likewise, the type or source of collateral also varied by region, especially between the North and South. Industries have traditionally acquired credit based on signed contracts or purchase orders. On the other hand, farming was, and remains, akin to a crapshoot or gambling. A host of unforeseen and uncontrollable factors can either lower yields or destroy crops. Traditionally, plantation owners borrowed money to purchase equipment and seeds, secure payroll, and cover other operating costs prior to planting seasons with the intention of repaying the debt and accruing a net profit after the harvest. Credit or loans were often secured from banks in New York, Boston, and London, England. As collateral, plantation owners frequently put up their "assets" in the form of land and slaves. When they defaulted on their loans, banks and some foreign investors became owners of both the land and slaves.[70]

Some of the oldest and wealthiest financial institutions and families in the U.S. can trace their riches back to growing, processing, and selling hundreds of thousands of bales of cotton. Yet, they seldom credit any of their profits or wealth to African slaves and their descendants.

Post-Civil War Financial Transactions

Now imagine the challenges faced by blacks between the end of the Civil War and the 1950s as they planned to apply for bank loans. For sure, they had to identify the right banker; create a positive first impression; present a cogent request or application; offer up something as collateral; and secure a trusted guarantor or co-signer. Does that scenario seem familiar?

Prior to the last two to three decades, financial institutions had unbridled discretion in approving or denying loans. Loan decisions were subjective and made by a relatively small group, primarily males who possessed indisputable prejudices and opportunities to allow their attitudes to influence their actions. It is reasonable to assume that bank officials could have been correctly profiled as mostly fair, conditionally fair, or mostly unfair.

For years in black communities people have heard "you got to have money to borrow money." Also, numerous accounts indicated that financial institutions were far more willing to finance quickly depreciating automobiles for

70 https://economics.yale.edu/sites/default/files/banks_and_slavery_yale.pdf

blacks than home mortgages or other real estate that often appreciate over time. There could be race-neutral justification for those alleged patterns or practices, but on the surface, it seems counterintuitive in terms of risk aversion for the banks. The point here is that during a period in which blacks were trying to assimilate and become capitalists, financial institutions were "free" to deny them loans without cause, demand exorbitant collateral, and charge predatory interest rates.

Consumer Credit Protection Act

The federal government regulates financial institutions through related laws. However, historically, banking practices related to extending credit and making loans did not bode well for blacks. According to the Federal Reserve, a series of laws, with a majority being passed in the wake of the 1964 Civil Rights Act, has been passed to protect consumers and to expand the customer base of lending institutions. A couple of these laws are summarized below.

In 1974, the Equal Credit Opportunity Act (ECOA) was passed and aimed to eliminate discrimination related to awarding credit. The Act specifically made it illegal for credit to be denied solely based on marital status, race, sex, age, religion, country of origin, and receipt of public assistance.

Prior to the ECOA, financial institutions had unlimited discretion in terms of the information applicants had to provide and the criteria for credit approval. Because of this, credit application requirements were particularly challenging for African Americans. In the wake of the ECOA, applicants seeking credit were provided expanded rights including the following: 1) Creditors could grant loans to qualified individuals without requiring a spouse to be a co-applicant; 2) creditors were required to inform unsuccessful applicants in writing of the reasons credit was denied; 3) married individuals were allowed to have credit histories on jointly held accounts maintained in the names of both spouses; and 4) prospective borrowers had a right to copies of real estate appraisals prior to purchases.

Community Reinvestment Act (CRA)

During and in the wake of the 1960s Civil Rights movement, black leaders in urban centers lobbied the federal government to force financial institutions to end discriminatory lending practices. Specifically, they urged financial institutions to approve more home mortgages and startup capital for businesses at competitive interest rates. In terms of home mortgages, black leaders wanted relief from a system called "redlining," the practice of drawing a red line around areas in which blacks were routinely denied government-backed home loans. The practice facilitated the emergence of blighted and racially segregated residential areas. Moreover, it thwarted black home ownership rates, collateral or lines of credit, and wealth accumulation.

The federal government in the mid-1970s felt compelled to encourage financial institutions to increase their lending, investments, and services in low to moderate income (LMI) neighborhoods within their service area. Legislation was drafted and passed that created the Community Reinvestment Act (CRA). Using local ward maps and/or congressional districts overlaid with relevant quality of life indicators, financial institutions can readily identify target areas and mobilize efforts to develop relationships with residents. Recent reviews of CRAs suggest that they have not been fully embraced and intentionally utilized by financial institutions.

Credit Scores and Race

Financial institutions are in business to make money and they do so primarily by approving loans with expectations of being repaid with interest. Unfortunately, but understandably, the latter is a function of prospective borrowers' incomes and credit histories. Just those two factors alone place the poor and people of color at a severe disadvantage regarding large purchases or investments, thus causing additional stress and strain. Data reviewed here showed that even controlling for years of education and relevant experience, blacks earn significantly less than most whites, while possessing similar capitalist aspirations.

A term that has tormented millions of Americans is their "FICO" score. History and purpose of the FICO are relatively short. Some accounts credit the Fair-Isaac Corporation for launching the first credit risk scores in 1981; this tool has become the umbrella or brand for a host of similar rating schemes. People who have applied for credit quickly find out the importance of their FICO scores which can range from a low of 300 to the maximum of 850. Combined with income inequality, among a lot of blacks, a critical number is 630 because it represents the lowest credit score for which traditional credit is extended. It has been reported that nearly fifty percent of blacks have credit scores of 620 or less and their credit comes with devastatingly high interest rates. In the general population, about seventy percent have credit scores that range from 650 to 850. The naked truth is that credit scores impact every aspect of our lives. They influence the cost of credit, employment decisions, business investments, insurance eligibility and cost, apartment rentals, home mortgage rates, contracts for utilities, and unexpected emergencies (e.g., auto repairs).

Evidence of racial disparities related to credit scores was found in a study conducted in sixty (60) economically diverse cities across the U.S. Some of the relevant findings are provided below:

- Thirty-eight of the 60 cities have differences in median credit scores of 100 points or more between predominantly white and nonwhite areas. Nationally, the difference in median credit scores is nearly 80 points (697 versus 621, respectively), which, for a conventional mortgage, can cost families an additional $100 or more a month and thousands of dollars over the life of the loan.
- Predominantly nonwhite areas in more than 50 of the 60 cities have below-prime median credit scores (660 or lower), and most of these are subprime (600 or lower).

- Conversely, predominantly white areas in only 4 of the 60 cities have below-prime median credit scores."[71]

Loan Origination Experiments

For decades, researchers have generated circumstantial evidence of discriminatory patterns or practices inherent in lending institutions. In 2016 an investigative journalist presented results of a related study entitled "Discrimination in Mortgage Lending: Evidence from a Correspondence Experience." The paper was delivered at the Federal Reserve Bank of Cleveland Policy Summit). According to the journalist, the investigation uncovered evidence that corroborated claims of racial discrimination related to loan approvals.

Repeatedly, experiments have been conducted to help determine the effects of race on decision-makers' approval or disapproval of consumer credit. The most frequent design involved scripts that engaged black and white actors in negotiation or interviews with bank loan officers. To create a level playing field, the actors were identical in terms of educational attainment, work histories, net worth, age, and income. In most experiments, black applicants were either denied credit more often or were approved but charged higher interest rates, thereby automatically decreasing their purchasing power and potential wealth accumulation.

Credit and Consumer Debt

Studies have been conducted to determine the percent of household monthly incomes that go to pay creditors by race. Results of a recent survey found that whites dedicated forty-seven percent of their income to creditors each month compared to a whopping 53% among blacks. Furthermore, a survey of over 7,500 respondents showed that nearly thirty percent (30%) carried consumer debt associated with credit cards.[72] The percent of white, Hispanic, black,

71 https://www.urban.org/urban-wire/credit-scores-perpetuate-racial-disparities-even-americas-most-prosperous-cities

72 https://www.debt.org/faqs/americans-in-debt/demographics/

and Asian was 28%, 25%, 24%, and 24%, respectively. Blacks recorded the lowest total credit card balances hovering around five thousand dollars, approximately twenty-five hundred dollars less than Hispanics and whites.[73]

73 https://www.debt.org/faqs/americans-in-debt/demographics/

CHAPTER 6

Homeownership, Housing, and Race

This chapter is intended to reveal and examine at minimum circumstantial evidence pertaining to systemic barriers faced by many blacks in their attempts to make the unthinkable transitions from being merely house dwellers to renters to ultimately homeowners. Arguably, homeownership is one of the primary images or aspirations related to the American Dream. A preponderance of evidence indicates that decision-makers perpetuated patterns or practices that systematically thwarted African slaves and their descendants' homeownership rates thus strengthening President Trump's rigged system theory in yet another consequential sector of the U.S. economy.

Factors related to black homeownership varied by region and over time. Stark contrasts were evident before and following the Civil War. Homeownership has always been a manifestation of several interrelated factors and multiple decision-makers. As "free blacks," indentured servants, or chattel slaves, blacks needed individuals to agree to give, bequeath, or sell them land and/or homes. In most cases, they were required to have steady and sufficient income, collateral, and co-signers before being approved for loans.

During slavery, black homeownership was virtually impossible even in free states, but certainly there were a few exceptions. A review of related literature suggests that housing for blacks was different by region or southern versus northern states. In the South, prior to the Civil War, slaves lived in dwellings constructed on plantations. By all accounts, they resided in substandard structures even for that time period.

In the North or free states, blacks were primarily renters and resided in lofts above restaurants/kitchens, stores, and production facilities where they worked. Consequently, blacks accrued little equity or wealth related to home ownership for approximately two hundred and fifty years.

Post-Civil War employment opportunities and demand for cheap labor helped to spur black home ownership rates in both the North and South. In the South, most of the free slaves remained renters as they transitioned to tenant farmers, sharecroppers, or contract laborers. Housing was provided in many of those contractual agreements.

In the South where a majority of blacks resided, most were afforded deplorable living conditions. In 1934, about seventy years following the end of the Civil War, the Southern Tenant Farmers Union (STFU) was established primarily to protest and collectively demand improvements in both living conditions and employment practices particular to agricultural enterprises in former Confederate states.

Blacks who opted to move off the southern plantations faced numerous challenges. There were few employment opportunities, and a vast majority of available homes for sell or rent were owned by non-blacks. Having no feasible housing options, many blacks were forced to accept often inhumane living quarters. A small fraction was able to somehow navigate the system to gain ownership of houses.

1930's New Deal

Based on historical records, the U.S. government did not provide financial assistance for building homes and supplemental rent payments until nearly seventy years following the end of the Civil War. Historians credit Franklin D. Roosevelt's New Deal movement with institutionalizing government support for public housing through the Public Works Administration (PWA) that came about through an executive order in 1933. The PWA was charged with the construction, demolition, and renovation of low-income homes and clearing slum areas. A year later in 1934, the Federal Home Administration (FHA) was created to help first time homeowners qualify for home mortgages with the government being a guarantor of the loan which also lowered interest rates.

Subsequently, during President Truman's administration, the Housing Act of 1949 was enacted which increased the role of FHA backed mortgage insurance, increased government's footprint in both public and private housing developments, and fueled a renewed drive to address the eradication of slum or blighted areas through an initiative that became known as "urban renewal." Prior to the establishment of the U.S. Department of Housing and Urban Development (HUD) in 1965, public housing was under the auspices of the National Housing Agency (NHA).

Redlining and Gentrification 1930s

Following the end of the Civil War and during Reconstruction, challenges arose when newly freed slaves sought both public and private housing accommodations. Blacks were not welcomed in white neighborhoods in both the North and South.

In urban areas, restricting black home ownership and rentals to specific areas reflected systemic decisions and actions by the government, financial institutions, homeowners/neighborhood covenants, and real estate agents. In the 1930s and 40s, the federal government, through the Federal Home Administration (FHA), allowed its surveyors to draw red lines around certain areas in which loan guarantees to banks would not be approved. In those areas, both home sales and remodeling were virtually nonexistent, thereby causing a precipitous decline in home values and familial wealth in those areas. The systematic discriminatory practices involved both government regulators, lending institutions, and real estate agents.

Between the 1920s and 1970s, to keep blacks out of higher income neighborhoods, some deeds included restrictive covenants blocking sales to blacks.

Real estate agents systematically restricted showings to their black clients to designated areas. According to some accounts, realtors faced stiff repercussions for failing to adhere to the racist practices of limiting African Americans' access to faster appreciating properties.

Blockbusting and Race

Realtors and even their associations have been instrumental in perpetuating racial segregation in the U.S. for decades. Their contributions or efforts involved steering blacks from white neighborhoods and whites from black neighborhoods.

Prior to the 1960s, the National Association of Real Estate Board's code of ethics contained the following mandate: "Don't try to sell houses in white neighborhoods to black homebuyers." Upon further investigation, several sources claim that realtors were asked to take the following pledge:

> "A realtor should never be instrumental in introducing into a neighborhood a character of property or occupancy, members of any race or nationality, or any individuals whose presence will clearly be detrimental to property values in that neighborhood." [74]

Allegedly, the scheme that generated the most profit for realtors was commonly referred to as "blockbusting." According to several online sources, blockbusting is a strategy that plays on racial biases and aspirations related to the American Dream. The first step is to spread rumors of a black wave of home purchases in an all-white subdivision or neighborhood to generate fears of an invasion by "them," thereby creating a selling frenzy at below market prizes by white homeowners. The next step is to pitch homes in predominantly white neighborhoods to middle- and upper-income blacks for above current market values. Over time, the racial composition of the previously

74 https://www.citylab.com/equity/2015/03/how-real-estate-brokers-can-profit-from-racial-tipping-points/386674/

predominantly white neighborhoods is tipped with people of color. Finally, realtors work with fleeing white sellers in their search of usually more expensive homes in virtually all white subdivisions. The process is repeated as more blacks find ways to earn more or acquire collateral to purchase homes in the most high-valued subdivisions.

Not all realtors followed through on the race-based code of ethics, but no doubt some did. As such, blockbusting is an example of the power of realtors (i.e., decision-makers) who can employ racial biases to influence homeownership patterns across the U.S.

While redlining created black enclaves, gentrification has been employed to dilute or eliminate black neighborhoods. The latter has traditionally been primarily an urban phenomenon but can take place in suburbs.

Northern cities were characterized by major industries that spurred local businesses and a demand for cheap labor. Void of public transportation, workers had to reside in close proximity to their job sites, so black enclaves were allowed to develop. Over time, blacks purchased property and created small businesses. Then, something happened. Industries began relocating to the suburbs and more rural areas, leaving behind a disproportionate fraction of the poor, elderly, and people of color. In the wake of resulting high unemployment rates, major purchases and discretionary spending plummeted. Subsequently, small businesses went under, and tax revenues took a downward spiral resulting in inadequate city services and enormous infrastructure challenges. In some of the cities those areas became blighted, having little new investments.

Developers rushed in and bought up properties for pennies on the dollar and secured properties that were available because of accrued unpaid taxes. Elderly and low to moderate income populations who owned homes or rented got hit by a new economic challenge. Developers initiated redevelopment plans that have often included up-scale residential, retail, and commercial amenities. Land values and rental prices skyrocketed, forcing the poor and blacks to relocate.

Fair Housing Act

It is important to remember that laws are intended to satisfy compelling government interests. Promoting and encouraging homeownership and untethered rights to secure homes in neighborhoods regardless of race, sex, and country of origin surfaced as a compelling government interest. Despite passage of the proposed transformative 1964 Civil Rights Act, blatant discriminatory patterns or practices remained in the housing sector. So, on April 11, 1968, the Federal Fair Housing Act was passed to help decrease discriminatory practices that limited or blocked blacks' access to mortgage loans and both home sales and rental contracts in some neighborhoods.

The bill was passed reluctantly in the wake of Dr. Martin L. King's assassination on April 4, 1968. It might seem unimaginable to some younger Americans that a little more than fifty years ago, laws were required to give blacks the right to live where they wanted even if they had the money.

Unlike prior anti-discrimination laws, the Fair Housing Act included accountability measures. Persons or entities found guilty of violating the law faced both fines and possibly incarceration in a limited number of cases.

A decade following the passage of the Fair Housing Act, discriminatory patterns or practices of financial institutions were addressed. As stated previously, the Community Reinvestment Act (CRA) of 1977 was passed to force banks to actively seek customer relations from all segments of the community in terms of both deposits and loans. Unfortunately, recent news reports have indicated that directives from the Trump administration have relaxed CRA requirements or goals. [75] In their defense, banks have maintained that credit histories and credit scores, not race, are related to lower mortgage approval rates among blacks.

---

75 https://eji.org/news/banks-deny-home-loans-to-people-color

Housing Bubble

Between 2008 and 2012, working- and middle-class Americans witnessed what could be considered a violent assault on homeownership and equity accounts. Gains previously made in homeownership by many blacks were wiped away. It has been estimated that during that time, 5.5M homes were lost along with approximately $6.5T of equity.

Whether intended or unintended, the poor and people of color were disproportionately affected when they found themselves in new homes that lost a third to half of their original loan value in a matter of months. In addition, many were blinded by adjustable interest rate loans that caused their monthly payments to skyrocket when interest rates increased. The situation was devastating. People or young families had done everything prescribed to become legitimate homeowners, only to find that a "system" had been put in place that literally robbed or defrauded them of all their money and ruined their credit.

A huge fraction of affected black mortgage holders were first-time home buyers who did not have much equity in their homes to cushion the blow. Moreover, loss of their homes will have widespread and long-term negative implications for their children and subsequent generations. A lot of Americans access the equity in their homes via a second mortgage credit line that is used to help pay for college, purchase automobiles, make home repairs, and even start small businesses. That capacity no longer exists for a lot of blacks who were already disadvantaged.

Homeownership by the Numbers

For most Americans, their homes account for much of their net worth. According to the 2016U.S. Census Bureau Quick Facts, there were 135,697,926 homes. Of the total homes in the U.S., owner occupied housing equaled 63.6%. In terms of assets, the median value of owner-occupied housing was $184,700.[76]

A Wikipedia article reviewed in November of 2017 contained excerpts from a study of homeownership by race in 2005 and 2015. Shifts in homeownership were as follows: 1) white (75.8% v 71.9%); 2) Asian (60.1% v 56.1%); 3) Native American (58.2% v 50.3%); 4) blacks (48.2% v 42.3%); and 5) Hispanics (49.5% v 45.6%). It warrants noting that the black homeownership rate was not too far behind those groups that have faced far fewer historical barriers in the U.S.

Recent cultural changes fueled by economic forces have helped to depress homeownership among younger Americans. More and more, millennials are opting to delay purchasing homes and are instead opting to stay at home with parents or rent.

Researchers have attempted to explain the decline in millennials' homeownership in terms of social learning or modeling. A *New York Times* article published February 10, 2017 reports that young adults who grew up in a home owned by their parents were three times as likely to own homes compared to those who lived in rental units.

Interestingly, among the study sample, income did not account for racial gaps in homeownership between individuals reared in family owned houses and those who resided in rental units. Millennials age forty and earning over one hundred thousand dollars a year who were reared in family owned houses were far more likely to own a home than their counterparts.

The idea that homeownership is partially a "learned" aspiration executed through modeling is potentially insightful. However, giving priority to current income ignores other structural or legacy challenges facing some black, eligible homeowners. For example, the study potentially did not control for lack of familial wealth or collateral, familial financial obligations, student

76 www.census.gov/quickfacts/fact/table/US/PST045216

loan totals, and higher loan interest rates found among blacks who earn over $100,000 per year.

Median Home Values

According to U.S. Census quick facts for 2013-2017, the median home value in the U.S. was $193,500. In addition, the median monthly household expenditures including a mortgage was approximately $1,500 or about $18,000 annually. Data showed that median home values have declined by about seven percent overall; however, there are sharp differences by race. According to an Economic Policy Institute online article,

> "Between 2010 and 2013, inflation-adjusted median home values fell by 4.6 percent for white households and 18.4 percent for African Americans but increased by 3.7 percent for Hispanic households. Since respondents reported their highest home values in the 2007 survey, the median value reported by whites has declined 20.3 percent, compared to 37.7 percent for African Americans and 25.8 percent for Latinos." [77]

The report suggests that some of the disparity and losses in home value can be explained by geographical differences. Home values grew more in large western cities and were the most sluggish in the South where blacks are more heavily concentrated.

Despite corroborating evidence of the existence of discriminatory system forces (e.g., income inequality, limited employment opportunities, low FHA loan guarantees, unethical realtors, redlining, and gentrification), data reviewed suggest that nearly half of eligible blacks had successfully navigated barriers to become homeowners. Their progress related to homeownership is simply stunning.

---

77 https://www.epi.org/publication/home-values-starkly-disparate-recoveries/

CHAPTER 7

Rent Subsidy and Race

If in 2018 nearly fifty percent of eligible blacks own their homes, then it is reasonable to estimate that the remaining fifty percent were renters, boarders with family or friends, incarcerated, and/or homeless. Here is the catch. As with discriminatory patterns or practices that thwarted black homeownership rates, the same factors have forced more blacks to become renters of private and public housing units in mostly racially segregated areas.

Rental costs and rent assistance programs have not only influenced where some blacks could live, they also helped to determine the capacity of blacks to influence election outcomes as they facilitate "packing" and "cracking" of voting districts at local and state levels. Whether intended or unintended, information uncovered indicated that the system put in place to help the poor and blacks secure rental property of their choosing was rigged.

Gautreaux v Chicago Housing Authority

In the mid-1960s, Dorothy Gautreaux, who lived in Chicago and wanted better living conditions for her children, was forced to file a lawsuit to gain relief. It was the first ever class-action lawsuit filed against a city and a federal agency. The case was summarized as follows:

> "The Gautreaux lawsuit charged that by concentrating more than 10,000 public housing units in isolated African-American neighborhoods, the Chicago Housing Authority (CHA) and the U.S. Department of Housing and Urban Development (HUD) had violated both the U.S.

> Constitution, which guarantees all citizens equal protection of the laws, and the 1964 Civil Rights Act, which outlaws racial discrimination in programs that receive federal funding. Decisions at the district, appellate, and, ultimately, the U.S. Supreme Court levels affirmed the Gautreaux plaintiffs' position, finding both CHA and HUD guilty of discriminatory housing practices."[78]

After the ruling, housing vouchers were provided to black families that were comparable to their white counterparts who also needed public assistance to live in the suburbs. In addition, scattered-site public housing developments were mandated, forcing the construction of public housing units across Chicago based on the existing architectural designs in those areas so that they did not look and feel dissimilar.

Rent Payment Trends

Rent payments have been increasing for decades, especially in urban areas. Justin Feldman in 2014 summarized the trend as follows:

> "The cost of renting a home has increased throughout the United States in recent years, most notably in urban areas. According to an April 2014 analysis by Zillow Real Estate Research, between 2000 and 2014 median household income rose 25%, while rents increased by nearly 53%. The U.S. Department of Housing and Urban Development considers housing to be unaffordable when its costs exceed 30% of a family's income. A 2014 report from Harvard's Joint Center for Housing Studies found that just over half of U.S.

78 https://www.bpichicago.org/programs/housing-community-development/public-housing/gautreaux-lawsuit/

households paid more than 30% of their income toward rent in 2013, up from 38% of households in 2000."[79]

There is a thriving rental market that benefits from past discriminatory practices, poverty, unemployment, and low credit scores. When African Americans cannot obtain home mortgages at competitive interest rates for any number of reasons, many are forced to pay the equivalent of a mortgage note for rent. As a result, they do not build equity in the property nor are they allowed to deduct a portion of the payments in tax returns. In most cases, renters help increase their landlord's wealth that they subsequently transfer to their heirs.

---

79 https://journalistsresource.org/studies/economics/real-estate/gentrification-urban-displacement-affordable-housing-overview-research-roundup/

SECTION XI: CRIMINAL JUSTICE SYSTEM (CJS) AND RACE

The purpose of this section is not to deny or downplay the fact that blacks, like all other Americans, commit crimes. Instead, the goal is to critically examine data and information that could be used by President Trump and others to corroborate their rigged system theory. Specifically, the investigation looked for laws, social policies, and practices that could help explain racial disparities throughout the criminal justice system.

Guiding Assumptions

Several guiding assumptions provide the blueprint for trying to clearly layout evidence in a case. First, decision-makers (i.e., lawmakers) create laws that are intended to satisfy a compelling government interest. Second, lawmakers and other members of the CJS fall into the mostly fair, conditionally fair, or mostly unfair personality types. Fortunately, it is believed that a majority fall into the "mostly fair and "conditionally fair" camps with a small minority falling into the "mostly unfair" grouping. Third, members of all races commit crimes/delinquency. Finally, after laws are passed, patterns or practices surrounding their enforcement contribute to observed racial disparities found in official data.

To be clear, the CJS is a complex system consisting of several decision points. At each gate or entry port, decision-makers execute some discretions that could contribute to racial disparities. The remainder of this section contains results of investigations of each component of the CJS in terms of their capacity to influence the racial composition of the CJS pipeline.

CHAPTER 1

Laws and Criminals

Scriptures in the Holy Bible unveil an indisputable truth—-laws create sin or earthly crimes. Absent of laws, there are no crimes or criminal offenders. Moreover, enactment of laws created a need for a Criminal Justice System to deter, surveil, apprehend, arrest, charge, prosecute, determine guilt or innocence, prescribe prison sentences, manage a prison/jail system, selectively award parole, and maintain permanent criminal history records.

Colonial Laws and Race

A review of historical and archived documents revealed the scope and nature of rigged colonial laws that helped to solidify and perpetuate a chattel slavery system in the South. According to the U.S. Law Library of Congress, Virginia was one of the first states to pass slave laws that were recorded, publicized, and enforced. [80] Below are examples of laws passed by the Virginia General Assembly:

Loitering and Vagrancy

- 1680 – It became illegal for slaves to congregate alone even at funerals. [81]

Fugitive Slave Laws

80 https://memory.loc.gov/ammem/awhhtml/awlaw3/slavery.html

81 https://www.history.org/history/teaching/slavelaw.cfm

- If an outlying slave is killed while resisting capture, the owner receives financial compensation for the laborer;
- 1680 — It became legal for all whites to kill a slave attempting to escape and resist apprehension or capture; and
- 1705 — Escaped slaves who were captured and could or would not identify their owners were placed in a local jail.

Defiant Behavior

In addition, the following were considered crimes with corresponding punishment that consisted of lashes on their bare backs:

- Possess firearms (20 lashes);
- Exit the plantation without permission (20 lashes); and
- Display or exhibit an offensive gesture, especially against a Christian (30 lashes).[82]

The point here is that laws must be critically examined to discern both intended and unintended potential consequences. During colonial times, specific laws were passed that only applied to African slaves and their descendants. There were two legal systems prevalent during that time.

Constitutional Law and Race

During the decades between the ratification of the Constitution and end of the Civil War, only two federal laws specifically addressed criminal offenses by slaves. Lawmakers passed the Fugitive Slave Law of 1793 and a more restrictive version in the 1850 Compromise. Both were designed to make the act of a slave trying to escape or escaping a criminal offense. Bounty hunters and law enforcement armed with search warrants, bloodhounds, and extradition papers hunted, captured, and returned some runaways to their owners. In

82 https://www.history.org/history/teaching/slavelaw.cfm

addition, northern sympathizers and abolitionists faced criminal prosecution for aiding run-away slaves. Imagine that.

Due Process Denied

Prior to the end of the Civil War and ratification of the 14th Amendment, African slaves and their descendants did not have any due process rights as either plaintiffs or defendants. They had no "standing" in the courts.

Law enforcement, mobs, plantation owners, and justices of the peace served as juries, judges, and punishers, and/or executioners. In "1692, the Virginia assembly passed a law that made it illegal for free and enslaved blacks to testify in court proceedings.[83]

Post-Civil War CJS

After about two hundred and fifty years, in July of 1868, the 14th Amendment was ratified, giving former African slaves and their descendants the right to equal protection by the law and due process in criminal proceedings. So, for only about one hundred and fifty years, blacks have had the constitutional right to file charges against alleged offenders. For the first time, as alleged criminal offenders, blacks were afforded the following: right to legal counsel; trial by a jury of "their" peers; opportunity to present exculpatory evidence; and right to cross examine witnesses. This was significant progress on paper, but the implementation remained in the hands of decision-makers harboring different prejudice-discrimination personality types.

Essentially, prior to the 14th Amendment, blacks could only appear in courts as offenders or defendants as they had no legal standing as victims. Suddenly, laws relating to both offending and victimization were applicable to newly freed blacks who slowly transitioned from being "property" to needing public safety assurances and help to protect and retain ownership of their property.

---

83 https://www.history.org/history/teaching/slavelaw.cfm

Domestic Terrorism and Black Lynching

Blacks' 14th Amendment rights were frequently violated. Mob lynching of blacks have been documented and described in both oral and printed histories. They were performed to threaten, extort, humiliate, and deter blacks, especially men. The body of knowledge related to lynching in the U.S. was displayed on a digital map in a project initiated by Monroe N. Work, a Tuskegee Institute sociologist who began documenting cases dating back to the 19th century. His pioneering work continues through a research group, Monroe Work Today. Professor Work spent decades inventorying documented lynchings including dates, locations, and circumstances.[84]

Lynching victims included members of all races and ethnicities. [85]

According to the National Association for the Advancement of Colored People (NAACP), between 1882 and 1968, 4,743 lynchings were documented and blacks accounted for 3,446 (72.7%). However, it is widely believed that many black lynchings went undocumented. In comparison, whites were the victims of 1,297 (27.3%) of lynchings. It was reported that some whites were lynched for trying to assist blacks in some way.

There were geographical variations in the number of lynchings. The investigation uncovered the following overview:

> "Mississippi had the highest lynchings from 1882-1968 with 581. Georgia was second with 531, and Texas was third with 493. 79% of lynching happened in the South."[86]

As of January 31, 2019, Congress nor the executive branch have felt compelled to offer and pass anti-lynching laws. By some accounts, approximately two hundred anti-lynching bills have been introduced, but only three bills

---

84 https://www.smithsonianmag.com/smart-news/map-shows-over-a-century-of-documented-lynchings-in-united-states-180961877/#WFXMtKecpDIiOpgS.99

85 http://www.monroeworktoday.org/explore/map2/indexif.html

86 https://www.naacp.org/history-of-lynchings/

were passed in the House and none in the Senate. Many lynchings of blacks were never thoroughly investigated, and interestingly, those lynchings cannot be defined as "cold" cases.

Vagrancy, Loitering, and Interracial Marriages

Following the end of the Civil War, laws were passed that made the following criminal offenses: standing around in public (loitering), defiant or disrespectful behavior, and interracial relationships. Violations of those laws led to a lot of blacks being beaten, jailed, and lynched. Nonviolent misdemeanor acts carried relatively large fines that many blacks could not pay, so they were often jailed and then rented out to local plantation and other business enterprises. The criminal justice system was used to generate a supply of cheap labor and to help fund public or municipal budgetary obligations.

Little attention has been given to racial disparities that existed throughout the CJS prior to the 1960s. It is possible that there was insufficient standardized data collected by law enforcement and other CJS personnel to be analyzed scientifically. Examination of available official CJS data showed that the passage of several crime bills beginning in the 1960s exacted a disproportionate toll on blacks, especially young males.

CHAPTER 2

Crime Bills and Race

The U.S. Congress, executive branch, and state legislatures have enacted and implemented laws that created criminal offenses and new types of offenders/perpetrators. In general, crimes are broadly categorized as status, property, violent, or drug related. Status offenses generally are restricted to underage children and include truancy, runaways, and incorrigibles. Property crimes are as follows: burglary, larceny, and theft. Violent crimes include murder, manslaughter, rape, assault, and armed robbery. Drug or controlled substance crimes usually refer to possession and/or trafficking. Another, less publicized, suite of criminal offenses has been called "white collar" crimes. In general, white collar crimes include embezzlement, fraud, bribery, and insider stock trading. Curiously, arrests and conviction statistics related to white collar offenders by race/ethnicity are seldom reported.

Based on numerous reports, African Americans' quality of life has been disproportionately, and adversely impacted by the passage and enforcement of a host of crime bills, especially drug related laws. Both intended and unintended negative consequences have caused stress/strain in black families and entire communities. Briefs regarding several crime bills were outlined below.

Omnibus Crime Bill (1968)

According to the British Broadcasting Corporation (BBC), Lyndon B. Johnson's Safe Streets Act of 1968, more commonly known as the "Omnibus Crime Control and Safe Streets Act," was the "crippling shot" heard and felt throughout black communities in both the North and South.

Allegedly, lawmakers wanted to "crack" down on black unrest and civil disobedience and looming black-on-black drug related crimes. The legislation created a block grant program to increase the number of police and established the Law Enforcement Assistance Administration (LEAA). The legislation introduced widespread wiretappings, electronic surveillance, and harsh sentences related to harming or killing police canines or "drug sniffers."

Control Substances Abuse Act

Less than five years following passage of transformative civil rights laws, the Control Substances Abuse Act was signed into law by President Richard Nixon on October 27, 1970. The Act specified the federal government's rules and guidelines regarding the production, importation, possession, use, and distribution of narcotics, stimulants, depressants, hallucinogens, anabolic steroids, and other chemicals. The Act also allows the Drug Enforcement Administration (DEA) and the Federal Drug Administration (FDA) to request a change in the schedule of a drug or controlled substance on a scale from one (1) to five (5). Schedule 1 drugs are defined as highly addictive and have no medical benefits. Schedule 2 drugs have a greater probability of addiction and have accepted medical benefits along with strong restrictions. Schedule 3 drugs have medical use and a lower probability of addiction than schedule 1 and 2 substances. Schedule 4 substances have medical use and even lower addiction probabilities than lower scheduled substances. Finally, schedule 5 drugs have medical uses and low addiction probabilities.

At the federal level, marijuana and cocaine, including its derivatives such as "crack," are Schedule 1 drugs. Today, medical and recreational marijuana possession and use statutes vary from state to state. So, marijuana use in one state can result in a jail or prison term for possession while smoking a "blunt" on one's front porch would be legal just across the state line. The point here is that elected officials determine which drugs are legal, thereby expanding the criminal justice net as more drugs fall into Schedule 1 and 2 designations.

Cocaine-Crack for Guns Dilemma

In 2014, the *Huffington Post* essentially reopened a cold case that was nearly twenty years old. The stories surrounded Pulitzer Prize-winning journalist Gary Webb's revelations in a series of newspaper articles that shed light on an alleged crack-for-guns conspiracy. According to reports, participants in the offense included the Central Intelligence Agency (CIA), Nicaraguan rebels, and a street-level drug trafficking gang in South Los Angeles in the early to late 1980s. [87]

During the Reagan administration, the U.S. backed rebels seeking to overthrow the socialist Nicaraguan government. Allegedly, the Contra rebels were allowed to partner with at least one black drug trafficker to distribute and sell cocaine-crack in the U.S. Profits accrued by the Contras were used to purchase guns and other weapons. It has been surmised that the cocaine-for-guns conspiracy was a strategy that helped to achieve a U.S. government objective without its direct involvement.

In 1986, an investigation was launched by a sub-committee of the Senate Foreign Relations Committee that was chaired by then Senator John Kerry. The results of his investigation revealed that there was questionable financial support given to Contra rebels. According to a published source, the committee concluded the following:

> "'The Contra drug links included,' among other connections, '[...] payments to drug traffickers by the U.S. State Department of funds authorized by the Congress for humanitarian assistance to the Contras, in some cases after the traffickers had been indicted by federal law enforcement agencies.'"[88]

---

87 https://www.huffingtonpost.com/2014/10/10/gary-webb-dark-alliance_n_5961748.html

88 https://www.c-span.org/video/?102219-1/cia-drug-trafficking-allegations

For decades, the government and mainstream media adamantly rebuffed Webb's claims. A number of related investigations concluded that Web's earlier reporting was not credible. On the other hand, both a feature film and a documentary were released in 2014 and 2015 that provided additional corroborating evidence for Webb's investigative reports.

The cocaine-gun conspiracy was not subjected to a trial in a civil court. Based on evidence obtained from Webb and the Kerry Committee, the following question could be posed: "Was it more likely than not that the U.S. government facilitated drug trafficking by a foreign entity?" If there was a preponderance of evidence against one or more government agencies, the federal government might be found at least partially liable for a host of negative related outcomes. For example, some street-level drug traffickers were arrested, fined, paid bonds, and even served prison sentences. Moreover, the cocaine-crack epidemic devastated entire black families and neighborhoods.

Asset Seizures and Race

Reagan era anti-drug abuse acts established mandatory minimum sentences. They also included more vigorous enforcement of laws related to the possession of a controlled substance such as marijuana. Imagine that. In addition, the bills created a new funding stream for law enforcement agencies.

Drug-related asset forfeitures were introduced during the Reagan administration. They had both intended and unintended consequences. The process followed a similar sequence in most jurisdictions. First, drug traffickers were monitored over a period of time. Second, drug traffickers could accumulate conspicuous assets (e.g., cars, jewelry, guns, and even real estate). Third, after links between drug sells and the property were verified, drug traffickers were arrested and charged. Finally, if found guilty, all related property was awarded to all participating law enforcement agencies based on some predetermined allocation formula. Asset forfeitures have yielded cars and SUVs that have been incorporated into police motor pools or sold. In addition, seized cash, jewelry, and real estate have generated hundreds of millions that have gone into operating budgets.

Violent Crime Control and Law Enforcement Act

Another sweeping anti-violent and drug crime bill was passed by President Bill Clinton in 1994. Provisions of the bill were arbitrary and seemed to target certain offenses and specific drug users and traffickers. According to the BBC's "Clinton Crime Bill: Why Is It So Controversial" (2016), the major components were punitive in nature:

> "Its provisions implemented many things, including a 'three strikes' mandatory life sentence for repeat offenders, money to hire 100,000 new police officers, $9.7bn in funding for prisons, and an expansion of death penalty-eligible offences. It also dedicated $6.1bn to prevention programs designed with significant input from experienced police officers"...[89] States were also incentivized to pass harsher crime bills.

Patients and Communities Act (Opioids) and Race

In late 2018, a bipartisan funding bill was signed into law by President Trump aimed at decreasing or thwarting the toll opioid use and abuse was having on individuals and families. It was dubbed the Support for Patients and Communities Act. Lawmakers agreed that opioid use/abuse and related criminal offending were a public safety crisis, uniquely and materially different from alleged cocaine, crack, and marijuana use/abuse and criminal offending. Interestingly, they apparently favored treatment of opioid addicts over arrests, fines, and incarceration.

A case could be made that decision-makers are influenced by their perceptions, attitudes, and beliefs regarding both the types of drugs abused and the faces of drug users. During the past two decades, increasing attention

89 https://www.bbc.com/news/world-us-canada-36020717

has been given to the proliferation of drug overdoses and related deaths in the U.S. The cause has been attributed to increases in prescriptions for pain-killers that apparently serve as gateway drugs or precursors to heroin and other drug addictions. The Center for Disease Control (CDC) collected and analyzed data from thirty-one states and the District of Columbia between 2015 and 2016. [90] Results of the study revealed that over sixty-three thousand (63,000) deaths related to drug overdoses were reported in 2016, and two-thirds (66%) involved either prescribed or illicit opioids. Overdose deaths increased by nearly twenty-two percent (22%). Death rates increased by ten percent (10%) from prescription drugs only and were highest among males twenty-five to forty-four.

According to the CDC report entitled "Overdose Deaths Involving Opioids, Cocaine, and Psychostimulants in the United States 2015-2016" (2018), the overall spike in overdose deaths is related to synthetic opioids, "primarily those boosted by illicitly manufactured fentanyl (IMF)." Recent trends were described as follows:

- The prescription opioid-related overdose death rate increased by 10.6 percent.
- The heroin-related overdose death rate increased by 19.5 percent.
- The cocaine-related overdose death rate increased by 52.4 percent.
- The psychostimulant-related overdose death rate increased by 33.3 percent."

Public optics and narratives related to the prescription drug and opioid epidemic suggest that stress/strain related to pain generates different individual modes of adaptation. Patients either build up resistance to the medication and require larger doses or they are refused refills and turn to illicit drugs. In other cases, drug users are lured by the addition of IMF to their schedule 1 or 2 controlled substance(s) of choice.

---

90 https://www.cdc.gov/media/releases/2018/p0329-drug-overdose-deaths.html

Unlike previous urban-based, alleged drug crises, the opioid epidemic is not restricted to specific geographies. The distribution was described by the CDC as follows:

- Death rates from overdoses involving synthetic opioids increased in 21 states, with 10 states doubling their rates from 2015 to 2016. (New Hampshire, West Virginia, and Massachusetts had the highest death rates from synthetic opioids.)
- Fourteen states had significant increases in death rates involving heroin, with Washington D.C., West Virginia, and Ohio having the highest rates.
- Eight states had significant increases in death rates involving prescription opioids. West Virginia, Maryland, Maine, and Utah had the highest rates.
- Sixteen states had significant increases in death rates involving cocaine, with Washington D.C., Rhode Island, and Ohio having the highest rates.
- Fourteen states had significant increases in death rates involving psychostimulants; the highest death rates occurred primarily in the Midwest and Western regions.[91]

Elected officials and other decision-makers have determined how drug users and offenders have been treated by the criminal justice system. Unlike government responses to previous so-called marijuana and crack epidemics, official reactions to opioid users and abusers have included calls for treatment, not "lock 'em up." It should be noted that drug addicts who lack the financial wherewithal to purchase drugs often engage in criminal activities (e.g., burglary, robbery, prostitution, etc.). So, why have the reactions of elected officials or law makers to opioid-related crimes and offenders been seemingly more understanding and sympathetic? Is it reasonable to speculate that elected

91 https://www.cdc.gov/mmwr/volumes/67/wr/mm6712a1.htm

officials' responses might be a function of the increasing number of public faces of opioid death victims and offenders who look like them? Their greater similarity with opioid victims and offenders might lead to more emphasis on diversionary programs and substance abuse prevention and intervention oriented public policies.

In state legislatures across the U.S., lawmakers have been hard at work trying to find help and solutions related to the opioid crisis. An African American lawmaker in a rural southern state claimed that his white colleagues appropriated funds to only treat opioid users. He and some of his colleagues had to fight long and hard to get the target population expanded to include treatment for other addicts (e.g., cocaine-crack, marijuana, and so on). Readers are encouraged to review state and local budgets for drug treatment and diversionary programs to assess their "inclusiveness" in terms of the range of drug-related offenses for which treatment has been the preferred sanction.

To summarize, elected officials have enacted laws to satisfy compelling public safety needs. The fact is that each additional law inevitably creates more crimes and by default more offenders. Americans assume and expect laws to be applied uniformly to all suspected offenders regardless of race, sex, age, income, religion, zip code, and/or country of origin.

The following chapters contain the results of investigations related to the roles played by personnel in each of the major components of the CJS (i.e., law enforcement, prosecuting attorneys, defense lawyers, judges, and parole boards). Specifically, evidence was sought to corroborate claims of a rigged CJS.

CHAPTER 3

Law Enforcement-Police

This chapter contains evidence of potential patterns or practices among law enforcement that could help explain a portion of racial disparities in arrest rates. Again, the foundational assumption is that law enforcement personnel fall into one of the three prejudice-discrimination personality types (i.e., mostly fair, conditionally fair, or mostly unfair).

Similarities have been observed between pre-Civil War law enforcement and present-day policing. In fact, some reports suggest that photographs of organizations established to implement the notorious "slave patrols" and other vigilante type entities of the pre-Civil War era resemble present day sheriff and police departments. Prior to and after the Civil War, state and federal laws existed to protect the interest of landowners, businesspersons, and the social hierarchy among the races.

Certainly, a vast majority of law enforcement officers are professionals and honorable; they actually serve and protect. Today, it is estimated that there are approximately 18,000 police departments and over 750,000 sworn law enforcement officers in the U.S. It is difficult to uncover racial and gender distributions among officers. In most cases, departments are predominantly male and white. Prejudgments should not be made based on that fact alone. However, given the history of police type organizations and race relations in the U.S., it would be naïve of local stakeholders to assert that some police officers do not allow their prejudices to influence their contacts with blacks in some instances.

Job Security and Immunity

Reviews of literature and public discourse have revealed at least two major advantages that law enforcement has regarding job security and being shielded from personal liability; these advantages are even extended to criminal charges related to their behavior while on duty. Their protection from immediate termination and liability have come by way of powerful unions and qualified immunity.

Police Unions

Efforts among rank-and-file officers to unionize peaked in 1919 as police in Boston went on strike, protesting against relatively low pay and poor working conditions. Early attempts to unionize were defeated; however, organizations that worked to shield officers, including the Patrolmen's Benevolent Associations and the Fraternal Order of Police, grew in size and influence. It is important to note that it was not until 1964 that the first recognized police union was established in New York City.

Similar to other labor unions, police unions provided a mechanism for "collective bargaining" regarding compensation, benefits, pensions, training, safety and health, and disciplinary policies and procedures. Union contracts usually specify the nature and scope of alleged infractions that can be proposed as cause for termination. Union members who face termination must be afforded "due process," for which the review and appeal system can take months to complete. During that time period, some officers who had been accused of wrongful use of deadly force have remained employed with pay.

Qualified Immunity

In 1967, during the height of the fight for racial equality and civil unrest, the U.S. Supreme Court ruled that government officials were covered by a legal doctrine of qualified immunity which a basic Google search defines an as follows:

> "Qualified immunity is designed to protect all but the plainly incompetent or those who knowingly violate the law. Law enforcement officers are entitled to qualified immunity when their actions do not violate a clearly established statutory or constitutional right."

The court's ruling was allegedly intended to protect government personnel from frivolous lawsuits and civil liability judgements. Prior to the court's ruling, reports and televised scenes of police abuse and use of excessive force (e.g., beatings, unleashing of attack dogs, etc.) against men, women, and youth persisted. In general, police officers who have been accused of employing excessive force resulting in serious injuries and/or deaths have avoided criminal charges and civil lawsuits by evoking the qualified immunity defense.

To void a qualified immunity defense, prosecutors must prove that the accused officer "knowingly or intentionally" violated clearly stated rules and procedures and/or committed a criminal offense. It should not be surprising to learn that qualified immunity has been the overwhelming defense of officers involved in shootings unarmed black men.

Police Discretion

Americans cannot deny that patrol officers and other law enforcement personnel possess some discretion in their responses to suspects and offenders. They can ignore criminal offenses, issue verbal or written warnings, issue fines or summons, or take suspects into custody. It is that discretion that allows racial biases to influence the severity of their official responses. There is little doubt or debates regarding police discretion, but there is not consensus in terms of its impact on arrest rates by race.

Patrol Patterns and Arrests

A saying among some police, which might help explain some of their patterns or practices, is "seek and you will find probable cause."

Racial justice supporters have argued that disproportionate patrolling or surveillance in certain neighborhoods increases those residents' contacts with police and arrests. As a result, a commonly held view among African Americans is that enforcement of laws is disproportionately focused on them and their neighborhoods. Local stakeholders have routinely reviewed maps that contained the distribution of 911 calls and patrol stops by the police to understand the scope and nature of policing in different neighborhoods. Analysis of those data have revealed trends in terms of the following: impetus for police contacts; address/location; time; purpose of contacts; demographics of suspects and/or victims if applicable; and outcomes of contacts (e.g., no official action, detained, etc.).

Discriminatory Practices

According to a 2016 Public Broadcasting Service (PBS) documentary entitled "America in Black and Blue," several law enforcement practices appeared to have targeted the poor and communities of color. Broken windows was the name of a law enforcement strategy whereby people were stopped for minor offenses with anticipations of finding major infractions. Deferred maintenance on cars such as broken or inoperable tail lights, brake light malfunctions, and/or cracked windshield were probable causes for stopping residents in poor neighborhoods. Critics of broken windows argued that it was not similarly implemented in higher income areas.

In addition, New York City employed a "stop and frisk" practice. Police routinely stopped and searched men of color without "probable cause." During some of the illegitimate searches, drugs and/or firearms were uncovered that resulted in arrests. Critics of the "stop and frisk" initiative argued that similar arrest rates would materialize if other non-blacks were targeted in a similar fashion. Unfortunately, that hypothesis will never be tested. Elected officials and business leaders will not stand by and subject their children, family members, and friends to that type of law enforcement tactic because of what they might find.

Black versus white gathering patterns can also influence contacts with law enforcement. Just "lurking" or standing around is often defined by police as a form of intelligence gathering regarding an anticipated criminal offense. Where youth generally lurk also varies by race. Black boys and young men of color (BYMOC) in some neighborhoods appear to have a "herd' instinct. They tend to frequent street corners, abandoned structures, and other unsupervised outdoor spaces. In comparison, white youth display a similar herd instinct in large homes, private clubs, life centers, parking lots, and malls.

Operating Budgets and Black Gold

Recall that when "cotton was king," blacks were equal to gold in terms of their value. In addition, southern states generated the bulk of their operating budgets from taxes based on assessed value of slaves.

For decades, African Americans have alleged that police have monthly goals in terms of revenue derived from tickets and fines. Recently, investigations in some urban areas have uncovered law enforcement practices that appear to target blacks for a host of revenue generating offenses. In Ferguson, Missouri, research revealed that a significant portion of the city's operating budget was fulfilled by traffic related citations and fines for misdemeanor violations.

Drug-related Arrests and Race

To avoid the appearance of a conflict of interest, blacks and other criminal justice reform advocates have pointed to the results from official government research that has provided evidence of linkages between drug-related arrests and law enforcement practices. In October of 1995, Patrick A. Landon, a Bureau of Justice Statistics (BJS) analyst, authored a report entitled "The Racial Disparities in U.S. Drug Arrests." His research offered plausible explanations for the overrepresentation of blacks in marijuana and other drug-related arrests. Data were gleaned from two government sources.

First, data were obtained from face-to-face interviews during which subjects were asked, with assurances of anonymity and confidentiality, to indicate their use and/or possession of drugs that could be justification for arrest. Type of drug use was coded as follows: 1) heroin or cocaine/crack; 2) marijuana; and 3) psychotherapeutic or hallucinogens. Drug trafficking or sales was measured by asking respondents if they had sold illicit drugs during the previous year. Blacks accounted for thirteen percent of those admitting to drug use/possession and sixteen percent of admitted sellers.

The second source of data was the Federal Bureau of Investigation (FBI) nationwide arrest counts for drug possession and drug trafficking for 1991-1993. Arrest data included race, age, and sex.

Landon compared self-reported, drug-related offending rates from the survey to FBI arrest counts by race/ethnicity. Specific findings were shocking. For example, while representing only sixteen percent of admitted drug sellers, blacks accounted for nearly fifty percent or half of all drug sale arrests during the time frame in question. Similarly, blacks accounted for thirty-six percent of arrests for drug possession but only represented thirteen percent of respondents who reported drug possession and use in the general population. According to the author, several factors could help explain disparities in drug possession arrests including frequency of use, type of drug use, and place of use. Blacks reported more frequent drug use, preferred heroin/cocaine/crack, and were concentrated more heavily in urban areas.

Overall, the researcher concluded that:

> "Drug law enforcement is heavily concentrated in large urban places——To illustrate, large metropolitan areas are where forty-four percent of Americans live, and where forty-seven percent of illicit drug use occurs, but where sixty percent of drug arrest occur."[92]

92 https://www.bjs.gov/content/pub/pdf/rdusda.pdf

Again, the executive branch and Congress pass laws and the police are responsible for enforcing them. Critics of the 1995 study will potentially argue that self-reported drug-related behavior is unreliable, and data were based on conditions and practices that existed over twenty-five years ago. On the other hand, supporters of the findings will argue that things have not changed significantly in terms of drug use/abuse, racial segregation in housing, and police patrol patterns.

Words and Non-Verbal Communication Matter

While the U.S. Constitution gives citizens the right to freedom of expression and speech, it does not define how those expressions and speech will be perceived, received, and responded to in different situations and across different cultures. Many blacks believe they have been subjected to racial stereotyping by retailers, prospective employers, and the police. The scope and nature of contacts between police and blacks, especially BYMOC, are influenced by what Ervin Goffman in his book *The Presentation of Self in Everyday Life* termed "expressions given" and "expressions given off." The former refers to language or vocabulary, while the latter refers to non-verbal and/or outward appearance. It is imperative for parents/guardians and local stakeholders to work collaboratively to increase both police and youth awareness of the role language and non-verbal play in determining the nature of encounters with one another. The sad reality is that police have been wounded and killed by blacks and the reverse is also true. So, members of each group must deal with that possibility each day and it generates stress and strain on both sides. Caution is required to prevent stereotypes. Not all white police officers have been involved in shooting unarmed blacks, but an overwhelming majority of those involved in such shootings have been white. Similarly, everyone who wears a hoodie is not a convenient store robber, but 60% of convenient store robbers wear hoodies. Therefore, is it unreasonable for law enforcement to surveil blacks wearing hoodies in the aftermath of an offense for which the description included a hoodie? The point here is that in this scenario, the hoodie becomes "probable cause" for police contact; however, it is the possession of firearms and/or illegal substances that transform a benign contact into a criminal apprehension. All Americans have a right to wear hoodies but are generally not authorized to carry firearms or possess controlled substances.

African Americans must be taught early in life how to manage interactions with the police. There are literally untold numbers of arrests of blacks due to disagreements regarding words and gestures employed or exchanged during daily, routine interactions with law enforcement. Miscommunications undoubtedly account for only a fraction of arrests made in black communities.

The Talk (TK911)

A pattern of unnecessary, violent contacts with police has been the impetus for blacks, especially young boys and adults, to complete a "required" course designed to teach "get home safe" tactics and methods. In most American households, "the talk" still refers to the "birds and the bees;" however, in black households, the talk refers to the mandatory course on how to interact with law enforcement, commonly referred to as Talk 911. Attendance is mandatory, especially for BYMOC. During the talk, parents/guardians normally identify and discuss best practices for successfully negotiating contacts with law enforcement. Some parents go as far as creating role plays or entire scripts to reinforce the lesson.

The talk is a lesson in showing respect, humility, and an abundance of caution. Boys and young men are told where to place their hands and hold them; what to say; what not to say; what to ask; and what not to ask. For some young black men, the talk is a bitter pill to swallow. A gut-wrenching account was included in an HBO documentary:

> A black mother talked about moving to a white neighborhood with her teenage black son. They were out driving and were pulled over by the police. The mother described the anger in her son generated by being stopped for no apparent

> reason or violation. She observed his tone when asking the officer "What did I do?" His response was natural and normal but his tone and non-verbal were recorded and analyzed in a split second by the officers. Even the mother observed the anger and frustration in her son and thanked God for being there with him to calm him down. She wondered what would have been the outcome of her son's contact with the police if she had not been present.

By no means is the account above an indictment against the police or the teenaged black driver. It simply described how some police contacts can quickly go wrong because of mistrust and different definitions of situations.

To test the assumption that a natural and normal response to police contact is to ask, "What did I do?" or "why are you stopping me?" A role-play was enacted during a MBKC mentoring session:

> An adult mentor engaged a group of boys (n=24) ages 8 to 17 in a role play between a police officer and one of the participants. The goal of the role-play was to demonstrate the step-by-step exchanges that often take place on the streets. A second goal was to critically examine the language and gestures of all participants in the encounter. The adult mentor asked for a volunteer, and a sixteen-year-old agreed to play act with him. In a stern voice, the adult mentor said, "Come over here boy." The youngster immediately asked, "What did I do?" For many BYMOC when confronted by police, that is a natural and predictable response or inquiry. Each time the adult mentor gave a verbal command, the boy posed the question, "What did I do?" Consciously or unconsciously, the teenager failed to comply with the directive of the mentor who was playing the role of a police officer.

The role-play pointed out a couple of things. First, several of the boys noted that the use of the word "boy" showed prejudice or disrespect. Recall, the participants were between the ages eight and seventeen. Second, it is natural for a person to inquire about why they are being stopped or questioned, even if they are "dirty." From their perspective, they do not know if the police had an objective cause to stop the black teenager or was just profiling. Finally, police can avoid some negative encounters by immediately informing citizens of the reason(s) they are being confronted, and citizens ought to comply with reasonable requests or directives.

When educating youth, talks about both safe sex or abstinence and contact with police are important and have long-term consequences. Errors in one case could produce life while errors in the other might result in the loss of money to pay fines, time in jail/detention, or even loss of life.

Police Subculture

Is it unreasonable for Americans to expect to see and encounter diverse police departments? For decades, in a lot of municipalities both law enforcement and fire safety were controlled by families and/or ethnic groups. Unions were used to restrict employment and promotions of out-group members. Those hiring practices facilitated what has been referred to as "police subculture." The concept refers to a subset of beliefs, values, and norms that exist among and in some police departments. A primary norm is called a "code of silence," meaning that fellow law enforcement personnel keep silent about real and alleged improprieties of officers. At the departmental level, the code of silence is cloaked in the assertion that a matter is under investigation; therefore, information cannot be disclosed.

Alleged wrongdoings of police officers have been investigated by fellow law enforcement personnel in units commonly referred to as "Internal Affairs" (IA). Note that it is an internal entity. There are also Review Boards that were intended to hold officers accountable. A review of published accounts or reports revealed a paucity of cases in which alleged wrongdoings or crimes by police officers have resulted in firings and/or criminal charges. In most cases, officers having multiple serious complaints in their files have been allowed to resign and secure employment in other jurisdictions.

Screening of Applicants and Race

Supporters of police reforms point to several areas that should be examined, stressing that the recruitment and screening of applicants must be revised. Specifically, they question the weight or appropriateness of having a certain credit worthiness score. How does one's credit history relate to or predict future performance as a police officer? Second, misdemeanor law violations are also used to screen or eliminate applicants from search pools. In some jurisdictions, drug/alcohol, child support, traffic violations, and status offenses result in lower screening scores or outright rejection of applicants. Yet, there is no empirical research showing relationships between minor, non-violent criminal records and efficacy as a police officer. In fact, such experiences might facilitate empathy with some "would be" or "suspected" offenders. Third, education requirements including a minimum of sixty college credits or a postsecondary degree also has negative implications for an inclusive department. There is consensus that all police officers should have at least above average communication skills (e.g., read and comprehend material, use technology, and master applied math). By no means should illiterate applicants be hired to serve and protect; however, requiring a minimum number of college credits or a degree has not been shown to be related to police efficacy on the streets.

Finally, among a lot of black applicants, stress and strain are exacerbated by the fact that departmental screening committees, if established, are usually racially imbalanced with few if any people of color involved. In those circumstances, the chances of having an advocate in the interview process is drastically decreased. The composition and operating policies of screening and selection committees matter.

Reformers have also recommended additional sensitivity pre-service training for prospective police officers. Growing up in segregated neighborhoods and schools could have facilitated beliefs regarding racial stereotypes by members of all races. To decrease or eliminate racial stereotypes, trainees should be required to undergo an immersion in different neighborhoods within the jurisdiction prior to being hired. The experience should not be too structured or controlled; instead, it should mirror what he/she will encounter during their shifts. A fraction of their pre-service evaluation should be based on the results of their immersion experiences.

Video Recordings and Policing

For years, training specialists have developed videos to teach concepts and to demonstrate "best practices." The summer of 2016 witnessed a transformation in how police gather and report information regarding contacts with offenders of all types. After several videotaped police shootings of unarmed black men in 2016, calls for police to video their contacts with engaged individuals were deafening. In many police departments today, videocams capture both optics and audio.

Still, there was significant differences in the definition of some of the deadly encounters even though the scene was videotaped in living color.

Videotaped violent encounters with police have often generated opposing interpretations and conclusions. Unfortunately, video and audio recordings do not reveal the perceptions and emotions experienced by police officers and suspects. The "ace" card held by police has been their legal and justifiable right to take action to protect themselves when a threat is "perceived."

From a Mertonian perspective, decisions emanating from the intersection of prejudicial attitudes and predispositions to act must be at least considered as contributors to some of the police shootings of unarmed assailants. That realization might help explain divergent definitions of those situations viewed concurrently by members of different racial/ethnic groups. It is not uncommon for viewers who disagree about the justification for the shootings to ask, "Did you see what I saw?" This situation is reminiscent of famed comedic genius Redd Foxx who after being caught in the act of a wrongdoing told his wife, "Go ahead, and believe your old lying eyes," and Judge Marilyn Milano of the People's Court who observes, "There is no man so blind as he who will not see." Prejudicial attitudes and/or racial stereotypes can and do influence how observers define or explain some videotaped deadly interactions between some police officers and some people of color.

Consent Decrees

Without a doubt, a majority of police departments do not violate the constitutional rights of the citizens they are sworn to serve and protect. But for decades, some departments have been found guilty of doing so and entered consent decrees involving a blueprint or plan to achieve compliance. In 1994, during the Clinton administration, the U.S. Attorney General was authorized to enter consent decrees to remedy systemic, constitutional violations by police departments. Many of the consent decrees were entered into by urban or inner-city police departments.

Nearly twenty-five years later, one of the final actions of former Attorney General Jeff Sessions in late November 2018 was to modify the consent decree tool. According to media sources, Session stated that it sometimes takes the force of the federal government to make police departments do right. However, he mandated several modifications that appear to weaken the decrees: 1) stop justice lawyers from approving consent decrees and only allow higher level officials to do so; 2) require evidence of other violations in addition to those involving constitutional rights; and 3) limit the time of the consent decree on the front-end instead of it being contingent upon demonstrable progress towards compliance.[93]

93 https://www.justice.gov/opa/pr/justice-department-releases-memorandum-litigation-guidelines-civil-consent-decrees-and

Arrests by Race/Ethnicity

Without a doubt, laws, criminal offending, and patterns or practices of law enforcement have influenced official crime statistics. According to a recent Federal Bureau of Investigation (FBI) report entitled "Arrests, by Race and Ethnicity, 2016," arrest rates do not necessarily mirror the images portrayed in the media. Highlights copied from the report are as follows:

- In 2016, 69.6 percent of all individuals arrested were White, 26.9 percent were Black or African American, and 3.6 percent were of other races.
- Of all juveniles (persons under the age of 18) arrested in 2016, 62.1 percent were White, 34.7 percent were Black or African American, and 3.2 percent were of other races.
- Of all adults arrested in 2016, 70.2 percent were White, 26.2 percent were Black or African American, and 3.6 percent were of other races.
- White individuals were arrested more often for violent crimes than individuals of any other race and accounted for 59.0 percent of those arrests.
- Of adults arrested for murder, 52.0 percent were Black or African American, 45.4 percent were White, and 2.6 percent were of other races.
- Black or African American juveniles comprised 52.0 percent of all juveniles arrested for violent crimes.
- White juveniles accounted for 58.4 percent of all juveniles arrested for property crimes.
- Of juveniles arrested for drug abuse violations, 74.8 percent were White.

- White juveniles comprised 64.7 percent of juveniles arrested for rape and 60.2 percent of juveniles arrested for larceny-theft. [94]

There are no legitimate excuses or justifications for criminal offending regardless of race, sex, age, or country of origin. However, results of this investigation suggested that certain practices of law enforcement might have contributed to observed racial disparities in terms of arrests.

94 https://ucr.fbi.gov/crime-in-the-u.s/2016/crime-in-the-u.s.-2016/tables/table-21/#overview

CHAPTER 4

Post-Arrest System

After suspects have been taken into custody by police, their fates are generally in the hands of people with law degrees. Most defense counselors, prosecuting attorneys, and judges have law degrees.

According to the American Bar Association (ABA), there were over 400,000 practicing lawyers in 2016. Of practicing lawyers in the U.S., men accounted for approximately sixty-five percent (65%). In terms of the racial breakdown among lawyers, blacks accounted for a mere five percent (5%), and whites commanded a whopping eighty-five percent (85%). [95]

Prosecuting or District Attorneys

Prosecuting attorneys (PAs) determine consequences of arrests in most cases. They have the authority to prosecute an offender, plea bargain, or dismiss the case due to a lack of evidence. At district and state levels, they are elected by voters. An article that appeared on the National Public Radio website posed an interesting question: "Does it matter that over ninety-five percent of elected prosecutors are white?" [96] The question was prompted by the results of a 2014 survey of approximately twenty-four hundred prosecuting attorneys across the U.S. Surprisingly, survey data revealed that an overwhelming majority or ninety-five percent (95%) were white and mostly men.

---

95 https://www.americanbar.org/content/dam/aba/administrative/market_research/national-lawyer-population-10-year-demographics-revised.authcheckdam.pdf

96 https://www.npr.org/sections/itsallpolitics/2015/07/08/420913118/does-it-matter-that-95-of-elected-prosecutors-are-white

The decision to have eligible voters elect PAs was made in 1832 and about thirty-three years prior to the end of the Civil War. Decision-makers at that time believed elected PAs would be held accountable by the men who could vote for them.

From a rigged system perspective, it is important to remember that blacks could neither vote nor run for the office until the 1870s.

With over ninety percent of PAs being white, how realistic is it that an overwhelming majority are void of racial biases that influence their decisions to prosecute or not? Below was a view obtained from a study led by Brenda Choresi Carter of the Reflective Democracy Campaign:

> "Having women and people of color represented more fully in these positions is no guarantee of equality in the criminal justice system, but I do feel very confident that we're not going to get equality with these numbers," Choresi Carter said. "These are numbers that if we saw them in any other country, or pretty much any other context, we would say, 'Wow, something is really seriously wrong with the system.'"[97]

Of course, there is the counter argument that race of PAs does not automatically lead to injustices. But based on historical practices and rigged system allegations, one cannot help but question the potential for the combination of racial prejudices and power to influence prosecuting attorneys' decisions. The appearance of possible impropriety has been unavoidably linked to a racially monopolized PA system.

For decades, some prosecuting attorneys have campaigned on a "get tough on crime" platform and paraded their conviction rates as the sole measure of their effectiveness. There have been documented cases of overzealous PAs

97 https://www.npr.org/sections/itsallpolitics/2015/07/08/420913118/does-it-matter-that-95-of-elected-prosecutors-are-white

who used their decision-making authority to win erroneous convictions of mainly poor and black defendants. Fortunately, only a small fraction has been found guilty of witness tampering, withholding exculpatory evidence, and extorting false confessions in exchange for proposed shorter prison sentences.

Defense Counsel

It is often asserted that blacks, especially youth, receive longer confinements and harsher treatment than their white counterparts after initial contact with police. Tracking data has shown that on average, black youth flow further through the juvenile justice system (JJS) pipeline than their counterparts.

Unlike in education, the JJS pipeline appears more porous, leaking out more whites and higher income youth. In plain talk, the percent of whites who avoid legal processing is greater than the percent of blacks. In 2016, the National Juvenile Defense Counsel (NJDC) analyzed related data and argued that reforms should be implemented in all jurisdictions to ensure early, quality defense counsel regardless of race/ethnicity, criminal history, sex, age, income, and/or type of status or delinquency. According to the report, structural impairments remain that limit or block a lot of blacks and the poor from receiving quality defense counsel and justice.

After being arrested on initial charges, suspects are forced to engage in a form of competition between two teams, PAs and defense counsel. PAs and suspects and their defense counsels are on opposite sides in the courtrooms. Invariably, PAs are on offense and seek bond and/or detention/jail. Suspects who retain or are appointed legal counsel engage in defensive tactics to have the initial charges dropped or reduced, eliminate or decrease bond, and/or avoid detention/jail. During hearings or trials, it is the responsibility of defense counsel to present sufficient evidence on behalf of their clients to create doubt in the minds of jurors and judges.

Children having familial resources to engage effective legal counsel are undoubtedly advantaged over those not being represented. Juveniles without effective legal counsel were far more likely to be held in excess of twenty-four hours. In addition, lack of effective legal counsel has also been found related to both improper convictions and longer prison sentences among black adults.

From a Mertonian perspective, intersections of racial biases and discriminatory practices exist even among lawyers. Admitting that lawyers can be accurately categorized as "mostly fair," "conditionally fair," or "mostly unfair" raises some serious questions about effective defenses and prevalence of plea bargains among defendants of color. There have been widely publicized cases of lawyers essentially encouraging the poor and black defendants to accept plea bargains instead of going to trial for a crime they did not commit. In addition, a lot of black defendants do not have the money to hire legal counsel and are represented by more inexperienced and overworked public defenders. Lack of effective legal counsel cannot explain all the racial disparities related to initial charges, amount of bond, pre-trial detention/jail time, conviction rates, probation, parole, and/or prison sentences. However, it is reasonable to assume that a fraction of observed racial disparities can be linked to the lack of or ineffective legal counsel.

Bail, Class, and Race

Today, PAs have authority and discretion regarding whether non-capital suspects are allowed pre-trial bail. On the other hand, defense attorneys generally argue for their clients' release on their own recognizance or the lowest bail possible.

The U.S. bail system dates back to the 18th century. In 1789, framers of the U.S. Constitution worked concurrently to draft and pass the Judiciary Act and the 8th Amendment which made excessive bail unconstitutional. The bail concept was borrowed from England. Crudely, bail is the value or amount of money pre-trial suspects must pledge to the courts in order to remain free until their court dates. A similar system was also implemented for some convicted offenders to allow them to remain free during their appeals or for other approved reasons. The point here is that a lot of blacks do not have incomes or wealth to secure bail through bail bondsmen. In general, bail bondsmen require at least ten percent (10%) of the bail imposed by the court. For example, a bail of $50,000 requires about $5,000 in cash or liquid assets to be deposited before pre-trial or post-trial release.

Critics of the bail system have argued that it penalizes the poor. In general, higher income persons were more capable of being bonded out of jail prior to their court dates than the poor and most black suspects. The bail system has caused some racial justice advocates to characterize some facilities as debtor jails and prisons. Reports have documented the fact that literally thousands of "innocent" individuals have remained in pre-trial detention because they were unable to secure money for bail.

Peremptory Challenges and Rigged Juries

The 6th Amendment of the U.S. Constitution guarantees accused offenders the right to a trial in front of an unbiased jury of their peers. For centuries, researchers and racial justice supporters have highlighted the practice among some PAs to exclude certain residents from serving on juries based on their race and other factors.

Batson v. Kentucky

Batson v. Kentucky was a landmark case that affirmed blacks' right to the equal protection clause of the 14th Amendment. The court ruled that prosecutors and defense lawyers can ask to dismiss an unlimited number of prospective jurors for cause that can be substantiated and approved by presiding judges. In addition, each side has a limited number of peremptory challenges (PCs) for which no cause must be given. Zealous prosecuting attorneys have been accused of employing peremptory challenges to disproportionately eliminate blacks from juries in racially sensitive criminal cases.

James Batson, a black man, was accused of burglary and receipt of stolen goods. The prosecutor used his peremptory challenges to dismiss all four prospective black jurors, resulting in Batson being found guilty by the racially skewed jury. On an appeal, the U.S. Supreme Court in a 7-2 ruling found that the PA violated the equal protection clause of the 14th Amendment. Justice Powell authored the majority ruling:

> "The harm from discriminatory jury selection extends beyond that inflicted on the defendant and the excluded juror to touch the entire community. Selection procedures that purposefully exclude black persons from juries undermine public confidence in the fairness of our system of justice."[98]

Defendants are not guaranteed a jury consisting of members of their race/ethnicity, but prospective jurors cannot be excluded based solely on their race. In appeals filed in response to alleged discriminatory use of peremptory challenges, the burden of proof shifts to the state to disclose race-neutral causes for excluding black jurors.

On February 15, 2019, the Public Broadcasting System (PBS) posted a story online regarding another high-profile and racially sensitive criminal case in Mississippi. After a number of court cases and appeals, the U.S. Supreme Court agreed to hear the case of Curtis Flowers, a black man who was charged and found guilty of the murders of four whites in Mississippi in 1997. However, in five subsequent appeals, Flowers' verdicts and death penalty had been either thrown out or resulted in hung juries. His lawyers argued that the physical evidence and faulty witness testimonies were not sufficient for a conviction and the death penalty. Still, he had remained behind bars for at least twenty-two years. Tirelessly, his lawyers repeatedly appealed his convictions on the grounds that the prosecuting attorney had systematically employed peremptory challenges to eliminate all black prospective jurors, five in one case and 15 in another. At least one state court found that the blatant

---

98 https://www.uscourts.gov/educational-resources/educational-activities/facts-and-case-summary-batson-v-kentucky

exclusion of blacks was at a minimum prima facie evidence of biased jury rigging by the prosecuting attorney.

After hearing and reviewing evidence in the case, in June of 2019, the U.S. Supreme court reversed both Flowers' 2010 conviction and death penalty. In a 7-2 ruling, the court stated that Flowers' equal protection right covered in the 14th Amendment had been violated by the systematic elimination of black jurors for no reason other than race.

Racial justice advocates have examined PAs' patterns regarding peremptory challenges over specific time periods or their careers. In general, researchers have collected and analyzed data from cases that were similar in terms of the following: 1) the race of both victims and alleged offenders; 2) racial make-up of jury pools; and 3) the number of peremptory challenges used to dismiss prospective jurors by race. Results of empirical research show that some PAs used PCs at a significantly higher rate to exclude blacks from juries than whites, particularly when victims were white, and the defendants were black.

Judges and the Courts

Judges at local, state, and federal levels are decision-makers who influence convictions, fines, restitution, and incarceration rates. In 2016, the American Constitution Society reported that white men were about one third of the population but were over fifty-eight percent (58%) of state judges. In addition, people of color accounted for about twenty percent and women less than thirty-three percent. [99]

To be clear, there is nothing inherently wrong with white judges; however, questions do arise when Merton's modified personality types are considered. To what extent do their biases influence their discretion regarding pre-trial bonding decisions and sentencing of black defendants? Given the history of race relations in the U.S., is it reasonable for black defendants to experience

99 https://www.americanprogress.org/issues/courts/news/2016/09/15/144287/racial-and-gender-diversity-sorely-lacking-in-americas-courts

anxiety or strain in courtrooms, whether innocent or guilty? Their perceptions and beliefs regarding blind justice might influence their decisions to accept plea bargains to avoid longer prison/jail terms, especially those having previous criminal history records.

Sentencing Guidelines and Race

Discourse surrounding what is often characterized as black overrepresentation in jails and prisons must include examinations of judges and sentencing guidelines when applicable. Ultimately, the goal should be to decrease criminal offending rates of all races and to offer restorative justice models as alternatives to jails and prisons.

For several decades, at the federal level and in some states, mandatory minimum sentencing guidelines for repeat offenders of all types led to skyrocketing federal and state prison populations. Until about 2004, federal judges had no discretion in terms of length of prison sentences. They were mandated to utilize a numerical weighting system that did not allow for consideration of mitigating circumstances. A convicted offender's numerical score was the sole determinant of her/his minimum prison sentence.

Later, the guidelines became only advisory, giving the discretion back to judges. Keep in mind that a significant body of research has documented glaring racial disparities in prison sentences by race for identical crimes. Much of that research focused on the race of both offenders and their victims. Invariably, blacks received longer sentences for crimes against whites than whites who committed the same offense against blacks. An indisputable truth is that judges, who are humans too, possess biases and the authority to make life-altering decisions for defendants they encounter in their courtrooms.

Without a doubt, PAs, defense lawyers, and judges are major determinants of the treatment accorded those arrested by law enforcement at local, state, and federal levels. They have the authority to make decisions including the following: 1) who goes free; 2) who receives pre-trial bond and the amount of bail; 3) type of pre-trial legal counsel; 4) guilty or innocent verdicts; and 5) length of jail/prison sentences. While rendering decisions, they expect Americans to assume that they are objective and impartial. In other words, they want Americans to believe that they do not allow their prejudices or biases to influence their decisions. Is it reasonable to assume that CJ personnel can be accurately profiled as being mostly fair, conditionally fair, or mostly unfair? If yes, what are the possible implications for blacks given the racial composition of CJ decision-makers?

CHAPTER 5

Prison System

This chapter contains the results of an investigation of the U.S. prison system regarding the plight of African Americans. The investigation focused on the following: 1) racial composition of U.S. prisons; 2) treatment of inmates; 3) penological experiments; 4) commercialization of prisoners; and 5) parole and its implications.

Historically, it has been asserted that a prison sentence was designed to accomplish different goals. First, it was solely punishment for a crime. Second, it was a form of retribution or pay-back for a crime. Third, prison sentences were thought to deter would-be or prospective offenders. Finally, it was offered as a time for inmates to engage in rehabilitation programs that could give them a fresh start upon their release.

Based on observations, documentaries, and official statistics, most Americans agree that a prison sentence functions to exact punishment, dehumanize, and strip away citizenship. Clearly, prison sentences were not designed to provide treatment or to rehabilitate. In many cases, individuals are a lot worse-off after serving a prison sentence than when they entered. That fact has serious implications for groups who are disproportionately represented in the system.

Unbeknownst to most Americans is the fact that the 13th Amendment to the U.S. Constitution states that prisoners/inmates are "slaves." Below is the text of the 13th Amendment for review:

> "Neither slavery nor involuntary servitude, except as a punishment for crime whereof the party shall have been duly

convicted, shall exist within the United States, or any place subject to their jurisdiction."[100]

Many prisons in the U.S. have been characterized by inhumane living quarters and slave labor. In some Deep South states, life inside prisons appear analogous to conditions that existed on large plantations prior to the end of the Civil War.

Profile of U.S. Inmates

Ironically, the world's model democracy has the highest imprisonment rate. Reports reiterate that while the U.S. represents a little under five percent of the world's population, it accounts for at least twenty percent of the world's prisoners. Furthermore, reports reveal that glaring racial/ethnic disparities exist with blacks accounting for at least twenty percent of U.S. prisoners while only being about thirteen percent of the general population. That fact means that African Americans have been and continue to be disproportionately exposed to dehumanizing living conditions in some prisons, mandatory free or cheap work, inadequate rehabilitation programs, and loss of some of their constitutional rights and privileges.

Compared to pre-Civil War times, though horrific, the current racial composition of U.S. prisons reflects significant progress. Absent of equal rights and protection under the U.S. Constitution, blacks have been overrepresented in jails and prisons for centuries. Plantations were nothing but prison camps for slaves. The point here is that records regarding racial disparities in prisons have been standardized for only about seventy years. As a result, the "true" magnitude of black overrepresentation among prisoners between 1865 and the 1950s is unknown.

As slaves of the government, inmates are forced to undergo resocialization upon their arrival to prisons. They receive instructions regarding rules of

100 https://www.law.cornell.edu/constitution/amendmentxiii

conduct and their daily routines. In a lot of cases living quarters are wide-open, barn-like areas with hundreds of metal cots and open toilets and shower areas. However, some living quarters are steel cells that house one, two, or more inmates and are equipped with bunk beds and a metal vanity-toilet unit placed in plain view of everyone. In general, meals consist of food raised on the farms, where applicable. The average day begins around 5:00 AM beginning with breakfast before inmates proceed to work assignments or return to their living quarters. In some prisons, inmates are forced to work in the fields and around the facilities if they have relevant skill sets (e.g., painting, construction, plumbing, and back office). Some prisons operate production facilities that build or renovate furniture and/or create leather-products (e.g., belts, caps, sun visors, and wallets/purses). In a few cases, inmates are compensated for their labor, however, usually far less than the minimum wage.

Prison life breeds a subculture. For protection, inmates often join racially segregated gangs. Weapons or shanks are made from anything that can cause harm or even death to a fellow inmate. Perceived weak inmates are often subjected to rape or assaults; however, hope for some inmates is found in religion. Despite the dehumanizing prison environment, a majority of inmates appear to adopt conforming, innovative, and ritualist modes of adaptation.

Education and the Prison Connection

Readily accessible official data draws a direct, causal link between low educational attainment and the probability of being imprisoned. Approximately sixty-six percent (66%) of state inmates did not have a high school diploma in 2015.

It has been estimated that a ten percent (10%) increase in high school graduation rates would potentially coincide with a nine percent (9%) drop in arrests and eventually imprisonment rates. Moreover, policy analysts suggest that it costs about $15B to imprison about half of all non-violent offenders in the U.S. If diversionary programs were offered to non-violent offenders, a large portion of prison budgets could be reallocated to help improve poor and isolated public schools.

In July of 2016, the U.S. Department of Education (ED) published a report entitled "Trends in State and Local Expenditures on Corrections and Education" that revealed spending priorities over the past three decades. Results of their analysis showed that expenditure budgets have favored corrections over education in 48 of the 50 states. On average, increases in per capita spending for state corrections and jails have tripled that of rates for public PK-12 education. A key finding was that: ["During the past three decades, between 1979-80 and 2012-13, state and local expenditures for P-12 education doubled from $258B to $534 billion. On the other hand, total state and local expenditures for corrections quadrupled from $17B to $71 billion."]

Penological Experimentations

Whether intended or unintended, a disproportionate percent of African Americans has been forced to participate in government sponsored penological experiments that have become models for other nations. On August 10, 2016, a segment appeared on C-SPAN's Book TV that disclosed results of a comparative study of prisons and incarceration around the globe. It was reported that many countries have adopted practices previously implemented in the U.S.; however, only two of them, the proliferation of super max prisons and for-profit corrections, are reviewed here.

Solitary Confinement

Despite the psychological trauma caused by solitary confinement, the U.S. has been a leader in building and operating what are termed "super max" prison facilities. The units feature extended length of severe isolation for up to twenty-three hours per day. Unlike drug trials, policy makers have not even demanded "animal experiments" to identify and assess short and long-term impacts of extended social isolation on prisoners. On the surface, it appears that blacks have been disproportionately subjected to treatment previously reserved for persons with severe mental challenges and treatment used to punish and/or obtain valuable intelligence from prisoners of war. Such treatment is likely to result in post-traumatic stress disorders (PTSD) that will likely go untreated upon their re-entry into society because of their prison records.

Commercialization of Incarceration

During the last three decades, governmental agencies and private and public institutions have "outsourced" different functions or operations to external providers to cut costs, which is reflected in personnel-related costs and less strict federal regulations.

In most cases, when private corporations contract prison functions, they reduce the number of full-time employees and their fringe benefits. Hiring and firing decisions also undergo less scrutiny and are devoid of meaningful due process in terms of employee appeals.

Privatization of jails/prisons is sold to the public as cost-cutting measures to combat skyrocketing state and federal prison/corrections budgets. Essentially, private companies are awarded contracts to provide facilities, staff, and all other necessities to carry out prison sentences. Australia adopted this model and has outpaced the U.S. in recent years.

Stakeholders at all levels should ask why private prisons are theoretically more efficient and less costly than government-run prisons while providing comparable services. As a business enterprise, private prisons develop a supply chain to obtain necessary goods and services to operate their facilities. The supply chain includes food, utilities, telephone, healthcare, waste management, and recreation/exercise equipment. Because of this, it is easy to see why communities lobby heavily for the construction of a jail/prison in their area. Local businesses welcome family and friends of prisoners who routinely show up and often buy food, beverages, fuel, and some even stay overnight.

Private prison corporations invest their assets based on the assumption that if they build a prison, the federal government or state will ensure that they place a minimum number of inmates in their facilities to satisfy their cash flow and profit margins. Here is how it works. Unlike hotel guests, prisoners do not pay for their room and board in cash. They merely serve as a headcount for per diem reimbursements from the government. The model is similar to that of "choice" in public education. Funding for each child goes to where they are enrolled. There is an agreed upon daily per diem placed on the head of each inmate held. Ironically, blacks' overrepresentation in private jails and prisons generate hefty profits for private investors or stockholders.

Some real estate operations often say, "Build it and they will come." In terms of private prisons, the saying is likely "guarantee a minimum number of inmates per year and we will build it." Like any other enterprise, for-profit prison companies secure construction and other loans and must produce a viable business plan showing sufficient profit margins. Financing is contingent or likely when prospective borrowers have service contracts in hand to generate income to repay loans. In terms of private prisons, the first and most critical milestone is to obtain an official estimate of the number of inmates and the daily per diem rate the government is willing to pay over a specific number of years.

They will not construct a jail or prison without some assurances that they will be given custody of a minimum number of inmates each year. For example, to build a two hundred bed prison, developers would reasonably need to have the assurance of at least one hundred inmates per year, equaling a projected fifty percent (50%) annual occupancy rate.

Here is another indisputable truth. From a free enterprise or capitalist perspective, there is literally no incentive to develop and implement criminal justice reforms to divert non-violent and drug-related offenders or to decrease prison sentences for such offenses. Private jails/prisons are enterprises that generate income and wealth for stockholders who look like the decision-makers responsible for literally ensuring a minimum headcount. Imagine that. To test the assertion, take some time to examine and compare photographs of state and federal officials who negotiate outsourcing contracts and private prison executives. It would not surprise most Americans to find that photographs of the two groups of decision-makers would look very similar.

Prisoners and Politics

In some voting districts, black headcounts carry more political weight than their votes. From a geo-political perspective, black inmates help to increase population counts in primarily rural areas. The U.S. census counts inmates in the district in which they are held captive, resulting in artificial inflation of population counts that influence the drawing of political boundaries or districts.[101]

Prison counties or districts benefit from having hundreds if not thousands of "residents" who they do not have to consider when formulating public policy. In most states, inmates do not vote. Some readers will immediately be reminded of the Three-Fifths (3/5) Compromise that allowed slaves states to count each slave as only 3/5 of a person in census counts to ensure a greater number of southern congressmen at that time. Things seem to change but remain undeniably the same.

So, is there a preponderance of evidence of blacks' amazing perseverance and resiliency in avoiding prison despite system forces? According to some analysts, the odds of a black American being imprisoned are relatively high. Experts who analyzed criminal justice data and demographics have calculated the odds of going to prison in the U.S. by race/ethnicity. An article that appeared in the *Denver Post* on May 4, 2016 revealed some startling projections. According to the article: ["The U.S. Department of Justice reports that boys born in 2001 face the following odds of going to prison: 1 in 17 for whites; 1 in 6 for Latinos; and 1 in 3 for African-Americans."][102]

---

101 https://www.prisonersofthecensus.org/faq.html

102 https://www.denverpost.com/2016/12/22/colorado-race-arrests-prison-report/

Parole and Race

After serving a portion of their prison sentences, some inmates who meet certain criteria become eligible for parole or early release from prison. Criteria for earning parole include staying out of trouble; satisfactorily performing work assignments; and increasing their academic attainment. Considering conditions in a lot of prisons, the percent of inmates who become eligible and granted parole is astonishing.

Parole is often a two-edged sword or a blessing and a curse. It is a privilege, not a constitutional right. In most jurisdictions, parole boards are appointed by governors and charged with assessing each applicant's readiness to return to society.

Usually parole is contingent upon an applicant having a stable, post-incarceration living environment, a viable sponsor, and a job or employment prospects. After their early release they are required to meet with their parole officer regularly, submit to random drug tests, and pay a fee and/or restitution each month. Failure to satisfy any one of those requirements could result in reincarceration. In addition, all subsequent criminal violations can result in parole revocation.

Parole related payments and fees are major obstacles for the poor and many black former inmates. Their prison record, relatively lower educational attainment, and lack of 21st Century job skills limit their competitiveness for employment, thereby making parole related payments extremely difficult. The inability to earn wages causes some parolees to turn to crime to finance their parole.

Disenfranchisement of Ex-Felons

Michelle Alexander argued in her book entitled *The New Jim Crow* that the ex-con label serves to further segregate the U.S. population. She argued that the practice of "unmasking" criminal history records has helped to perpetuate a 21st Century caste-like existence among African Americans in the U.S. The primary evidence in her prosecution of the caste-like case focused on the pattern of treatment afforded ex-felons who are essentially stripped of all their civil rights, even after completely serving their sentences.

There is general agreement, regardless of race/ethnicity, that if you commit the crime, you should pay the fine or do the time. When debt to victims and society is paid or satisfied, punishment should end completely, and ex-offenders should be afforded equal rights as all other citizens.

However, consistent with Alexander's observations, in the U.S. a prison record serves as a permanent stigma or master status. It limits and blocks access to a host of opportunities including student loans, certain employment sectors, and public assistance. Ironically, ex-cons have been mandated to check a box on applications indicating that they had been incarcerated. After obtaining jobs, some former inmates have been fired for failing to check the "ex-con" box on their applications.

Literally tens of thousands of ex-offenders who did their time and want to work are forced to settle for less than living wage jobs without benefits and unfavorable work conditions. Rather than accepting low wages and no benefits, some ex-offenders turn to illegal acts that eventually cause their return to prison. This burden is disproportionately felt in poor and communities of color. If merely being black in the U.S. is a challenge, imagine what life is like for African Americans who have been imprisoned.

Unfortunately, a large percentage of ex-inmates return to jail/prison. Recently, the Bureau of Justice Statistics reported that about sixty-seven percent (67%) of inmates released were re-arrested within three years. Extending that time to about five years, a whopping seventy-six percent (76%) were re-arrested.

Those sentenced initially for property and drug related offenses had recidivism rates ranging from about sixty-two percent (62%) to seventy-six percent (76%).

Expungement

Ex-cons often see themselves as physically free but socially, politically, and economically chained or held captive. For decades some connected and/or higher income ex-cons have masked their criminal records by applying for a little-known legal tool called expungement. In most states, expungement options are available to wipe criminal records clean. Eligibility criteria often include type of offense and criminal history. However, those meeting eligibility requirements encounter another roadblock. The cost of retaining a lawyer is prohibitive in many cases, ranging from about six hundred to twelve hundred dollars. While twelve hundred dollars might not seem like much, to clear an ex-offender's criminal record, their past contacts with the justice system might have exhausted their resources along with those of family members and friends. In addition, expungement is not a right and is awarded by judges who potentially issued the prison sentence.

Fortunately, civil rights advocates have been proposing criminal justice reforms intended to restore some rights to ex-cons. Recently, advocates pushed for Amendment 4 in Florida that restored voting rights to more than an estimated 1.5M convicted felons who had successfully completed their sentences. Restoring voting rights to convicted felons will potentially change the landscape of some voting districts at local and congressional levels.

First Step Act

Lively debates continue regarding the effects of get tough on crime bills at state and federal levels on moral, racial equality, and economic grounds. The enormous costs to taxpayers for housing non-violent and drug-related offenders for decades just does not make sense.

Arguably, now that the faces of drug-related offenders are becoming unavoidably "diverse/inclusive," decision-makers appear to be more inclined to show compassion and advocate for diversion and treatment instead of a chorus of "lock 'em up."

It is imperative that readers keep in mind that laws and statutes are passed to satisfy a compelling government interest. President Trump signed the First Step Act a bipartisan, criminal justice reform bill in December of 2018. Its intended impacts were summarized by a Fox News post as follows:

> "The legislation would give federal judges more discretion when sentencing some drug offenders and boost prisoner rehabilitation efforts. It also would reduce life sentences for some drug offenders with three convictions, or 'three strikes,' to 25 years. Another provision would allow about 2,600 federal prisoners sentenced for crack cocaine offenses before August 2010 the opportunity to petition for a reduced penalty. The changes were aimed at addressing concerns that the nation›s war on drugs has exploded the prison population without helping people prepare for their return to society."[103]

The criminal justice reform bill should be perceived as being analogous to a constitutional amendment based on unanticipated consequences of enacted laws. It can also be viewed as corroborating evidence of President Trump's rigged system theory.

---

103 https://www.foxnews.com/politics/senate-passes-criminal-justice-reform-bill-sends-to-house

CHAPTER 6

Wrongful Convictions and Imprisonments

Corroborating evidence of a rigged CJS was found in the literature regarding wrongful criminal convictions. Recall that the 14th Amendment contains the rights of the accused and victims in a court of law. They were intended to prevent wrongful convictions and imprisonments and to make crime victims "whole again."

Criminal cases are characterized by competing teams. Defendants are defined as the accused and, they are presumed innocent until proven guilty in a court of law. On the opposing side are PAs who represent the government and eligible victims. As stated earlier, prosecuting attorneys in collaboration with law enforcement are tasked with presenting evidence that prove "beyond a shadow of a doubt" the guilt of the accused. There are untold dollars and human resources expended to ensure guilt in local, state, and federal courts. As a result, patterns or practices in so-called "wrongful convictions and imprisonments" must set-off alarms. If errors are made in more high-profile cases, what is the error rate among non-violent and drug-related criminal cases?

In general, at least two or more CJS officials are required to "fix" a case to ensure conviction. Information gleaned from a *New York Times'* article indicated that police investigators, prosecuting attorneys, expert witnesses, racially skewed juries, and trial judges play varying roles in wrongful convictions. [104] Zealous investigators, prosecuting attorneys, and judges have employed one or more of the following to fraudulently strengthen their cases:

104 https://www.nytimes.com/topic/subject/false-arrests-convictions-and-imprisonments

1) planted evidence; 2) witness tampering; 3) dubious line-ups; 4) withholding of exculpatory evidence; and 5) offer of a reduced sentence for a guilty plea. In addition, many wrongful convictions can be partially attributed to ineffective legal counsel.

Innocence Project

Fortunately, numerous non-profits, social justice advocates, and the mass media have helped to illuminate the growing number of wrongfully convicted and imprisoned U.S. citizens. The Innocence Project has a storied record of freeing wrongfully convicted African Americans from U.S. prisons. Overall, it has led efforts to exonerate and gain the freedom of more than three hundred wrongfully convicted suspects based on new DNA test results. Its more recent successes were summarized as follows:

> "In 2018, together we've exonerated nine innocent people, the most ever in the Innocence Project's 26-year history and helped pass 17 wrongful conviction reforms in 14 states. After spending more than 215 years in prison combined, our clients are where they belong: home with their loved ones."[105]

While there is no claim that a majority of inmates are innocent, one wrongful conviction, imprisonment, and/or execution is too many. Among the more than two hundred and sixty [106] "overturned" convictions since 1989, almost all were men and a whopping seventy percent were men of color. [107] Shockingly, over twenty wrongfully convicted men were sentenced to death.

On March 7, 2017, an article appearing in the *New York Times* summarized results from the National Registry of Exonerations. The project has been managed by the University of Michigan law school and was designed to create

---

105 https://www.innocenceproject.org/justice-2018/

106 https://www.naacp.org/history-of-lynchings/

107 https://www.naacp.org/history-of-lynchings/

profiles of those wrongfully convicted and subsequently exonerated. Data related to nearly 2,000 exonerations over about thirty years were analyzed. The research team found striking racial disparities among persons wrongfully convicted of murder, sexual assault, or drug trafficking crimes. The percent black or white wrongfully convicted for specific crimes was as follows: 1) murder—black (50%) and white (36%); 2) sexual assault—black (60%) and white (33%); and 3) drug related—black (55%) and white (25%). Ironically, African Americans have had the dubious distinction of having both higher conviction and exoneration rates for those offenses. [108]

According to published reports, blacks have spent more years in prison due to wrongful convictions than any other race of Americans. Unfortunately, victims of wrongful convictions and imprisonment can never be made "whole" again. They suffer immeasurable losses in terms of "free time," unrealized income and wealth accumulation, and quality time spent with family and friends that cannot be recouped.

---

108 https://www.nytimes.com/2017/03/07/us/wrongful-convictions-race-exoneration.html

SECTION XII: MASS COMMUNICATION SYSTEM AND RACE

The impetus for this component of the rigged system investigation was the suspicion that mass communication platforms have facilitated the emergence, dissemination, and perpetuation of negative racial stereotypes. It is reasonable and logical to assume that the way blacks have been portrayed in the media has served as justification for their treatment in different sectors of society. The investigation focused on types of communication platforms and the optics and narrative they have employed to define African Americans.

Without question, freedom of speech and the free press are cherished and unique rights inherent in true democracies. However, mass media decision-makers who harbor racial biases help determine the scope and nature of how blacks were and continue to be portrayed on different platforms. It is that power or authority that can be employed to influence race relations in the U.S.

CHAPTER 1

Birth of Black Stereotypes

Stereotypes can be either positive or negative. In the past, racial/ethnic stereotypes have been generated by a single or few alleged acts committed by a member(s) of a group. The real or alleged acts/behaviors were strategically publicized to characterize or typecast most or all members of that group.

In 2016, Suzane Jardim published an online article that systematically traced the origins of an array of black stereotypes. The author employed a similar research design utilized in this endeavor as online sources were examined for common themes but not all sources were cited. Readers were encouraged to conduct follow-up investigations.

According to Jardim, most of the early stereotypes were born out of unfounded and exaggerated allegations. Or, they were based on mythical black characters depicted in books authored by slave owners and/or like-minded persons. Some of the most frequently deployed stereotypes or type-casting of blacks included Jim Crow, Uncle Tom, Uncle Remus, sex-crazed black bucks, and Jezebels. The latter, according to the author was based in part on biblical scriptures regarding a Jewish Queen who was ruthless and seductive. European explorers and early settlers likely encountered African women who appeared nearly naked. In addition, many possibly practiced polygamy and enthusiastically worshipped an array of idols in public through dance.

In comparison, African men were portrayed as being unintelligent, wild, strong, lazy, and easily frightened. The most prominent and lethal stereotype of black men was the "black buck" who was allegedly obsessed with sex and young white girls. The buck stereotype was justification for untold numbers of beatings and deaths of black men.

CHAPTER 2

Dissemination of Stereotypes

This chapter chronicled the introduction of communication platforms in the U.S. The investigation focused on print, radio, television, and internet-based platforms. Particular attention was given to observed patterns or practices related to content regarding blacks. It was assumed that Americans are apt to believe what they frequently hear, read, and see.

Print Media

First, the print media was propelled in the wake of the introduction of the printing press in 1440. Mass production and distribution of both religious and government decrees helped solidify collective ideals and patterns or practices.

Early newspapers and newsletters were distributed by proponents of slavery and the opposition or abolitionists. Front page stories depicting blacks as immoral and violent rapists served to justify them being held captive and subject to cruel and unusual punishment.

In comparison, anti-slavery print media did just the opposite. They printed stories of black families being separated, rapes of young black women, and castrations and lynchings of black men. Those stories shocked the inner souls of some decision-makers, resulting in a sporadic freeing of some slaves, contributions to the Underground Railroad, and support for the Civil War.

Leading up to the Civil War, actions or decisions rendered by all three branches of the federal government resulted in both positive and negative consequences for slaves.

A thriving public campaign was waged by abolitionists primarily in the North and Northeast. William Lloyd Garrison is often credited with being an anti-slavery thought leader during his time. In 1831, Garrison began publishing *The Liberator,* a newspaper with a fairly large circulation. Optics and narratives included in the paper depicted the cruel, unusual, and inhumane treatment of slaves. Abolitionists established social networks and used them to distribute *The Liberator.* Garrison was credited for helping to mobilize anti-slavery associations including the Massachusetts Anti-Slavery Society, the New England Anti-Slavery Society in 1831, and the American Anti-Slavery Society in 1833.

Of course, black abolitionists were also publishers of anti-slavery newspapers and newsletters. Frederick Douglass published the *North Star* beginning in December 1847 in New York City. The name, North Star, was chosen because slaves followed it to escape to freedom from southern plantations. By some accounts, he funded the paper initially from proceeds from his speaking tour throughout Ireland and Great Britain.

Douglass and Garrison were collaborators but had philosophical differences. Around 1851, it was reported that Douglass and Garrison parted ways as Garrison, not Douglass, began advocating for violence. [109]

In the early 1850s Harriet Beecher Stowe wrote a series of articles that appeared in an anti-slavery newspaper. Overtime, they were combined and published under the title of *Uncle Tom's Cabin* in 1852. The book, depicting cruel, unusual, inhumane treatment of blacks, became enormously popular in the U.S. and around the world. [110] Some accounts indicate that upon meeting Ms. Stowe, President Lincoln stated that her book helped to mobilize an aggressive anti-slavery movement.

Similar to earlier forms of print media, front page stories in a lot of today's newspapers contain images and narratives gleaned from filed police reports

---

109 https://www.britannica.com/topic/The-North-Star-American-newspaper

110 https://www.historynet.com/causes-of-the-civil-war

that invariably showcase alleged crimes by the poor and black boys and young men of color (BYMOC). Front-page and daily coverage of a small segment of the black population evidently sells newspapers, while helping to perpetuate racial stereotypes.

Radio and Television

Advances in the study of electromagnetic waves and the revelation that they could propagate through free space enabling both audio and video to be transmitted and received by billions around the globe ushered in the widespread ownership of radios and subsequently televisions.

When the radio became an affordable technology in American households, it also became a preferred source of both news and entertainment. Content was determined by station owners who in terms of racial justice were either mostly fair, conditionally fair, or mostly unfair. Even on radio, blacks were more often than not portrayed as criminals, illiterate, and childish.

Prior to the introduction of social media platforms, television, which was introduced in the late 1920s and early 1930s, was the only source of both optics and narratives related to African Americans. Ownership of radios and television sets was related to income and race, yet television became the primary disseminator of negative black stereotypes. Early on television executives allowed programming that almost exclusively depicted blacks as illiterate, domestics, unemployed, pimps, drug abusers and traffickers, rapists, and murderers. Those descriptors are eerily similar to those recently employed by President Trump to characterize illegal immigrants. To combat the blaxploitation genre in sitcoms and motion pictures, a small number of black movie-makers, directors, and writers began producing programs that reflected the full range of black life, eventually leading to the successful launch of Black Entertainment Television (BET) and more recently, the Oprah Winfrey Network (OWN).

Newspaper, radio, and television executives or decision-makers are in business to make money. Their content is determined in large part by what business owners believe will get the largest share of consumers' attention or viewership. Apparently, the plight of African Americans is attractive to a large segment of the general population. On major networks, blacks have been both the alpha and omega of newscast programming. Prior to COVID-19 coverage, they literally monopolized breaking news stories at the top of the hour as well as the sporting news segment at the bottom of the hour. A compelling case can be made that network news stories primarily cast blacks in one of two roles, criminal offenders and/or athletes.

Social Media and Race

The introduction of social media platforms (e.g., Facebook, YouTube, Apple, Snapchat, and Twitter) have given people and organizations with differing ideologies related to race in the U.S. tools to disseminate their views to millions each day. It has been estimated that nearly one-third of Americans receive their news online. The power of social media is reflected in how it has been employed to recruit foreign fighters to the Middle East, promote white supremacists' groups, and interfere with the 2016 presidential election. So, it is no surprise that online campaigns that attempt to "shame" and belittle blacks have been at least somewhat successful.

Furthermore, advances in artificial intelligence have enabled "fake news" generators to manipulate videos and audios to spew disinformation or "alternative facts" to hundreds of millions of unknowing viewers. An investigative report and video released by CNN on February 2, 2019 showed the potential threats posed by deep fakes in terms of the upcoming 2020 elections, national security, and race relations. [111]

The technology allows perpetrators to superimpose the faces and voices of elected officials, business leaders, and everyday Americans in a virtual

111 https://www.cnn.com/2019/01/28/tech/deepfake-lawmakers/index.html

environment that could set off potential conflicts and wars. As a result, Americans have been encouraged to be cautious of information or news gleaned from video and audio that cannot be substantiated by other trusted sources. Deep fakes require consumers to view but verify news stories and other posts.

A plethora of empirical studies have found that the negative representation of blacks in the media influences out-group members' attitudes and behaviors toward them. Those studies are readily accessible in scholarly journals and online. Moreover, similar findings have been gleaned from surveys of people in the U.S. and Great Britain. Nearly fifty years ago in 1974, Hartman and Husband published their book entitled *Racism and the Mass Media* that is still regarded as one of the definitive empirical studies in this space. It is based on a survey of British citizens that was designed to measure their attitudes and beliefs regarding immigrants of color, primarily blacks. Subjects reported their reactions to the images of blacks in the media during that time frame. Results of the study found that the mass media was a powerful force that had influenced public opinions, biases, and behavior. Similarly, Ronald Weitzer and Steven A. Tuch reanalyzed data from several surveys regarding U.S. citizens' perceptions of police biases. The researchers found that public attitudes and beliefs regarding police encounters with blacks was primarily a function of personal contacts with law enforcement and frequency of their consumption of daily news, especially those alleging racial profiling and other discriminatory patterns or practices.

Unfortunately, the proliferation and perpetuation of racial stereotypes can influence the perceptions and beliefs of even African Americans. In 2014, Valerie Adams-Base published results of a study that was designed to measure the effects of the stereotypical representation of blacks in the media. The Black Media Messages Questionnaire (BMMQ) was administered to over one hundred and twenty black youth. Items on the survey were designed to measure subjects' social media engagement, body-image ratings, awareness of related historical facts, racial socialization, and their identities. The effects of black representation in the media on black youth well-being and self-concepts differed by age, gender, television viewing patterns, and whether subjects rejected or endorsed the images. The point here is that negative images consumed daily by black youth can lead to anti-social self-concepts and lower self-efficacy. [112]

Mass Media Field Experiment

For decades, it seems that the business plans of mass communication enterprises have been partially based on a demand for negative content regarding African Americans. Examinations of content programming in print, television, and online suggest that negative optics and narratives regarding African Americans attract billions of dollars in advertising revenue from business/industry annually.

Circumstantial evidence of a biased mass communication system can be easily obtained. Readers are encouraged to conduct a weeklong observational study of the news on different platforms (e.g., print, radio, television, and/or online). Step 1: Create three columns and assign one of the following labels to each: positive (e.g., non-criminal); negative (e.g., unemployed, criminal offenders, etc.); and neutral or balanced portrayals. Step 2: Closely examine all stories featuring African Americans on the chosen platform. Step 3: Evaluate each story and assign them to the most appropriate category/column. Step 4: At the end of the experiment time frame, add the totals in each category together to get the sum of all stories contained in the experiment. Step 5: Divide the total in each column/category by the sum of all the stories to obtain the percent of positive, negative, and neutral portrayals or images. For the purpose of this crude observational study, thirty-four percent (34%) or greater signals overrepresentation in a category. Based on the results of your

112 https://journals.sagepub.com/doi/abs/10.1177/0021934714530396

investigation, you will either provide corroborating or exculpatory evidence in the alleged "rigged" communication system case. [113]

113 Weitzer, Ronald, and Steven A. Tuch (2005). "Racially Biased Policing: Determinants of Citizen Perceptions." *Social Forces*, 83(3), 1009–1030. https://doi.org/10.1353/sof.2005.0050.

SECTION XIII: RELIGION AND RACE

Extrapolating from President Trump's rigged system thesis, religion or faith could be intentionally or unintentionally employed to obtain social and economic advantages over illiterate and new converts. This section contains the results of an investigation of the possible role Christianity or scriptures found in the Holy Bible might have directly or indirectly played in the etiology and perpetuation of chattel slavery in the U.S.

Particular attention was given to the treatment of religion by the framers of the Constitution. The 1st Amendment denied the government the right or authority to form or establish a religion. In addition, it could not dictate how religion was practiced. The point here is that African slaves had or should have had freedom of religion following the ratification of the 1st Amendment that occurred on December 15, 1791.

CHAPTER 1

Biblical Scriptures and Slavery

For the purpose of this investigation, information or evidence was sought in scriptures contained in the Old and New Testaments. A careful examination of Old Testament scriptures revealed statements that instructed nations on who they could attack, capture, purchase, and hand down from one generation to the next as heir-property. In Leviticus 25:44-46, the following decree is found:

> "...Your male and female slaves are to come from the nations around you; from them you may buy slaves. 45 You may also buy some of the temporary residents living among you and members of their clans born in your country, and they will become your property. 46 You can bequeath them to your children as inherited property and can make them slaves for life."

Papal Bull of 1493

Fast forward to the 15th Century. During that time, the Roman Catholic Church issued laws and decrees that addressed colonizing foreign lands and slavery. Roughly one year after Portugal built its trading post in West Africa, a decree came down from the Catholic Church that would set the stage for slavery in the U.S. Historians have credited Pope Alexander VI for issuing the 1493 Papal Bull or Inter Caetera that authorized European explorers, primarily Spain and Portugal, to colonize, convert, and enslave non-Christians in both Africa and the Americas.[114]

114 https://www.nlm.nih.gov/nativevoices/timeline/171.html

CHAPTER 2

Religion in Africa

For centuries, treatment of blacks around the globe and in the U.S. has been influenced by decision-makers' interpretations of selected biblical scriptures. This chapter contains the results of an investigation related to the scope and nature of religion in Africa.

In Genesis 10, Noah's son Ham had several sons including Cush. His sons became kings of nations. Biblical scholars have traced the names of nations and people to Noah's sons.

The connection between Ham and Africa has been described as follows:

> ["...Ham was the second son of Noah and the father of Cush, Miriam, Phut and Canaan. Ham's descendants are interpreted by Flavius Josephus and others as having populated Africa and adjoining parts of Asia."] A more detailed account of Ham's connection to Africa is documented in "Hidden Africans of the Bible and Early Church."[115]

Biblical scholars appear to have agreed that references to Cush have referred to some or all of Africa, except Egypt. Much of that area today is referred to as the Sudan. Cush, Niger, and/or Ethiopia were cited nearly sixty times in the Holy Bible but are not clearly identified as Africa.

---

115 https://www.cbeinternational.org/resource/article/priscilla-papers-academic-journal/hidden-africans-bible-and-early-church/

References to Cush or Cushites were found throughout the Old Testament: Psalm (68:31); Psalm (87:3-6); Isaiah (4; and 11:11); Zephaniah (3:10; and 18:1-8); Jeremiah (38:7, 10, 12; 39:16); and Amos (9:7).

African women were described as both beautiful and powerful. Moses had a Cushite wife (Numbers 12:11-16) who was despised by his brother Aaron and his sister Miriam.

King Solomon, who married an Egyptian princess, was afflicted by what Spike Lee called "jungle fever." In his Song of Solomon, his love was described as "black and beautiful" (1 Kings 9:16; 2 Chronicles 8:11). In addition, King Solomon had a delightful visit from the Queen of Sheba (1 Kings 10:1-13; 2 Chronicles 9:1-2) as they exchanged numerous pleasantries and gifts.

It is important to note that scriptures contained in the New Testament described God's love for all people regardless of their race, sex, and/or nation of origin. Questions surrounding the role of blacks in the New Testament were prompted by information contained in an article found online: https://www.cbeinternational.org/resource/article/priscilla-papers-academic-journal/hidden-africans-bible-and-early-church.

While not explicitly identified in the New Testament, Africa and/or Africans, played significant roles with several references to the nation called Cyrene (Libya). According to an online source:

> "Cyrene was located in northern Africa in eastern Libya. A Greek city in the province of Cyrenaica, it had a Jewish community where 100,000 Judean Jews had been forced to settle during the reign of Ptolemy Soter (323–285 BC) and was an early center of Christianity."[116]

In the New Testament, Cyrene was introduced in the books of Matthew, Mark, and Luke. According to Luke 23:26, "As the soldiers led him away,

---

116 https://www.cbeinternational.org/resource/article/priscilla-papers-academic-journal/hidden-africans-bible-and-early-church

they seized Simon from Cyrene, who was on his way in from the country" and forced him to carry the cross as he trailed Jesus. He was arriving to celebrate Passover in Jerusalem. Next, Cyrene was mentioned several times in the book of Acts. Some Cyrenians opposed the ministry of Stephen who was stoned to death for spreading the gospel while Saul looked on with approval (Acts 6:9). In Acts 8:26-39, Phillip explained Isaiah's prophecy regarding the crucifixion of Christ to the treasurer of Ethiopia (Nubia). On his return home, the African stopped in his chariot to read scriptures. He asked Phillip to interpret the scriptures and later convinced Phillip to baptize him. Scholars have reasoned that he had been sent to Jerusalem bearing gifts by Nubia's Queen Candace.

In Acts 10, 11, and 13, native Cyrenians were credited with being instrumental in spreading the gospel of Jesus the Christ in Cypress and later in Antioch. At least two of the disciples who were first called Christians in Antioch were either from Cyrene (Lucius) or Africa (Simon of Niger— (Latin for black). It has been theorized that Simon of Niger was called Simon of Cyrene during the crucifixion.

Religion in West Africa

Surely, cultural conflicts occurred when European explorers landed on the coast of West Africa and when slaves off-boarded ships in the colonies. Race and religion or faith rituals fueled Europeans' ethnocentrism and xenophobic reactions to Africans.

In 2012, the British Broadcasting Corporation (BBC) published an online brief regarding traditional and neo-paganism forms of religion. [117] Many early societies can be characterized as polytheism as they practice religion that focused on idolizing things found in their natural environments. However, the most prominent distinctions are that they lack a single leader, written doctrine, and a uniform philosophical foundation. Pagans made idols and

117 http://www.bbc.co.uk/religion/0/20693321

worshiped birds, cows, snakes, the sun, moon, and stars. Witchcraft, spells, and burning incense were prevalent practices. In Africa, idol worship was common until formal religions were introduced. In addition, there was likely music, dance, and a whole lot of shaking going on. Upon observing novel religious rituals involving worshipping images of birds, snakes, and other carved works of art, European explorers were probably shocked. Just think of the differences among Americans today in terms of observed rituals and practices during worship services.

Islam in Africa

Even other organized religions were foreign to some European explorers and traders. Islam was propagated by the prophet Muhammad who is believed by some to be the last of God's prophets. He has been credited with the uniting of Arabia into a geopolitical force governed by a religious doctrine. The written doctrine is called the Quran, and followers believe that it contains revelations from God as recorded by the Prophet Muhammad until his death.

The introduction of Islam was accompanied by Shari'ah which is composed of a system of laws and punishments. [118] According to most sources, the Arabic term shari'ah (Arabic: شريعة) "refers to the revealed law of God" and originally meant "way" or "path." The system primarily focuses on rituals and social relationships having varying levels of priority and punishment for violations. Recently, several states have passed legislation making the implementation of sharīʿah in the U.S. a criminal offense. Some precepts of the system appear remarkably consistent with prescriptions found in the books of Deuteronomy and Leviticus in which stoning was a form of capital punishment or the death penalty. Specifically, in Deuteronomy (19:19-20) it is stated that a person found guilty should be subject to an equivalent punishment: an eye for an eye, a tooth for a tooth, a life for a life. As a source of deterrence, justice was traditionally carried out in well attended and public spectacles. The point here is that Europeans most likely found both pagan

118 https://www.islamreligion.com/articles/304/viewall/spread-of-islam-in-west-africa/

and Islamic practices different and foreign. Those perceived differences facilitated the emergence of dehumanizing characterizations and/or "them v us" mindsets that served as justifications for slavery.

CHAPTER 3

Enslavement Systems

Most Americans have erroneously believed that Africans were a monolith. However, Africa was home to untold numbers of tribes, or nations, each having its own language and culture. As in other societies, Africans fought among themselves for land, power, and status. Tribal warfare resulted in those being conquered to be either killed or enslaved for a specific amount of time. Generally, captives were not enslaved from one generation to the next. Basil Davidson, in his book *The African Slave Trade*, stated that ["slavery in Africa and the brutal form of slavery that would develop in the Americas were vastly different. African slavery was more akin to European serfdom —the condition of most Europeans in the 15th century. For example, in the Ashanti Kingdom of West Africa, slaves could marry, own property and even own slaves. And, more importantly, slavery ended after a certain number of years of servitude. [119]

The West African slavery system was remarkably similar to Old Testament scriptures regarding the year of jubilee that gave parameters for the scope and nature of the enslavement of fellow Christians. Essentially, after a specific amount of time, all debt would be forgiven, land would revert back to its owners, and slaves would be set free. Imagine that.

In contrast, chattel slavery was implemented in the southern colonies. It was characterized by stripping slaves of their social institutions, tribal hierarchy, languages, norms, values, and gender roles. Moreover, in the colonies, most slaves and their offspring became heir-property that was transferred from one

119 http://www.pbs.org/wgbh/aia/part1/1narr1.html\

generation to the next. Imagine the shock and stress realized by African slaves when it became clear that they would never experience freedom again as they would have in their homeland. To them, the system of enslavement was no longer temporary but for life.

CHAPTER 4

Weaponization of Biblical Scriptures

For a moment, consider the possible implications of slave owners serving as missionaries and using biblical scriptures to convert their slaves to Christianity. Surely, if taken out of context, some scriptures could be employed to convince slaves that their treatment and circumstances were commanded by God, the omnipresent and omnipotent one. As such, why would slaves rebel against God's will?

After an exhaustive search, no evidence was found that identified specific biblical scriptures that were tactically used by slave owners and decision-makers to control slaves, but a few are presented here as purely speculations.

Obedience to Authority

The Apostle Paul in Romans (13:1-7) instructs citizens or believers to obey decision-makers or authorities and their enacted laws. Essentially, Paul urged restraint or avoidance of civil disobedience for fear of unfavorable divine judgement. It is no wonder that in the mid-19th century Karl Marx offered his belief that religion can be used to sustain the populace adherence to "unjust" laws.

Suffering

The bible repeatedly reveals all types of sufferings, trials, and tribulations endured by believers. The quintessential expectancy regarding suffering on earth can be found in the words of Jesus: "In the world you will have tribulation" (John 16:33). In 1 Peter (4:12-14) believers are told that suffering is a fundamental part of their walk with God. The ultimate example of God's expectations regarding suffering was reflected by his decision to allow his prophets and son to be surveilled, harassed, plotted against, publicly humiliated, tortured, enslaved, exiled, and killed.

In Romans 5 (NIV) believers were told:

> "…we also glory in our sufferings, because we know that suffering produces perseverance; 4 perseverance, character; and character, hope".

The promise of eternal life void of illnesses, pain, and persecution had to be attractive to African slaves, especially those on plantations.

Finally, several writings by the Apostle Paul, while imprisoned in Rome, instructed both slaves and slave owners regarding their treatment of one another. In Ephesians 6:5-9, Paul wrote:

> "5 Slaves obey your earthly masters with respect and fear, and with sincerity of heart, just as you would obey Christ. 6 Obey them not only to win their favor when their eye is on you, but as slaves of Christ, doing the will of God from your heart. 7 Serve wholeheartedly, as if you were serving the Lord, not people, 8 because you know that the Lord will reward each one for whatever good they do, whether they are slave or free".

Paul also instructed slave owners to treat their slaves fairly. He wrote:

> "9 And masters treat your slaves in the same way. Do not threaten them, since you know that he who is both their Master and yours is in heaven, and there is no favoritism with him".

The Apostle Paul must be credited with encouraging both slaves and slave owners to show one another love and compassion.

Imagine being a slave-owner for a moment. Which of Paul's scriptures would you more likely than not share with your slaves?

CHAPTER 5

Geo-Religion and Slavery

Based on published accounts, followers of different religious doctrines settled in different colonies. Some denominations believed that slavery was a violation of God's commandments. In general, those opposed to slavery were commonly referred to as abolitionists. [120] Specifically, abolitionists were guided by several beliefs: 1) All humans, regardless of race, were made in the image of God; 2) slave ownership was a personal sin; and 3) giving blacks freedom and equality would lead to redemption. The point here was that ownership of slaves was a personal choice allowed or condoned at the time by decision-makers.

Quakers have been identified as one of the denominations that opposed slavery. Early on, they were the overwhelming majority voting bloc in Pennsylvania. As a result, Pennsylvania was a "free" state. However, there are few accounts of black Quakers.

In comparison, throughout the southeast, or slave states, Christianity was the dominant religion. Recall that most West Africans were pagans; however, according to a 2016 Black Demographics article, up to thirty percent of the original slaves were Muslim.

By most accounts, southern slave owners defined themselves as Christians. They imposed their religion upon their slaves. It has been reported that a majority of slaves were converted to Christianity including some found in Louisiana who were converted to Catholicism by French settlers.

---

120 https://www.nla.gov.au/selected-library-collections/anti-slavery-movement-in-the-united-states

In the South, as more and more slaves were imported to the colonies and forcibly converted to Christianity, laws were passed to limit their rights as fellow children of God. Interestingly, only white Christians could purchase and own other Christians. In 1670, the Virginia General Assembly passed a law that disallowed baptized blacks and Native Americans from purchasing other Christian servants.[121]

121 https://www.history.org/history/teaching/slavelaw.cfm

CHAPTER 6

Early Churches and Race

An online source "The Black Church: A Brief History" chronicled the emergence of Afrocentric religion from the 1750s to post Civil War. [122] Apparently, pre- and post-Civil War decision-makers were suspicious and threatened by all forms of black organizations and associations. In fact, early on, African slaves were not allowed to congregate together in the absence of whites.

In both the North and South, integrated church services were common. Records suggest that blacks were not directly involved in church leadership and finances. In addition, blacks were generally assigned seating in the rear of sanctuaries or in balconies. This was a strategic racial desegregation tactic that was both effective and efficient. Slaves were taught selected scriptures while being under constant surveillance during regular worship services.

Conflicts in mixed churches led to blacks petitioning for independent religious associations. Early on, the Methodist church seemed sympathetic to the plight of free blacks in the U.S. Apparently black and white Methodists worshipped together until racial tensions, causing a split in 1787. The conflict led to the birth of the African Methodist Episcopal (AME) Church in Philadelphia, Pennsylvania. [123] Allegedly, black parishioners were attacked while on their knees praying. That vicious attack in church prompted free blacks to seek religious independence.

Richard Allen, a former Delaware slave, became pastor of Bethel AME Church in 1794. He filed lawsuits in Philadelphia in both 1807 and 1815

---

122 https://aaregistry.org/story/the-black-church-a-brief-history/

123 https://www.ame-church.com/our-church/our-history/

arguing that blacks had the right to an independent church. The court ruled in the plaintiff's favor and the AME Church became an independent black religious denomination, spreading to the northeast, Midwest, and Pacific coast between 1815 and the 1850s. Surprisingly, it also spread to some slave states including Maryland, Missouri, Kentucky, Louisiana, and even South Carolina prior to and during the Civil War. In fact, according to the AME, the church had its greatest gains during the Civil War.

Southern Baptist Association (Evangelicals)

Recorded accounts indicate that the Baptist denomination was present in England and was brought to the colonies in the 17th century. At that time, religious doctrines and practices were identical in the North and South, as they used the same commentaries and Sunday school books. But lingering disagreements regarding slavery created divisions in the church. Northern Baptists believed that God shows no favor, and all are equal in his eyes. For most southern Baptists, however, God intended for the races to be separate, and whites were apparently God's chosen people.

As usual, disputes over money led to a split. Southern Baptists argued that they were not receiving adequate funding to do mission work. Their relatively low allocation was explained as follows:

> "The Home Mission Society declared that a person could not be a missionary and wish to keep his slaves as property."][124] Apparently, there were suspicions of southern, white missionaries sharing only selected or strategic biblical scriptures with African slaves.

Prior to the Civil War, in 1845, the Southern Baptist Church met in Augusta, Georgia, broke ranks, and formed their own association. Following the Civil War, the Southern Baptist Convention established its own Sunday School

124 https://www.thoughtco.com/southern-baptist-church-history-700525

Board in 1891. It is currently headquartered in Nashville, Tennessee and develops and distributes its own literature. [125] It should be noted that in 1995 in celebration of the convention's one-hundred-and-fifty-year anniversary, the governing body issued an apology for its role in slavery and denying blacks equal rights. Moreover, they pledged to work intentionally to promote racial equality.

During Reconstruction, Independent black churches were established in the South with the Baptist denomination surging ahead of others. Black churches posed serious threats to social norms and Jim Crow patterns or practices that had benefitted non-blacks for centuries. The black church helped to mobilize members and non-members to seek their constitutional privileges and rights.

Following Reconstruction, evidence suggests some landowners gave former slaves provisions to worship and educate family members. Early black churches doubled as schoolhouses and many are still standing, and in some communities, those churches serve as the only connections that families have to one another and their deceased ancestors. Not surprising, some of the churches are literally still sitting on heir-property:

> The planning committee for the 129th Syrene Missionary Baptist Church anniversary, located in rural southeastern Arkansas, sought to locate historical records related to the church site. A deed search firm was hired because none of the current members could find documents. The firm found what they certified as the original deed. It was dated May 1888. A white couple deeded five acres to establish a church and school. Here is the catch. Many of those deeds that were signed in the 19th century had a claw back clause that states the land reverts to the owners/heirs if the site ceases to be used for religious or educational purposes. There have been recent cases of some of those sites being recouped by heirs

125 https://www.thoughtco.com/southern-baptist-church-history-700525

who worked to have the graveyards relocated because they were not specified in the contracts/deeds]

While many black churches were early owners of land and sanctuaries, a large number benefitted from the generosity of white landowners; however, their generosity had binding conditions. Most of those who gave land for building churches and schools for blacks did not want the land to be used for anything else.

Church Arson Prevention Act (1996)

In the eyes of some decision-makers, independent black churches posed a potential existential threat to a cherished, privileged lifestyle. According to historians, initially, church burnings were intended to intimidate, suppress voter registration and voting, and prevent efforts to mobilize resistance.

Published sources have repeatedly attributed a large fraction of church burnings to the Klan and other anti-black terrorist groups. Churches were vandalized, burglarized, burned, and bombed. Victims have included men, women, and children. Lists of these church burnings can be easily found.

In response to an increasing number of church arsons, Congress passed the Church Arson Prevention Act of 1996. The law made church burning a federal offense and mandatory prison sentences were implemented. Additional research is warranted to profile those who commit crimes against churches.

CHAPTER 7

Religion by the Numbers

Results of the PEW Foundation's 2007 U.S. Religious Landscape Survey showed that a higher percentage of blacks associated with an organized religion and rated religion as highly important. In addition, among African Americans, approximately eighty-three percent were Christians and fifty percent self-identified as Baptists.

The survey also asked respondents whether they believed in God; two response categories were summed together (Absolutely Certain and Very Certain). The percent "certain" by race were as follows: White (81%), black (94%), Asian (67%), Latino (85%), and other/mixed (84%). More than 9 out of 10 blacks stated that they believed in God.

Participation in collective worship is a common practice among different denominations. Respondents were asked to report their frequency of church attendance. They could select one of the following responses: 1) at least once per week; 2) one or twice a month; 3) a few times a year; 4) seldom/never; and 5) don't know. For those who reported at least weekly attendance, the results by race were: White (34%); black (47%); Asian (26%); Latino (39%); and other/mixed (34%). Nearly one in two blacks stated that they attend church at least one time per week.

Extrapolating from strain and general strain theories, among Christians, eternal life in paradise is their ultimate aspiration or spiritual dream. Black Christians remain cognizant of past and present trials and tribulations but find hope and joy in the gospel of Jesus Christ. They believe that realized advancements or progress has been gained through divine interventions. That belief system has fueled their persistence and resiliency. They persevere by faith instead of buckling under the weight of perceived or real injustices that they feel, see, and/or hear about every day.

NOTES

SECTION XIV: PUBLIC POLICY AND FAMILIAL SYSTEMS

This section presents evidence related to laws, public policies, and practices that could have altered gender role expectations, marriage rates, and family structures among African slaves and their descendants.

Throughout history, decision-makers at local, state, regional, and federal levels have intentionally or unintentionally created laws and public policies and supported practices that either limited or blocked black men from occupying traditional or Christian-based gender roles (e.g., protector and provider). Americans should attempt to assess the impact of past discriminatory patterns or practices on current statistics related to marriage rates, out of wedlock births, and percent of single female headed households by race/ethnicity.

CHAPTER 1

Marriage and Family in West Africa

To fully appreciate the black experience in terms of marriage and family in the U.S., it is imperative for Americans to learn about that institution in West Africa where most slaves had resided prior to their voyages to the colonies. According to information gleaned from a 2015 article by scholars at Emory University, marriage and family norms in West Africa were guided by paganism and Islam. The latter was the dominant faith prior to and during the slave trade era, in the more urban or commercial areas. West Africans were patriarchal meaning that men were the undisputed heads of households and children traced their ancestors through their fathers' family tree.

In terms of traditional marriage norms, girls were eligible for marriage following puberty between ages ten to thirty, depending on the ethnic group. In most areas, it was taboo for child-bearing aged women to be unmarried. It is also important to note that men could not marry until they were financially able to support a wife and children. As a result, most men were in their late 20s or early 30s before they married. Some marriages were negotiated by parents. Traditionally, men had to pay what is called a bride wealth or dowry to the family of the proposed bride. [126]

The point here is that African slaves had their own beliefs and customs related to gender roles and marriage. Southern plantation owners placed restrictions on traditional marriage and family dynamics among African slaves. Ironically, many of the restrictions were in stark contrast to Christian doctrine.

---

126 https://scholarblogs.emory.edu/islamic-family-law/socialcultural-information-by-region/west-africa/

Gender Roles, Family, and Religion

An overwhelming majority of the early settlers followed religious doctrines that made clear distinctions between men and women in terms of their roles. Christian doctrine provides guidance for gender roles within families. In the book of Genesis, Adam was created first and Eve was created from him and for him. In addition, it was the man who would leave his father and mother to find a wife and start a family, with him being the head of the household.

Regarding marriage and family, there are similarities between Islam and Christianity. Both assign men leadership roles and require them to be a protector and provider for the family. However, in the colonies, many West African beliefs, norms, values, rituals, and roles were forbidden.

Recall that in West Africa men served as kings, priests, warriors, farmers, hunters, builders, and heads of households.

So, imagine the emotional trauma experienced by African men who were transported to the colonies. To avoid cruel and unusual punishment, they had to appear docile, humble, and ignorant. Displays of intelligence, masculinity and pride often led to bare-back whippings or lynching in rare cases. Essentially, African men were forcibly denied their roles as heads of households or providers and protectors of their women and children. They had only two functions—work and procreate. That was the system, especially in slave states.

Pre-Civil War Laws

Since marriages between African slaves and their descendants were not recognized or had no standing, laws related to marriage and family only addressed mixed race or interracial unions. In Virginia, laws were passed to limit or block interracial marriages. Mixed race couples had to leave some jurisdictions and/or pay fines. European women who birthed a mixed child became an indentured servant along with her child; however, European men did not face strong rebuke for their fornication or adultery involving African women and/or young girls.

CHAPTER 2

Mixed-Race Children and Inheritance

Documents found on the Law Library of Congress webpage revealed laws that addressed the status and rights of African women and their mixed-race children in the colonies. Early settlers followed Great Britain's laws and practices related to marriage and family, known as a primogeniture system; whereby, familial lines were solely traced from their father's family, even when procreation occurred outside of marriage. Under British custom, mixed race children would also claim their father's blood line, certain rights and privileges, and heir-property.

To eliminate mixed race children's claims regarding their status and to their fathers' wealth upon his death, new laws were enacted in slave states. Virginia was one of the first colonies to legislate a change to the British custom. See below.

> "Act XII: Negro women's children to serve according to the condition of the mother.
>
> WHEREAS some doubts have arisen whether children got by any Englishman upon a Negro woman should be slave or free, be it therefore enacted and declared by this present grand assembly, that all children born in this country shall be held bond or free only according to the condition of the mother."[127]

127 https://memory.loc.gov/ammem/awhhtml/awlaw3/slavery.html

The law stipulated that the race and status of fathers did not matter when establishing whether his children were "free" or "slaves." The status of children was based solely on the status of their mothers. Specifically, the law made mulatto or mixed-race children ineligible as heirs to their fathers' familial wealth.

CHAPTER 3

Plantations, Marriages, and Rape

The investigation also focused on patterns or practices in the colonies that influenced the scope and nature of marriage and family among African slaves and their descendants here in the U.S. Attention was focused on slave owners' possible motivations for implementing rules related to marriages among slaves. Data and information were obtained from an expert on the subject. Professor Tera Hunter of Princeton University was interviewed February 11, 2010 by National Public Radio (NPR). The interview focused on results of her research related to gender roles and marriages among blacks during the 19th and 20th centuries.

Evidence obtained from Dr. Hunter was based on her exhaustive examination of case studies and oral histories provided by black domestic workers. Documents were found at the Freedman's Bureau Records of the National Archives that covered the time period between the Civil War and World War I (WWI). Results of her research were detailed in her 2010 book entitled *Bound in Wedlock: Slave and Free Black Marriage in the Nineteenth Century.* Several themes emerged from Dr. Hunter's investigation.

First, it appears that among blacks, marriage and family faced enormous challenges in both the North and South during the time period in question. While chattel slavery was mostly confined to the rural South, blacks in so-called free states did not enjoy most of the rights and freedoms promised in the Constitution. However, from most accounts, assaults on marriages among blacks were less vigorous in the North.

Second, according to Hunter, there were two schools of thought among slave owners toward marriage and family for slaves. For some, because slaves had no legal standing or citizenship, their marriages were null and void in the eyes of the law. And, members of black families could be separated at any moment and sold on an auction block. On the other hand, some slave owners encouraged or allowed unofficial familial structures to exist as a form of deterrence for potential runaways. It was far easier for a single or small group of slaves to escape than for an entire nuclear family consisting of men, women, and children. Anecdotal accounts of freed slaves going through extraordinary challenges to search and buy-back a sold spouse or child do exist, and an example was displayed on the big screen in *Django Unchained*, starring Jamie Foxx and Samuel L. Jackson.

Third, for some decision-makers, Christian based marriages and familial traditions among African slaves and their descendants would chip away at their dehumanization ideologies. Dr. Hunter observed that the legalization or legitimization of black marriage and family represented severe threats to the existing social order and racial hierarchy at that time. Fortunately for slaves, some abolitionists publicly indicted slave owners for their blatant assaults on black marriages and families. They argued restrictions related to marriages were a rebuke of religious doctrine.

Fourth, after passage of the 13th, 14th, and 15th Amendments, in an attempt to dissuade blacks from marrying, some states imposed marriage-limiting or blocking requirements including exorbitant fees, restrictions on access to court houses, and refusals to issue marriage licenses. Ironically, similar tactics or methods were used to depress voter registrations and voting among blacks.

Finally, Dr. Hunter found that due to previous laws and practices regarding black marriages, some freed slaves were ambivalent about having to officially register with the "government" to marry following the end of the Civil War. Despite their ambivalence, the number wanting to marry skyrocketed and challenged the Union Army's resources to process the paperwork. According to Dr. Hunter, marriage rates among blacks between 1865 and the 1960s outpaced rates for whites, suggesting that marriage was a priority among the newly freed slaves.

Rape and Post Traumatic Stress Disorder (PTSD)

Dr. Hunter's research found that black men and women overwhelmingly adhered to Christian doctrine and officially married following the end of the Civil War. While black men assumed the roles of heads of households, providers, and protectors of their wives and children, laws and discriminatory practices restricted their capacity to do so. Cross burnings, brutal whippings, castrations, and lynching were tools employed to deter blacks from using harmful defensive methods against non-black offenders.

Accounts indicate that both African slaves and those subsequently freed were often put in positions in which they either risked severe beatings or death or were forced to standby while their wives, daughters, nieces, and close family friends were raped. Public accounts suggest that rape was a power tactic employed to intimidate, demoralize, and hopefully shame both black women and their husbands or significant others. In addition, rapes and the threat of rape were employed to extort obedience and to satisfy pent-up, lustful desires.

Case studies, documentaries, and oral histories have described instances of black women, including wives, being forcibly raped by decision-makers or small groups of white men. Recall that some southern states passed laws specifically regarding mulatto or mixed-race children to protect the assets of out-race fathers.

Accounts of black women being raped following the end of the Civil War provide some indication of their plights prior to passage of the 13th Amendment. A documentary entitled "The Rape of Recy Taylor" was aired on HBO describing her horrifying ordeal at the hands of six young white boys in Abbeville, Alabama in 1944. The crime received national coverage in the media.[128] Sharecropping in Alabama, Recy Taylor's, courage and strength led her to press charges against her white assailants, an action literally unheard of in the Jim Crow South. The rape occurred nearly seventy-five years prior to the "Me Too" movement. Despite eyewitnesses, Mrs. Taylor's testimony, and even one admission, the six teenagers were never found guilty by all-white jurors. Similarly, an exhibit housed in the Mississippi Cultural Museum, in Jackson, Mississippi tells the story of a black woman who was raped by several white men in public. In addition, Danielle McGuire's book *At the End of the Street,* disclosed evidence related to the rapes of black women between the 1940s and 1960s.

For centuries, black men were forced to witness their wives and daughters ravaged and raped by men who felt free to do so. In fact, an overwhelming majority of rapists were never prosecuted or found guilty despite eyewitnesses and other incontrovertible evidence against them. Surely those brutal and inhumane offenses and the lack of justice or punishment caused a great deal of strain/stress or what could arguably be called the forerunner of untreated, post-traumatic stress disorders among both black women and men.

---

128 https://www.nbcnews.com/news/nbcblk/recy-taylor-alabama-woman-raped-six-white-men-dies-97-n833336

CHAPTER 4

Public Assistance and Marriage & Family

While the current investigation did not uncover laws that specifically limited or suppressed black marriages following the Civil War, discriminatory patterns or practices related to safety net or public assistance to the poor were investigated. Recall that majority of blacks in the U.S. between 1865 and the 1960s were existing at or below the poverty line due to no fault of their own. Still, they did not come close to being the majority of Americans who would ultimately receive public assistance or welfare.

In 1935, President Franklin D. Roosevelt launched the New Deal program that allocated tax dollars to help states aid "needy" segments of their populations including widows, the elderly, and households with children without fathers. The latter is important to keep in mind when thinking about the pros and cons of marriage and family among poor blacks due to extremely high unemployment and less than living wage jobs. It is reasonable to conclude that public welfare was not intended to elevate people out of poverty or to assist poor, black families. Despite their limited or blocked access to education and employment opportunities during that time period, black men were ineligible to receive public assistance and their mere presence in the household caused the mother of their children and their children to lose public assistance in a lot of cases. Decision-makers have traditionally been reluctant to make public assistance available to what they commonly referred to as "abled bodied men" regardless of past injustices levied against them.

Even among the poor, racial inequality existed in terms of the scope and nature of public assistance received. [129] Several discriminatory practices that eliminated or reduced the number and total dollars awarded to poverty-stricken blacks included the following: 1) Assistance was denied during times of high demand for labor; 2) two parent households were ineligible; 3) black women who received welfare could not have a man in the house; and 4) assistance could be revoked for what welfare staff deemed an unclean or unkempt home. Welfare workers possessing racial biases made life-altering decisions related to the plight of poor blacks.

Aid to Families with Dependent Children (AFDC)

During President John F. Kennedy's administration, welfare eligibility was expanded to include households with low or no income regardless of whether a father/spouse was present. The program was called Aid to Families with Dependent Children (AFDC), and the assistance came in the form of cash to those meeting the criteria. There were both federal and state funds and eligibility requirements. States were incentivized to cover a larger number of the poor in order to receive more federal funding.

Subsequently, public assistance was expanded during President Lyndon B. Johnson's administration. He introduced the concept of the "Great Society" in which he waged a war on poverty. Specifically, support was given to Medicare, Medicaid, Head Start, job training, and healthcare programs. It was estimated that in 1965, 4.3M Americans received some type of public assistance and that number more than doubled by 1972. Subsequent administrations, both Republican and Democratic saw the need to expand welfare programs.

Welfare Reforms

By 1996, under President Clinton, welfare reforms resulted in changes regarding level of support and duration of eligibility. Going forward,

---

129 https://people.eou.edu/socwelf/readings/week-2/welfare-expands-in-the-1960s/

unlimited time frames for receiving public assistance no longer existed, and work requirements became popular. The transformation of the welfare system under President Clinton was called the "Personal Responsibility and Work Opportunity Reconciliation Act" (PRWORA). The reform has been credited with helping decrease the number of welfare recipients by more than 300% in little over a decade or by 2009.

Temporary Assistance to Needy Families (TANF)

Under President Clinton, Temporary Assistance to Needy Families (TANF) was implemented in block grants to states based on their previous drawdowns for AFDC, thereby rewarding those states that had covered more of its poor. The primary change was that the federal government no longer recognized welfare as a "right" of the poor and gave states the responsibility of determining eligibility and type and nature of assistance given to the poor. Here is where voting participation and drawing congressional districts by state legislatures determined the nature and scope of public assistance. The only requirement was that at least eighty percent of federal funds had to be allocated to AFDC type initiatives. The federal share of the funding hovers around twenty billion annually with another match from states' TANF allocations.

Child Support Laws

About forty-five years following the end of the Civil War, newly freed black men were expected to have the capacity to pay child support. Child support laws have been on the books since 1910. The intentions of those laws were to hold biological parents financially responsible for the health and welfare of their children. The federal government led the way in holding parents accountable by authorizing agencies to seize income tax returns and employers to garnish paychecks of those in arrears for failing to make required child support payments. Specific laws included the following:

> "1992: The Child Support Recovery Act of 1992 (P.L. 102-521)

The Child Support Recovery Act allowed states to prosecute parents who willfully chose not to pay child support.

Personal Responsibility and Work Opportunity Reconciliations Act of 1996 (PRWORA)

This law transformed the government assistance program formally known as welfare to Temporary Assistance for Needy Families (TANF). Some provisions in the law also directly impacted child support collection, including the creation of a Federal Case Registry of Child Support Orders (FCR) and a National Directory of New Hires (NDNH). Both systems were implemented to track child support cases and locate those liable for child support payments. The law also streamlined the process for establishing paternity, allowing biological fathers to voluntarily acknowledge paternity.

Deadbeat Parents Punishment Act (DPPA)

This supplement to the Child Support Recovery Act (CSRA) of 1992 increased the consequences for parents who willfully choose not to pay child support. According to the Deadbeat Parents Punishment Act, parents can accrue fines of up to $10,000 and face up to two years in prison for failing to pay child support to a child who resides in another state."][130]

Without question, parents should provide for their children. However, as a result of century-long discriminatory employment practices and inequitable compensation, African Americans are forced to work harder and longer than their counterparts to satisfy child support requirements. Results gleaned from focus groups consisting of non-custodial fathers who owed child support in South Carolina shed light on either intended or unanticipated consequences of child support laws and prosecutions. Ironically, the researchers concluded that for fathers the law does more to

130 https://www.liveabout.com/the-history-of-child-support-in-the-us-2997821

> "...hinder his efforts to find stable employment than they do to provide economic security to his children. However, across the United States, destitute non-custodial parents are incarcerated for failing to meet child support obligations they have no means to pay. The end result is that indigent child support debtors fill jails across the country."[131]

According to the data, non-custodial parents who have an arrearage are routinely arrested and jailed about every eight to twelve months. In most cases, they have only two options, pay the arrearage or spend time in jail. What is interesting is that in some states, failure to pay child support is judged as civil contempt, not a criminal offense. The former does not command at least a public defender, while criminal defendants are assigned legal counsel. So, indigent, and destitute non-custodial parents, often fathers, are more likely to be jailed/imprisoned for non-payment, due in large part to a lack of legal counsel. [132]

131 https://racism.org/index.php?option=com_content&view=article&id=1514:fathersbehind-bars&catid=53&Itemid=176&showall=1&limitstart=

132 https://racism.org/index.php?option=com_content&view=article&id=1514:fathersbehind-bars&catid=53&Itemid=176&showall=1&limitstart=

CHAPTER 5

Geo-Public Assistance Benefits and Race

Surprisingly, the size of the black population in a state is related to the scope and nature of public assistance they can receive. On June 6, 2017, the *Washington Post* published an article entitled "States with More Black People Have Less Generous Welfare Benefits." The story contained excerpts from a study conducted by the Urban Institute where researchers found an inverse relationship between the percent of blacks in a state, the percent in the state that received assistance, and the amount of assistance given. Below is a synopsis of the results:

> "A poor family in Vermont, where 94 percent of residents are white and only 1 percent are black, is 20 times as likely to receive welfare as compared with if that same family lived in Louisiana, where 61 percent are white and nearly a third of residents are black, according to a previous analysis by the Center on Budget and Policy Priorities. Vermont has the most generous welfare benefits of all 50 states, with 78 out of every 100 families in poverty receiving cash assistance. In comparison, Louisiana, the least generous state, gives welfare cash assistance to only four out of every 100 poor families. The disparity does not end there. Vermont offers a maximum monthly benefit of $640 to a family of three, and allows families earning up to $1,053 to qualify for cash assistance. Louisiana only offers a maximum cash benefit of

just $240 a month, and families must make less than $360 a month to qualify." [133]

In addition, the researchers observed that while blacks make up about thirteen percent of the U.S. population, they accounted for almost thirty percent of TANF recipients. In comparison, whites represented about sixty-two percent (62%) of the general population and accounted for about twenty-eight percent (28%) of TANF recipients. The key revelation was that, in terms of headcounts, blacks were far from being the majority or "face" of TANF recipients in the U.S.

Void of historical context, statistics related to the distribution of public assistance by race can be misleading. Despite centuries of limited or blocked educational and economic opportunities, only three out of ten TANF recipients were black, meaning that a whopping seven out of ten (70%) were of other races. [134]

---

133 https://www.washingtonpost.com/news/wonk/wp/2017/06/06/states-with-more-black-people-have-less-generous-welfare-benefits-study-says/?noredirect=on&utm_term=.a226f3cb80a2

134 https://www.washingtonpost.com/news/wonk/wp/2017/06/06/states-with-more-black-people-have-less-generous-welfare-benefits-study-says/?noredirect=on&utm_term=.a226f3cb80a2

CHAPTER 6

Familial Trends and Race

Certainly, laws and discriminatory practices have influenced marriage and family dynamics in the U.S. Based on evidence presented here, blacks have had to overcome numerous obstacles to marry and for those unions to have standing. To be "fair and balanced," all discussions regarding racial disparities in terms of marriage rates, single female headed households, and out-of-wedlock births must include references related to historical or antecedent marriage suppression patterns or practices.

There are numerous sources of data regarding marriage and family by race. Below is an excerpt from Black Demographics:

> "Marriage has been a declining institution among all Americans and this decline is even more evident in the Black community. In 2016 only 29% of African Americans were married compared to 48% of all Americans. Half or 50% of African Americans have never been married compared to 33% of all Americans." [135]

Similarly, a review of recent U.S. Census data showed that in 2014 there were an estimated 123M household in the U.S. The percent of married households by race was white (51%); Latinos (47%); blacks (28%); and Asian (60%). In less than one hundred and sixty years, among blacks, marriage rates have surged despite not having legal standing in most states prior to 1865.

---

135 http://blackdemographics.com/households/marriage-in-black-america/

Single Parent Households

Declines in marriage rates have resulted in an increase in the percent of single heads of households and so-called "out-of-wedlock" children. The increase can be attributed to several factors. First, scholars observe that cultural change has decreased the stigma related to out-of-wedlock births. Second, women have made enormous progress economically and are no longer totally dependent on men for economic security. Third, massive jail and prison numbers limit "suitable" marriage candidates from the perspectives of some women. Fourth, young adults are opting to remain single longer than in the past. Finally, from a purely economics perspective, unemployed, underemployed, or less than living wage earners are not highly attractive, prospective spouses. That reality alone places a lot of black men and women at a disadvantage.

In 2016, a report produced by Downsizing Government.org indicated that during the past fifty years single female-headed households have skyrocketed, and out of wedlock births increased from a low of eight percent in 1965 to a recent high of thirty-nine percent. This sharp and often devastating increase has been attributed in part to welfare eligibility guidelines and alleged incentives. Those making that argument invariably do not factor in the impacts of other factors (e.g., increasing divorce rates, deaths, and "choice").

Public assistance eligibility has traditionally favored the elderly, persons with disabilities, and single parent households with children. In general, the latter has been linked to relatively low educational attainment, unemployment, working poor, and despair that routinely flows from one generation to the next.

Policy analysts have attempted to profile both single-female headed households and their children. According to information obtained from the 2016 Downsizing Government.org website, some characteristics were as follows: a) Out-of-wedlock children have traditionally been nearly six times more likely to live in poverty; b) 20% of single mothers initially received welfare; c) 75%

of government assistance via mean-tested assistance went to single parents; and d) tenure on welfare rolls was longer for single parents.

Admittedly, it is conceivable that some eligibility guidelines for public assistance have forced some mothers to make strategic choices. The economic dilemma that has confronted some mothers is the decision to either marry an unemployed or less than living-wage earner or remain eligible for public assistance to guarantee her children food, shelter, and healthcare.

While many will argue that a single female headed household poses no inherent or unavoidable threat to the growth and development of children, the overwhelming consensus is that a loving and nurturing two parent household would be preferable. Based on recent counts, approximately sixty-six percent of black children reside in single parent households. The rate for Asians/Pacific Islanders, whites, Hispanics, and Native Americans was 16%, 24%, 42%, and 52%, respectively.[136]

The reality is that many single-headed households must be credited with doing the most with the least. Despite being single parents, often living in poverty, and residing in public housing, many black women and a growing number of single fathers have done phenomenal jobs in helping to empower their children to become successful doctors, lawyers, entrepreneurs, teachers, plumbers, electricians, industrial personnel, sanitation workers, farmers, and professional athletes.

136 https://datacenter.kidscount.org/data/tables/107-children-in-single-parent-families-by#detailed/1/any/false/870,133/10,11,9,12,1,185,13/432,431

SECTION XV: PUBLIC EDUCATION

During President Trump's rigged system indictment, he specifically addressed the state of public education. In his attempt to lure black voters, he said "your schools are no good." However, he failed to provide evidence to corroborate his charge nor did he give specific examples as to the scope and nature of how the education system had been rigged.

This section contains results of an investigation regarding the U.S. public education "system" in terms of its history, purpose, organization, funding, leadership/decision-makers, teachers, policies and procedures, student support services, and student outcomes. In each area, it is important to remember that there were, and are, people making decisions and those decisions are based at least in part on personal prejudices that can lead to both individual and institutional discriminatory patterns and practices. The investigation also examined the black response or adaptations to a perceived or real rigged education system which can help explain or account for their gradually increasing educational attainment rates.

CHAPTER 1

History of Public Education

On July 29, 2013, Allison Stewart, author of "First Class," was interviewed on NPR's "All Things Considered." She provided expert testimony regarding the birth of public education for blacks in the U.S. prior to and following the end of the Civil War. Her thesis was based on the results of oral histories and case studies conducted to obtain insights into the scope and nature of public education during the time in question.

According to Stewart, grammar and elementary schools for blacks were operated in homes and churches as early as 1807 in the North. She noted, however, that prior to the Civil War, slaves in the South could have their fingers cut off if they were found trying to learn to read. So, it is reasonable to assume that disparities in educational achievement and attainment were gigantic and intentional between 1619 and 1870 or about one hundred and fifty years ago.

Prior to Reconstruction, state and/or local governments managed public education. Surely, racial segregation and budgetary implications influenced the availability of educational opportunities for blacks in the North. In slave states, limiting or blocking African slaves and their descendants from learning to read, write, and perform elementary math was strategic and functional in several ways. First, illiterate slaves were less likely to be able to devise and implement successful escape plans. Second, their owners or overseers were their only source of information. Finally, their alleged inability to learn or low intelligence provided the justification for their enslavement.

U.S. Department of Education (ED)

At the federal level, legislation signed by President Andrew Johnson in 1867, only a mere two years or so after the end of the Civil War, created the U.S. Department of Education (ED). Its original function was to collect, analyze, and report on the operations and effectiveness of public schools. However, the creation of the department did not eliminate past norms and consequences of centuries of prohibitions against blacks being taught to read, write, and do math. There is little mention of the interface between the ED and the Freedmen's Bureau related to the construction and operations of schools for blacks during Reconstruction. Much of the credit for increasing the number and quality of schools for blacks following the Civil War is commonly given to black churches, white abolitionists, and other faith organizations. Consistent with the time, the schools were racially segregated and unequally funded.

According to Stewart's research, Paul Laurence Dunbar High School in Washington, D.C. was the first recognized public school for freed slaves that opened in 1870, only about five years after the end of the Civil War.[137] Stewart credits both blacks and primarily Quakers for establishing Dunbar with an inaugural class of four students. The Dunbar School provided a glimpse into some advantages and disadvantages of school segregation. Stewart talked about early Dunbar graduates who earned doctorate degrees from some early Ivy League schools and returned to teach at Dunbar. It had a rigorous curriculum and teachers expected and demanded excellence from their students. However, challenges of adequate funding for staff, facilities, and equipment were commonplace.

Throughout Reconstruction, adequate funding for separate black schools faced strong and systematic challenges. Southern lawmakers at state and federal levels fought and voted against adequate funding for educating freed slaves. It is worth noting that unequal funding for black schools was also the norm in other regions of the country.

---

137 https://www.npr.org/sections/codeswitch/2013/08/22/206622688/the-legacy-of-dunbar-high-school

Supreme Court-Brown v Topeka, KS

The U.S. Supreme Court seemed ambivalent in their reviews and rulings related to the constitutionality of "separate but equal" public accommodation cases. As mentioned previously, in the 1896 Plessey v Ferguson case, the court ruled that separate public accommodations for races did not violate blacks' 14th Amendment rights. That decision encompassed both public secondary and postsecondary schools. With the passage of time, social activism, and changes among the justices, the U.S. Supreme Court became a catalyst for racial integration as they began to chip away at the "separate but equal" laws and social norms. The landmark ruling in Brown v Topeka, Kansas was the turning point in disallowing entities receiving government funding to discriminate based on race, sex, age, religion, or country of origin. The Brown family, who would become the plaintiffs in this case, purchased a home in what they thought was a "good" neighborhood with high performing schools, located only blocks from their home. There was only one huge problem. The nearby school was all white, and there was a "black" school in the city. Keep in mind that this case was brought forth in Kansas, not the Deep South. Mr. Brown, like Mr. Plessey, did not think the Jim Crow law was fair and violated his civil rights. He along with legal counsel filed a lawsuit to allow his daughter to attend the all-white neighborhood school. In 1954, nearly sixty years after the Plessey separate but equal affirmative ruling by the Supreme Court, the same court ruled that separate but equal facilities violated citizens' 14th Amendment rights. All public schools and higher educational systems were forced to allow black students to attend. Of course, this ruling meant that schools in the Deep South also had to desegregate. It is worth noting that the Brown decision was rendered only about sixty-five years ago.

Theoretically, in terms of guaranteeing future equality in public education, the 1954 Brown decision leveled the playing field by desegregating public schools. However, the ruling did not compensate blacks for centuries of patterns or practices that intentionally blocked or depressed their educational attainment.

Immediately following the Brown ruling, private academies, faith-based institutions, and home schooling increased. To achieve desegregation goals, elaborate and time consuming busing or transportation systems were implemented and led to unrest in some cities.

School desegregation was slow in both the North and South. In the latter, however, vestiges of extreme racial segregation and Jim Crow norms continued to fuel demands for states' rights and separate but equal education until the 1970s.

The scope and focus of the ED changed over time. For decades, it was not a high-profiled department. Beginning in the late 1940s and early 1950s, during the Cold War, its focus was on producing the next generation of skilled and scientific workforce to compete with the Soviet Union's space program.

During and in the wake of the mid 1960s Civil Rights Movement, the U.S. Congress began allocating federal funds to help improve educational opportunities in public secondary schools. For example, Title I, Part A was a program introduced that gave federal funding to schools that had a large population of low-income students. In general, those schools were in municipalities that suffered from high unemployment and relatively low tax revenue.

For decades following the Civil War, the cost of attending college made earning postsecondary degrees nearly impossible for a vast majority of African Americans. As part of the 1960s civil rights reforms, the federal government created two sources of financial aid: grants and student loans. PELL grants were introduced in 1965 and are based on a student's household income or "need." It is a grant not requiring pay-back as in the case of student loans. Less than sixty years ago, the Brown v Topeka, Kansas school desegregation ruling, Title I funding, and federal student financial aid combined to provide unprecedented opportunities for blacks to begin increasing their academic attainment.

The next major development in the federal government's role in shaping public education occurred in 1980 during President Jimmy Carter's administration. The ED became a cabinet level agency with a secretary of education at the helm. By 2016 the ED had roughly 4.5K employees and a budget of over sixty-three billion dollars.

In terms of policing discriminatory practices, the department is also responsible for ensuring equal access to quality education for all. Critics of ED have argued that through mission creep the department has taken away authority and discretion from the states and local school districts. On the other hand, advocates argue that it is essential that research-based, educational "best" practices be shared with the nation and rigorously evaluated. Moreover, all students should have access to quality public education regardless of their race, sex, religion, and zip codes. To ensure that quality education is available to all students, standards must be developed, and education leaders must be held accountable.

The ED employs a "big stick" and "carrots" to facilitate the adoption of research-based best practices. It provides guidance and incentives to districts based on outcomes related to academic success, statewide testing, support for special needs students, and access and use of technology.

Federal funding has been used to encourage diversity/inclusion in public education. Recipients of federal ED funding must agree and certify that they will not discriminate against students, teachers, staff, and administrators based on race, sex, age, religion, or country of origin.

Proponents of anti-discrimination policies believe that if such contractual agreements were removed, decision-makers at local and state levels might revert to pre-civil rights patterns and practices.

CHAPTER 2

Poverty and Student Success

This chapter reviewed evidence related to a link between poverty/income inequality and student success. Specifically, data and information were sought to determine the relative effects of poverty and race/ethnicity on academic performance.

A comparative study of student outcomes from around the globe is called the Program for International Student Assessment (PISA), which is managed by The Organization for Economic Cooperation and Development (OECD). The study began in 2000 and is administered every three years to fifteen-year-olds from over seven hundred and thirty countries. The core subject areas assessed are science, reading, and mathematics.

Results of the 2015 PISA found a potential link between low income and educational outcomes. Based on comparisons of mean scores by students' socioeconomic status, poor students all over the world had relatively lower test scores than their higher income counterparts. [138]

In the U.S., research regarding predictors of student success has primarily focused on either income or race. Analysis of student performance in different types of schools can be informative. Several schemes for categorizing or stereotyping schools are examined below.

---

138 https://nces.ed.gov/programs/coe/indicator_cnu.asp

Free Lunch and Academic Success

Invariably, multidisciplinary research findings have shown that food and nutrition or diet plays an important role in the capacity of students to stay focused and learn. For many public-school students, school nutrition programs are their only source for healthy foods. Without those programs, learning would be further depressed. Students are unable to concentrate, comprehend, and learn when they are hungry or juiced-up on an assortment of processed foods containing enormous amounts of natural and artificial sugars/sweeteners.

Results of empirical studies have consistently found negative relationships between percent of students eligible for free/reduced lunch and academic success. At local levels, researchers generally conclude that as the percent of students eligible for free/reduced lunch increases in schools, average scores on standardized tests decrease. Substitute "black" for "poor" and the statement would become, "In general, as the percent of black students increase in schools, the overall performance on standardized tests will decrease." There is no debate about scores on standardized tests; however, there should be open and frank discussions about the factors that contribute to relatively low scores. Is it low income (i.e. poverty) or race?

Free Lunch by the Numbers

According to a 2016 article found on the ERS.USDA.GOV website, in 2006 over 5B lunches were served. Of that 5B, almost half were free, approximately ten percent were reduced, and two-fifths were at regular prices. Recent figures regarding the raw numbers of free/reduced lunch recipients might shock the average American. In 2014, the National Center for Education Statistics (NCES) reported that the number of participants by race in 2011-2012 was as follows: whites (25,464,162); Hispanics (11,693,788); blacks (7,782,146); Asian (2,321,362); Mixed Race (1,265,222); American Indian/Alaskan Native (541,986); and Pacific Islanders (177,871).

In terms of raw numbers and cost associated with free/reduced lunch, whites outnumbered all other races combined. To deflect from that fact, narratives regarding free lunch recipients invariably contain only the percent within a race that receives free/reduced lunch. Those figures are as follows: Non-Hispanic Whites (68%); Non-Hispanic Blacks (78.2%); Hispanics (76.3%); and Other (76.3%). Exclusive focus on percentages instead of headcounts of recipients of free/reduced lunch is a form of misinformation or disinformation that can help perpetuate negative stereotypes. Nearly seventy percent of all races received free/reduced lunch. Greater challenges emerge when free/reduced lunch recipients are concentrated in specific school districts.

90/90/90 Schools

In 2003, Douglas B. Reeves launched his 90/90/90 thesis related to factors that contribute to student success in poor schools. He identified and researched schools that fit the following criteria: 90% free/reduced lunch recipients as a proxy for low socioeconomic status; 90% students of color; and 90% scoring basic or higher on a normed achievement test. Apparently, Reeves offered his study as a blueprint for raising expectations and standards for poor school districts. His research findings were in stark contrast to commonly held views regarding poor and students of color when assessing academic achievement. Poverty has long been identified as a major impediment or barrier to general or widespread academic achievement and attainment. If the 90/90/90 schools exist, then the burden is squarely on the shoulders of education leaders to review and revise their formulas for academic success. Education leaders would be forced to account for students of color relatively lower performance scores on factors other than race and/or poverty.

Critics of the 90/90/90 school thesis have pointed to what they refer to as low achievement bar or low criterion for success. Opponents argue that the inclusion of the "basic" performance scores as a desired or acceptable outcome is misleading because "basic" is not a desired or acceptable performance mark and it is achieved by a vast majority of students.

Isolated Public Schools

The results of a U.S. General Accounting Office (GAO) study released in summer of 2016 revealed some alarming developments in the area of public education. A synopsis of the study, published in the May 26, 2016 edition of *USA Today*, reported that from 2000-2014, the number of public schools in poverty-stricken areas with large concentrations of black students and students of color grew from 7,009 to 15,089. The report introduced the concept of "isolated" schools, which serve a whopping seventy-five (75%) of the most underserved students. The percentage of socioeconomic isolated schools grew from 9% to 16% during the time period in question. A profile of those schools included inadequate funding, challenges recruiting and retaining certified teachers, old or outdated facilities and technology, and fewer AP classes. In addition, they had a relatively higher percentage of students in "risk" categories including chronic absences, in and out of school suspensions, expulsions, and retained students. The surge in the number of isolated public schools reflects a gradual return to a "separate and unequal" era in the U.S.

Education Outliers

Not surprising, some minority serving public schools are outstanding. Educators, however, will define them as "one-offs" or "outliers." They are often ignored or devalued by those in power. Profiles of high performing poor and isolated schools must be studied to identify best practices:

[In a relatively small, rural county, there had been decade-long discussions and debates about under performing schools and students, combined with greater than average per pupil cost. As usual, informed people focused on the percent of students in the schools eligible for free/reduced lunch as a prime explanation for subpar performance. An ad hoc committee was formed to conduct an exploratory study of best practices among schools with a large free/reduced lunch student population at or above eighty percent. Several schools or districts were identified, and representatives or leaders of those schools were invited to a roundtable discussion. They were asked to list what they thought were their ingredients for success in getting poor black students to perform significantly above the state average. Invariably, they talked about effective and connected principals and teachers, clean facilities, clear rules, high expectations, and connected parents/guardians.]

This account suggests that connected educators can help overcome or weaken the hypothesized influences of poverty on academic achievement. Surprisingly, higher budgets or funding was not ranked as a top priority. Unfortunately, success stories defined as "one-offs" or "outliers" receive little if any media attention. Their superintendents, principals, and teachers are not appointed to related statewide boards or study groups. Colleges of Education do not routinely invite those leaders and teachers to their campuses and classrooms or use those schools as teaching and learning laboratories for prospective teachers and administrators.

CHAPTER 3

Architecture and Student Success

A casual tour of schools across the U.S. will reveal striking differences in their architectural designs and features in connection with the socioeconomic status of enrolled students. Many facilities housing black and poor students were built during the separate but "equal" era or Jim Crow. It is indisputable that schools constructed for blacks were vastly inferior. Even with renovations and some cosmetic upgrades, they still lag behind more modern schools in terms of creating positive learning environments for both teaching and learning.

Today, education leaders go through an elaborate planning process to design and construct schools and classrooms. At some point, they bring in professionals to design and program the space to achieve desired outcomes. When architects design buildings and specific spaces, they first determine how the space will be used. The design of schools, classrooms, labs, and other spaces is a creative work that involves thinking of the facility as a stage on which acts will be performed. The structures are designed to become objects with shared meanings and expectations from all stakeholders. So, after determining the purpose of the buildings, spaces are carved out to serve different functions such as classrooms, cafeteria, gym, labs, studios, offices, storage, common space, hallways, mechanical space, and toilets.

Design and construction of school facilities are determined by budgets. Public schools in higher SES communities generally have newer and more attractive physical plans than those found in poorer communities and communities of color. Below is an account that might help shed some light on the physical or structural conditions in some isolated schools:

> A poor and low performing school district had been taken over by the State and was being managed by a conservator. Some area leaders blamed the elected school board and superintendent for relatively low-test scores. When touring school facilities, it was like walking through the past. There were old wooden desks, an outdated science lab and toilets, inefficient window air conditioning units along with cracked windows, those little moon shaped metal seats in the cafeteria, and noticeable chipped paint. There was no visible instructional technology in the classrooms.

It is widely accepted that the design of physical structures and the internal, ambient environment are related to how teachers and students feel and behave. Dimly lighted classrooms and laboratories do not promote learning. Other features of schools including paint, flooring, types of seating, access to electrical outlets, windows, and of course size of classrooms and their locations related to natural sunlight all impact academic achievement.

Despite old and outdated physical structures, furnishings, and instructional technology, teachers are expected to excite, encourage, and empower students to learn and perform as well as students in more favorably built environments. That is a daunting assignment for even the most senior and productive educator/teacher.

CHAPTER 4

Financing Public Education

Public education is intended to satisfy a compelling government interest. At the state level, legislative bodies develop formulas to award funding to school districts. In general, allocations are based on headcounts, performance, and average daily attendance. Incentives are also given to reward high performance or to help improve test scores.

At local levels, property taxes generate the bulk of funding for public education.

Many Americans have little or no understanding of how their local schools survive on taxes paid by real estate owners. Locally, funding for education has been couched in terms of "millage rates," which a basic Google search defines as:

> "The tax rate used to calculate local property taxes. The millage rate represents the amount per every $1,000 of a property's assessed value. Assigned millage rates are multiplied by the total taxable value of the property to get the amount owed."

In general, those owning property get mobilized to either support or oppose tax hikes to fund public education. Turnout for a referendum to increase property taxes is usually relatively low, especially among blacks who traditionally own fewer properties and pay less property taxes. Business leaders, developers, owners of rental property, and high-end homes often oppose millage increases. They complain that they are disproportionately taxed for a "collective good" that many of them choose not to directly utilize. Institutional discrimination has both short- and long-term consequences.

In some circumstances, businesses and elected leaders will actively support a tax increase to improve public education in a city or county. Decision-makers at state and local levels engaged in the retention, recruitment, and creation of living wage jobs know the value of public education. Some prospective companies or employers rank quality of public education high on their priorities list in terms of site selections for new investments. They not only look at school ratings but also "curb appeal" of the school facilities because they know or suspect that some of their employees will choose public education, instead of an optional expenditure for a private school if they were equivocal in both curb appeal and performance. So, communities involved in trying to attract new, high-wage jobs will eventually invest tax dollars to offer competitive salaries for teachers, improve aging facilities, and acquire state-of-the-art technology.

CHAPTER 5

Academic Decision-makers

At state and local levels, academic decision-makers include advisory or oversight boards, superintendents, principals, and teachers. They all possess biases or prejudices and can be categorized as mostly fair, conditionally fair, or mostly unfair in terms of their support of policies and/or treatment of students.

Public education is a political endeavor. Funding, personnel decisions, and policies emerge from mostly partisan-led elected and appointed bodies. At state and local levels, appointed boards are charged with overseeing the administration and execution of policies and procedures to achieve desired educational outcomes.

At the state level, oversight boards are generally appointed by governors to help provide input and feedback regarding the status of education in the states. In most cases, appointments are made as a quid pro quo for their support or political connections. Again, politics and voting matter.

At city and county levels, a similar organizational structure exists. Elected leaders in most cases appoint oversight boards. In other jurisdictions, candidates must garner a majority of votes in designated districts.

Jurisdictions in which school board members are appointed, elected bodies screen and select members. In most cases, votes for applicants are often along racial lines. With gerrymandered local districts or wards, African Americans are generally in the minority thus unable to appoint school board members without one or more votes from other board members. There is nothing inherently wrong with having to persuade people from other parties or races to vote one way or another. Perceived or real discrimination is charged, however, when numerous consequential decisions are approved or defeated along racial lines.

Superintendents of Education

At state and local levels, superintendents, who are either elected or appointed, serve as chief executive officers (CEOs) of education. Governors generally appoint state superintendents. In comparison, at local levels appointments are usually made by an oversight board.

State education leaders, who manage the operations of the state department of education, make decisions that impact all public-school students. State superintendents oversee the development and implementations of policies and procedures in areas including teacher certification and licensing, state-wide testing, evaluation of school districts, dissemination of research-based best practices related to instruction and student success, and criteria for earning diplomas. Demographics of state superintendents were not readily accessible during this investigation.

Diversity/inclusion among school superintendents at local levels was examined. A 2006 article published in *Ed Week* contained the following related quote: "The nation's 14,000-odd district superintendents are overwhelmingly white and male. The most recent data from the American Association of School Administrators showed that in 2000, fifteen percent (15%) of superintendents were women and 5 percent were members of racial or ethnic minorities." [139]

Roughly seven hundred (700) or five percent (5%) of the more than fourteen thousand school districts had a non-white superintendent in 2000. Even if all were African American, the five percent is significantly lower than their representation in the general population. Surely, multiple factors contribute to the shortage of black superintendents. Empirical research is warranted to identify unintended or intended factors that contribute to their "underrepresentation."

---

139 https://www.edweek.org/ew/articles/2006/02/17/24supes.h25.html

Principals

Principals are division leaders who are responsible for outcomes associated with specific grades or schools. They help determine the culture and social climate, assign teachers to different classes and classrooms, and hold personnel accountable. Ironically, principals are primarily seen and heard when there is either good or bad news. Because a principal's workload can be overwhelming, schools generally have one or more assistant principals.

In concert with district priorities, principals have established mission statements, goals, objectives, timelines, strategic action plans, budgets, and evaluation systems. Overall, their goal is to facilitate effective instruction and support in order to encourage the mastery of increasingly complex materials by all students.

According to a 2016 report found on the RAND website, from 1999 to 2000, the number of principals in public schools was 84K. The breakdown of principals by race and gender was as follows: white (82%) or a little over 8 out of 10; female (approximately 43%) or 4 out of 10; and persons of color (17.8%). The latter suggests that black students may be cognizant of the fact that less than one out of five principals looks like them, even in schools where black students represent upwards of 60% of the population.

Again, for every action, there are generally intended and unintended consequences. For example, it has been alleged that black teachers who excel in their classrooms are frequently recruited to the assistant principal rank to serve as enforcers or disciplinarians. Stakeholders can quickly assess this allegation by inventorying principals in their local schools. Pay attention to roles and responsibilities written and observed. Which assistant principal appears to be assigned to help manage instruction and learning outcomes versus discipline and/or physical operations (e.g., buildings and transportation)? Case studies could help shed light on this hypothesis. Partial support is illustrated by the following account:

> A senior college administrator heard about a dynamic and effective black male teacher in the area. The young educator was driving up mathematics test scores the right way. He was engaging previously low performing students and motivating them to learn. The administrator immediately was saddened as he considered the implication of the young man's success in the classroom. Some school districts would promote him to assistant principal because of his success in the classroom. However, he would most likely become a "disciplinarian" instead of being placed in charge of instruction or curriculum, which would provide a significant raise and/or bonus. In these cases, students lose an effective teacher and gain an "enforcer," who then becomes marginalized. The senior administrator reached out to the young educator and found that indeed his principal had approached him about becoming an assistant principal.

In terms of career advancement, elevation to assistant principal would be a good and deserved promotion for people of color. The pay is higher, and the experience could lead to additional career advancements. Such decisions are difficult for some applicants of color because they understand the additional roles that they might be playing in their classrooms. They must weigh that consideration against higher pay and expanded career opportunities.

CHAPTER 6

Public School Teachers

After deliberate consideration, most Americans will agree that teachers are one of the country's most prized possessions. Effective teachers stimulate the minds and unlock the imaginations of millions of students each school day, thereby helping to sustain America's exceptionalism and global, economic competitiveness. Their interactions with students through words, gestures, and images/symbols play critical roles in students' lives particularly in the areas of academic self-concepts, academic self-efficacy, public identity, educational attainment, future employment opportunities, and wealth accumulation.

Public School Teachers by the Numbers

In 2013, the National Center for Education Statistics reported that the U.S. public school teaching core was predominantly female. Specifically, the percentage of women in the teaching core in 1987 was 70.5%. Recent reports indicated a gradual increase in female and slight decrease in male teachers by 2012. Women represented roughly 2.6M/76.3% of all teachers and men represented 802K/23.7%. That equals a decline in the proportion of men by six percentage points between 1987 and 2012. During the time frame in question, men accounted for only one out of four teachers in the U.S. This point will be thoroughly explored later.

Upon further examination of the teaching corps, a comparison of the racial composition of teachers between 1987 and 2012 revealed the following: black (191K/8.2% v 231K/6.8%); white (2.2M/81.6% v 2.8M/86.9%; Latino (69K/3% v 264K/7.8%). Analysis of the change in percentage by race shows a small decrease among black teachers, approximately a five-percentage point decrease among whites, and a significant increase among Latinos. While relatively small, the percentage of Asian teachers also saw a slight increase during the time period under review. These statistics suggest that black students are exposed every day to a disproportionate number of white teachers (4 out of 5) and only a sprinkling of black teachers (approximately 1 out of 10). The good news is that all other racial groups experienced increases in the number of teachers who looked like them over the twenty-five-year period in question. See Table 3 below.

Table 3: Teachers by Race/Gender

Race	Total Number	Number of Females	Percent of Males	Percent of Females
White	5 million	2.8 million	86.9	81.6
Black	422,000	231,000	8.2	6.8
Latino	333,000	264,000	3	7.8

Source: The National Center for Education Statistics (2013)

Teacher Pipeline

Teachers are decision-makers who determine whether students pass or fail. As decision-makers they fall into one of the three prejudice-discriminatory personality types (i.e., mostly fair, conditionally fair, or mostly unfair). The unknown is the extent to which their biases influence their treatment or evaluations of students.

Explanations for the overrepresentation of whites and women among public school teachers have not been thoroughly vetted. Several contributing factors need to be examined. First, Americans only aspire to become teachers, plumbers, architects, lawyers, brick layers, mechanics, and so on only after being exposed to those professions. Again, social learning or modeling theories help explain how seeing teachers who look like them influence students' academic self-efficacy. Critical to social learning is the stage where students observed teachers being officially recognized and adequately compensated.

Second, for a long time, uncompetitive salaries and benefit packages in education were unattractive to most men or heads of households. Relatively low wages or compensation has caused what some have called the "feminization of teaching." Accordingly, in the past, teachers' pay was often the secondary income in middle to upper class households. In recent years, teachers' pay has seen some gains due to strikes and public outcry.

Most public-school teachers did not pursue a career in education in anticipation of becoming rich; instead, they chose to teach for a variety of other reasons.

Data related to median salaries of teachers by type of school was obtained from Payscale.com on March 29, 2016. The breakdown was as follows: special education/preschool/kindergarten/elementary ($43,554); elementary ($41,706); middle ($43,528); and high school ($45,849). Of course, those median salaries would vary widely across local school districts. The median salaries listed above would be a milestone for some teachers and depressing for others. Recall that the median household income in 2016 was an estimated $56,000.

Third, among some students, especially young men, teachers, based on their observations and experiences, are generally women. Most effective teachers exhibit unconditional compassion and interest in their students. They unapologetically reveal their emotions and actively try to engage students. Those characteristics alone push some men, particularly black males, from the profession. They believe that to survive in their worlds, they have to appear "hard."

Fourth, colleges of education often lack sufficient diversity among both students and faculty members. For blacks, the education degree pipeline appears to be leaky. Reports have shown that an unexplainable high percent of poor students and students of color wash-out even after completing all degree requirements in good standing but are unable to secure full-time teaching jobs.

The reality is that a sizeable number of students earn education degrees and accumulate enormous student loan debt only to be denied full-time employment due to low scores on state certification or licensure examinations. Below is an alarming account:

> During a casual conversation with a young, black male on campus, an administrator/educator was astonished by the student's education pipeline horror story. The student stated that he had made only A's and B's. His grade point average was well above 3.0 on a 4.0 scale. He earned his degree in education but had failed the state certification test/requirement, so he could not find permanent employment as a teacher.

Unfortunately, this student's account is not an isolated or one-off case. Most readers will either know someone or have heard of similar cases. Additional empirical research is warranted to identify ways to help students improve their performance on state certification tests after performing above average or higher in their degree programs.

Education leaders will quickly state that new standards have been put in place to increase the quality and performance of teachers across the board. However, little attention and public discourse have been given to who determines what those standards ought to be and why. Ironically, educational outcomes have not increased significantly in the wake of "higher" pre-service standards.

CHAPTER 7

Typology of Teachers and Student Success

Teachers are often classified in terms of their specialty areas, certifications, and grades taught. Few investigations have examined social and cultural aspects of teachers that could be linked to student outcomes. Certainly, Merton's race-based personality types and the concept of social distance are potential determinants of instructional efficacy and student success.

Social Distance

Social distance refers to attitudes or beliefs of members of different races toward establishing relationships with out-group members. Traditionally, social distance has been measured by asking subjects to respond to a series of items relating to whether they would approve of having a person of a specific race as one or more of the following: co-worker, neighbor, church member, close-friend, teammate, or spouse. Those indicating "no" to most items were defined as desiring greater social distance between themselves and members of the target group. Conversely, those who responded "yes" to most items were determined to harbor less social distance. The point here is that public school teachers would have varying scores, but their scores would not necessarily be a strong predictor of their treatment of out-group students.

The idea of social distance being an impediment to instructional efficacy is not a novel one. According to a Public Broadcasting System (PBS) article dated March 28, 2016, cultural conflicts or clashes are prevalent in schools. The claim was based on a 2012 warning sounded by Professor Edin of the

Columbia University Teachers' College. He stated that work must be done to bridge the gap between cultures within schools and classrooms across the U.S. Research suggests a significant number of recent education graduates who become teachers in public schools only last for about two years due to cultural clashes with primarily poor students and students of color. As a mentor to some prospective teachers, Edin sounded an alarm regarding a phenomenon whereby well-meaning white and black teachers see urban and poor students as needing to be rescued or saved. He said that some of those teachers see themselves as "knights in shining armor," venturing into an unruly school system with a mission to convert and rehabilitate wayward potential learners. According to Edin, much of their despair arises out of failures to persuade students to adopt what might be termed white middle-class values and norms. As a reality check for pre-service teachers, he stated, ["If you're coming into a place to save somebody then you've already lost because young people don't need saving. They have brilliance, it's just on their own terms."]

Professor Edin proposed a form of "reality pedagogy" to help mitigate or alleviate cultural clashes in schools. First, he argued that teachers must endeavor to learn about their students' backgrounds and everyday experiences before embarking on teaching the curriculum. Second, teachers must be able to incorporate their students' life experiences into their instruction. Finally, colleges of education must be encouraged to make cross-cultural immersion experiences mandatory. Pre-service teachers should be given opportunities to see and hear what their students see and hear every day.

Additionally, social distance is created as the ratio of teachers to students increase in classrooms. Education experts invariably argue that small class sizes are more conducive for learning. Yet, in many public schools, it is not uncommon to have upwards of 25 students in a class being taught and managed by a single teacher/instructor. Stop and think about the typical learning environment with recent education graduates and twenty-five or so energetic, sugar fueled students in a reading or English class. How much individual attention can be given to students, especially those who might be experiencing some difficulty in grasping the material? Unfortunately, budget cuts primarily affect teaching assistants and reading coaches who provide enormous instructional assistance at exceptionally low costs. The key take-away from this discussion is that as the teacher-student ratio increases, so does social distance between teachers and their students.

In general, poor school districts are at extreme disadvantage in the recruitment and retention of high performing principals and teachers because their salaries, fringe benefits, and supplemental incentives are not competitive. In general, they have relatively high turnover rates among both teachers and administrators. Isolated schools often become "training sites" for recent graduates and/or second and third chance "placements" for lower performing teachers. It should be noted, however, that some effective and extraordinary teachers remain at lower funded schools because of personal ties to the area and a commitment to helping those less fortunate.

Surely, teachers use the same logic and justifications for seeking employment opportunities as all other professionals. They desire competitive compensation, favorable work environments, freedom to be creative, recognition when appropriate, and opportunities to advance their careers. Though underpaid and overworked, many teachers earn living-wages and maintain moderate to middle class lifestyles, and their household incomes are significantly higher than most of their public-school students'. They mostly live in different communities and neighborhoods and often socialize in different venues from the parents/guardians of their pupils, thereby sustaining social distance.

CHAPTER 8

Diversity Among Teachers and Student Success

A theme espoused by the 100 Black Men of America is that "Black boys will be what they see." A minor addition of "what they hear" seems appropriate in the context of teaching and learning. When applied to public schools, students are more likely to emulate the behaviors of people with whom they feel connected or share a master status and auxiliary traits.

According to a John Hopkins University news release on April 5, 2017, results of a multi-institutional study found evidence of a positive relationship between black students' access to black male teachers and academic achievement. The report entitled "The Long-Run Impacts of Same Race Teachers" was based on the results of a study designed to track the progress of over one hundred thousand black students who enrolled in third grade in North Carolina public schools between 2001 and 2005. A primary objective of the research was to assess the impacts of having at least one black teacher on their academic achievement. Students who were randomly assigned to at least one black teacher in third, fourth, or fifth grades had lower dropout rates and higher postsecondary aspirations. Black boys who were defined as low income because they received free/reduced lunch were twenty-nine percent more likely to express interest in attending college than those who did not have a black teacher in one of those grades. It should be noted that only half of the students had a black teacher during the study.

Somewhat surprised by the North Carolina findings, team members also looked at black students who attended kindergarten in Tennessee in the late

1980s and had at least one black teacher in K-3rd grade. Results of that study revealed that students who had at least one black teacher were fifteen percent less likely to dropout than those who did not have one.

Surely, just the mere experience of having a black teacher is not a sufficient explanation for the results cited. According to Professor Nicholas W. Papageorge, a co-author of the study, a plausible explanation is what he called the "race match or role model effect." Among low socioeconomic black boys in third through fifth grades, impacts of having just one black teacher (i.e., prospective role model) resulted in a 29% increase in college aspirations and a 39% decline in dropouts. Results were similar among black girls but not as strong.

According to Professor Papageorge, stunning results of empirical research has shown that "stubbornly persistent attainment gaps are not impervious to policy changes" that would result in having more black teachers in America's classrooms.

Intentionally affording black students' access to credentialed black teachers should not be defined as any form of discrimination. White students are literally guaranteed access to white teachers throughout their academic journeys. Could anyone imagine white students matriculating from pre-K–3rd grade without having a single white teacher to serve as a role model?

It would be grossly naïve of Americans to assume that racial biases and discrimination end at the entrance to public schools. Superintendents, principals, teachers, and other personnel possess biases and prejudicial attitudes to some extent, and only they have the authority to discriminate. Lack of diversity among school personnel limits true integration of perceptions, ideas, beliefs, and behavioral idiosyncrasies. In many cases, a type of social distance exists between school personnel, students, and parents/guardians that often stymie academic aspirations.

CHAPTER 9

Quality Early Childhood Education (QECE)

When some children receive quality early childhood education (QECE) and others do not, potential explanations for gaps in academic achievement between the two groups should not be questioned. For decades, educators have acknowledged and raved about the life-long positive effects of quality early childhood education. In fact, some go so far as to state that access to QECE is a major determinant of academic achievement and attainment. So, students whose access to QECE is limited or blocked face challenges in school, and without additional time and effort, often lag behind their peers.

To level the learning playing field, most educators have lobbied for public quality early childhood education for all children regardless of their zip codes and household incomes.

A 2010 report by the Southern Education Foundation entitled "A New Majority: Low Income Students in the South's Public Schools" reviewed the body of research related to QECE and several positive outcomes. According to the report, children's brains can be trained for achievement and learning at the early ages of three and four. They are also susceptible to developing characteristics necessary for success, such as persistence, aspiration, focus, curiosity, and the ability to cooperate. Other key findings included the following: 1) Preschool programs have a positive effect on cognitive development ability or skills; 2) students who received high-quality pre-school education were less likely than children who received no pre-K education to repeat a grade; and

3) QECE students were significantly more likely to attend a four-year college or university.

Formal early childhood education outside of the home often begins with nursery care. According to the U.S. census 2016 American Community Survey, nursery students numbered approximately 5.1M and by sex the breakdown was males (2.6M) and females (2.5M). By race the numbers were as follows: white alone (3.6M); white non-Hispanic (3M); black alone (723K); Asian (224K); and Hispanics (949K).

It has been estimated that less than 20% or 1 out of 5 black and Hispanic children have access to quality early childhood education. When access to quality early childhood education is measured in terms of months of reading skills, those who lack access lag behind their peers by an average of five to seven months.

While support for universal QECE is increasing, only a few publicly funded programs are accessible in heavily black populated states. Educators and researchers have encouraged parents and other stakeholders to establish "Local Learning Communities in which early childhood education is promoted, encouraged, and recognized. Pre-K coordinated competitions or showcases should be implemented in local neighborhoods, subdivisions, and public housing. People will do things in anticipation of recognition and/or positive reinforcements. Excelling in pre-K should be celebrated like winning a football championship."[140]

Kindergarten

In states without publicly funded early childhood education, kindergarten is the first milestone or phase of students' formal education. According to the U.S. Census 2016 American Community Survey, the number of kindergarteners in 2008 was 4.1M.

---

140 Ray, M. C., & Stevenson, T. (2016). *Why College Degrees Still Matter Success Strategies*. Ray & Stevenson.

The breakdown by sex was male (2.81M) and female (1.98M). By race the distribution was as follows: white (2.79M); white alone, non-Hispanic (2.21M); black alone (571K); Asian alone (171K); Hispanic of any race (930K). Labels used were adopted from the survey.

The lack of quality early childhood education can help partially explain children's low preparedness for kindergarten, which in turn, causes them to progress at a slower rate than other students. This slower progression often leads to loss of motivation and interest in learning.

Kindergarten is analogous to the ACT measure of college readiness. Children who attend kindergarten and perform well acquire the foundation for active listening and learning in grades 1-12. Essentially, kindergarten was designed to make children "school ready."

The point here is that if the absence of pre-K creates a learning gap equivalent to several academic months, then those students who do not attend kindergarten are likely to face even greater academic or learning challenges. Historically, African Americans have disproportionately not attended kindergarten due to a host of factors.

CHAPTER 10

Reading and Academic Success

Increasingly, reading proficiency at grade level is the criterion for academic attainment in most public schools, and it provides the trajectory for academic attainment in a lot of cases.

In a growing number of states, low reading proficiency has risen to crisis level among the poor and students of color. An excerpt from a White House initiative during the Obama administration provided a sobering assessment:

> "Mastering reading by the end of third grade is essential for school success since students begin to transition at that point from learning to read to reading to learn. Those who do not hit the proficiency mark by then are four times more likely to drop out of high school, research shows. Among those who do not read well, the dropout rates are twice as high for African-American and Hispanic students as they are for white students."[141]

In many states, failure to meet statewide standards in reading results in some students being held back to repeat third grade.

In 2017, the National Assessment of Educational Progress (NAEP), which has tracked educational outcomes in the U.S. since 1969, conducted its national assessment including reading comprehension among fourth and eighth graders. For the first time, digital tablets were used to collect student responses instead of the traditional paper and pencil format.

---

141 https://gradelevelreading.net/wp-content/uploads/2014/02/Young-Men-of-Color-and-the-Early-Reading-Gap.htm

Students can score from zero (0) to five hundred (500) and based on their scores they are assigned to different performance levels (i.e., basic, proficient, or advanced). Results of the 2017 reading assessment of fourth graders included the following: 68% scored basic or above; 37% proficient or above; and 9% were advanced. [142] For the official U.S. Department of Education overview see the assessment of the NAEP Reading Performance report.[143]

Reading scores were also examined by race/ethnicity. The breakdown was as follows for students scoring proficient or above: Asian (59%); white (47%); Hispanic (23%); black (20%); and American Indians (20%). Approximately 1 out of 5 black students scored proficient or higher, despite being less likely to have had access to QECE.

Nearly one-third or 1 out of 3 U.S. fourth graders scored below basic in 2017. In addition to not being able to "read to learn," in some states a relatively large percentage of poor students and students of color were held back. Unfortunately, being held back begins a negative labeling process by parents, teachers, close friends, and peers. Students who are held back are often attractive targets for bullies or they employ bullying tactics and methods as offensive tools to deter would be bullies.

Based on a plethora of scholarly research and anecdotal accounts, learning, and performing gaps by race are extremely narrow from pre-K through second and third grades, but the gap appears to widen thereafter. Empirical research is warranted to identify factors that help to exacerbate gaps between the races beginning in third and fourth grades.

---

142 https://www.nationsreportcard.gov/reading_2017/nation/achievement?grade=4

143 https://nces.ed.gov/programs/coe/pdf/coe_cnb.pdf

CHAPTER 11

Zero-Tolerance Disciplinary Policies

Policies and procedures implemented by decision-makers in school districts can intentionally or unintentionally help to decrease academic success and disproportionately impact certain groups of students. Recall from an earlier discussion that the justice department examines patterns or practices that appear to discriminate against groups of Americans.

Some education leaders and scholars have suggested that the flurry of school shootings during the past two decades prompted adoption of zero-tolerance disciplinary systems. In general, school administrators transitioned to a disciplinary system that included swift and mandatory sentencing for a wide range of behaviors. Alarms were sounded when disciplinary infractions were expanded to include the catch-all category referred to as "defiant behavior." The term was used to define just about anything that teachers and other decision-makers perceived as disrespectful, disruptive, and/or threatening. Defiant behavior is like pornography; teachers know it when they see or hear it but there is generally a lack of consensus as to specific actions or non-actions to create uniform policies. For instance, in some cases, the disciplinary infraction list was expanded to include wearing hats/caps, sagging, texting, listening to music via earphones, hair styles, talking back, chewing gum or eating in class, rolling eyes, moving in desks, and sitting in an unassigned seat. The defiant behavior "catch-all" gives teachers and school officials broad discretion when defining language and gestures as "cause" for some type of disciplinary action. While "sagging" should not be condoned or allowed in schools, depriving students of much needed instruction for such an infraction surely is not the most learning-oriented sanction. Critics of so-called "zero-tolerance" disciplinary policies have argued that they have unnecessarily increased the numbers of disciplinary infractions including suspensions and expulsions among students of color.

In 2015, Marion Wright Edelman, President, and founder of the Children's Defense Fund, called for major overhauls of zero-tolerance disciplinary policies:

> "…huge reforms are required in school discipline policies and practices across our nation as school push out has worsened in past decades with the criminalization of children at younger and younger ages aided and abetted by school expulsion and suspension policies which funnel children into the prison pipeline often crippling them for life."[144]

School disciplinary policies are developed and implemented at state and local levels. Oversight boards and superintendents are the primary decision-makers. In 2016, an *Ed Week* publication contained a stunning revelation by Dr. John King, former U.S. Secretary of Education:

> "Educators, schools, and states can do far more than the federal government can…to reduce incarceration. Every year, our schools suspend roughly 2.8 million students — the vast majority of them for non-criminal activities — and refer a quarter of a million students to police. Students of color, especially black students and those with disabilities, are suspended and referred to police at disproportionate rates. These students are more likely to fall behind academically, drop out of school, and wind up in prison."

Ironically, in a nation where most decision-makers self-identify as Christian, little consideration is given to allowing students to seek forgiveness and redemption for "defiant" acts observed in classrooms. Moreover, there is a

---

144 https://www.prnewswire.com/news-releases/childrens-defense-fund-releases-new-report-on-zero-tolerance-marian-wright-edelman-issues-call-to-action-for-mississippi-190375401.html

lack of intentional strategies to divert students from unnecessary contacts with the juvenile justice system. School disciplinary reforms must be engineered by a "community of stakeholders" and must be perceived as equitable and fair to all impacted, including teachers, students, parents/guardians, and youth development organizations.

Fortunately, decision-makers can modify policies. Some local school reforms have been implemented to address racial disparities related to issuing disciplinary infractions and suspensions. For example, in Los Angeles, based on results of an impact study conducted by the Public Counsel and the Labor/Community Strategy Center, citations for most non-injurious campus fights and some other infractions were discontinued. Instead, the time and effort school resource officers (SROs) were allocating to processing students were shifted to them being trained to seek appropriate referral services including mentoring, healthcare, and counseling.

Correlates of Zero-Tolerance Policies

To be clear, unruly, and disruptive students must be dealt with in a manner to decrease their negative impacts on learning environments. They must not be allowed to hinder other students' attention and progress in classrooms. However, critics of zero-tolerance disciplinary policies argue that the defiant category of infractions gave teachers and administrators too much discretion in terms of causes for in and out of school suspensions.

According to a 2015 report by the Center for Civil Rights Remedies (CCRR), impacts of zero-tolerance policies varied by race/ethnicity. From 2011-2012, among elementary students, the suspension rate was 2.6% and by race the results were as follows: Native American (2.9%); Pacific Islander (1.2%); Asian (0.5%); black (7.6%); Latino (2.1%); and white (1.6%).

Almost one out of ten black elementary students was suspended from school.

Without question, the attitudes, beliefs, and behaviors of principals, teachers, and students influence school disciplinary rates. As students grow larger, more verbal, and "defiant," the scope and nature of their interactions with the predominantly white female teaching corps is likely to be adversely impacted. The CCRR report that was released in 2015 showed that among high school students, the suspension rate was 10.1% and by race the rates were as follows: Native American (11.9%); Pacific Islander (7.3%); Asian (2.5%); black (23.2%); Latino (10.8%); and white (6.7%). When viewed across racial groupings and grades, Asians had the lowest and blacks had the highest suspension rates from 2011-2012.

Geography of Zero-Tolerance

Zip codes matter when implementing expanded or zero-tolerance disciplinary systems. In 2016, the U.S. ED published an online report stating that between 2011 and 2012, the highest rates of suspensions were in the Southeast and Southwest. In terms of black students, a similar geographical pattern was observed. The rates varied with the highest concentration in the Southeast, followed by the West, and the Rust Belt states or Midwest. The lowest rates for blacks were in the upper plain states and New England. In addition, states with relatively lower academic attainment reported higher suspension rates.

Certainly, students need rules and behavioral guidelines in order to increase both instructional effectiveness and student success. The goal should be to provide students more instruction, not less. Policies that intentionally, or unintentionally decrease students' instructional time serve to thwart learning and academic attainment.

CHAPTER 12

Guidance Counselors versus School Resource Officers (SROs)

Zero-tolerance disciplinary policies have created a demand for a type of policing in public schools. During the past two to three decades, there has been a surge in school budgets for "school resource officers" (SROs) and/or law enforcement personnel. In a lot of cases, isolated school students have greater contact with school resource or law enforcement personnel than counselors. Stakeholders need only to visit their local schools to make an informed judgement about this assertion.

Education leaders' priorities are reflected in their allocation of scarce resources. Data released in recent years showed that approximately "1.6M students attend schools that employ a sworn police officer but do not have a counselor on staff." That situation is an example of "displaced priorities," said former Secretary of Education John King.145 According to some education experts, to be effective the counselor to student ratio should be about 1:150. Little attention, however, has been given to the SRO to student ratio and its accompanying budget.

School counselors play important roles by helping students make informed decisions about school, college, and careers and dealing with socioemotional and mental health issues. In comparison, SROs or law enforcement officers are employed to serve and protect students and school personnel. Most adopt a community policing model in which they patrol the campus and monitor students. As one observer noted, the expansion of school policing inevitably

145 https://www.edweek.org/ew/articles/2016/07/26/us-secretary-of-education-lets-educate-not.html

extends the reach of the justice system yielding both intended and unintended consequences.

The debate about the role of an SRO versus school counselor is exemplified in the following account. An encounter involving an SRO and a student gained international attention. After repeated requests, a young black female student refused to put away or give her cell phone to her teacher and an assistant principal. A school resource officer was called in to address the defiant student. The officer used physical force to remove the student from the classroom. Hindsight suggests that a trained school counselor might have been able to diffuse the situation without the use of physical force.

CHAPTER 13

Broadband Access and Academic Success

Equality in terms of access to reliable and affordable broadband connectivity does not exist in the U.S. Oftentimes, it appears to be depressed or limited in poor and rural communities. Even in areas with broadband coverage, access is restricted by prohibiting cost structures and credit histories.

Students who have access to broadband connectivity are advantaged when it is used to augment instruction and learning. In 2016, Ray and Stevenson found that black college students who owned personal computers and had reliable access to broadband recorded significantly higher-grade point averages than those who had to utilize other means to study and complete homework assignments.[146]

While it is impossible to determine the impact of the digital divide on academic success, it is reasonable to assume that it depresses academic outcomes to some extent. For many poor students and students of color, if it were not for public libraries, after school programs, and close family members, they would be unable to access computers and broadband connectivity after schools dismiss.

---

146 Ray, M. C., & Stevenson, T. (2016). *Why College Degrees Still Matter Success Strategies.* Ray & Stevenson.

STEM and Race

To an extent, the digital divide can also help explain some of the variations in students' interest and pursuit of science, technology, engineering, and math (STEM) concentrations and careers. Most of the iconic social media companies constantly lament about the shortage of technology workers in the U.S. The severe underrepresentation of blacks in their workforces can be explained in part by a lack of related instruction in public schools.

School districts and teachers who have integrated technology across the curriculum are advantaged in their quest to engage and excite students. In many cases, exposure to and the use of technology spurs interests in STEM that can subsequently help bolster the U.S. in terms of its global economic competitiveness and national security.

Specifically, computer science related employment trends have indicated a growing demand for workers and a lack of diversity in the pool of prospective employees. According to an article that appeared in *USA Today* on October 18, 2016, Silicon Valley companies were dominated by white and Asian men, who accounted for about seven out of ten workers.

In 2015, Google reported that among its new hires the percent black and Hispanic was 4% and 5%, respectively. The company wanted to find out why they faced tremendous challenges in recruiting more women and people of color. Google teamed with Gallup to administer a survey to thousands of students, parents, and educators to identify barriers to increasing diversity in their workforce. Some of the major survey results included the following: 1) Black students were the least exposed to computer science education in K-12; 2) less than fifty percent of black students reported having a dedicated CS course; and 3) black and Hispanic students were less likely to have access to computers at home.[147]

---

147 https://csedu.gallup.com/home.aspx

The primary take-away from the study was that there were racial/ethnic disparities in terms of access to personal computers, broadband connectivity, and computer science education. CS instructional deficits, particularly in poor or isolated public schools, depress the number of black students who are afforded opportunities to acquire basic computer science competencies.

CHAPTER 14

Student Support Services and Race

Students of all races suffer from an array of medical and mental challenges and require additional support services. Most with sufficient support services can and do live normal lives and achieve aspects of the American Dream. This chapter contains the results of an investigation of selected mental and medical challenges among public school students that are often undiagnosed, untreated, and do not receive adequate student support services.

Attention Deficit Hyperactive Disorder (ADHD)

An Attention Deficit Hyperactive Disorder (ADHD) diagnosis labels or stigmatizes the student in question as incapable of focusing on classroom instruction and maintaining behavioral control without medication and/or behavioral therapy. Specific types of ADHD classroom behaviors include forgetfulness, interrupting classmates, and seemingly uncontrollable urges. Often, ADHD sufferers do not only impair their own learning, but they also interfere with other students' acquisition of knowledge and academic achievement.

During a *Washington Post* web chat in 2011, results of a study of ADHD were discussed. Data were obtained from the National Health Interview Survey which was conducted by the National Center for Health Statistics, an arm of the Centers for Disease Control (CDC). Results of the study showed that nearly ten percent of U.S. children had been diagnosed with ADHD. The methodology employed consisted of face-to-face interviews with over forty thousand households regarding health issues.

Some key findings were as follows:

- Within the last decade, the prevalence of ADHD was higher among white, non-Hispanics; however, by the end of the decade blacks and Puerto Ricans had surges and equaled the rate among non-Hispanic whites at approximately ten percent.
- Previously, ADHD prevalence was similar among all socioeconomic groups; however, in recent years, significant increases have been recorded among the poor. The increase was explained in part due to greater access to health care or more effective diagnosis in under-served communities.
- ADHD diagnoses vary by sex. The rate for girls was 5.5% and for boys 12.3%. Behaviorally, the researchers stated that girls are more likely to exhibit inattention patterns while boys are generally labelled as hyperactive. Those patterns have remained relatively stable over time.

Researchers have not consistently linked ADHD to intelligence or academic achievement. Based on reviews of relevant literature, it seems that academic success and ADHD can coexist. The key is to provide research-based student support services as needed.

There are different treatment models for ADHD sufferers by age. In 2013, the Centers for Disease Control (CDC) presented findings gleaned from a national sample of children ages 4 to 17 who were diagnosed as ADHD and have special needs. Results of the study included the following: 1) Less than a third of the children received both medication and behavior therapy; 2) roughly fifty percent of preschoolers (4 to 5) received behavior therapy; and 3) approximately fifty percent of preschoolers were prescribed some type of medicine, and one out of four were treated solely with medication. In general, based on available data, it appears that among children between four and five, behavior therapy is the initial treatment. Children ages six and older generally receive a combination of medication and behavioral therapy. As children age, medication appears to become more prevalent either as a standalone treatment or in conjunction with behavioral therapy.

While accepting the fact that some students may need medicine and/or behavior therapy, it is imperative that stakeholders carefully examine patterns and practices that may have inherent, unanticipated consequences. Access to prescription drugs is more readily available than sessions with behavioral therapists for a majority of the poor and communities of color. Counseling or behavioral therapy could be problematic for many poor and underserved children because it is less likely to be covered by insurance and government assistance programs. Also, transportation challenges might exist among the poor and rural populations. From an economics perspective, the drug model in some cases is associated with receipt of government assistance in the form of a monthly check to cover expenses, thereby making the medical model preferable to behavior therapy in some families.

The 2013 CDC report also found that the percent of ADHD diagnoses between 2011 and 2012 differed by state/region. The highest rates were recorded in the Southeast, followed by the Midwest with the lowest in the western quarter of the U.S. Prevalence rates ranged from a low of seven percent and below to a high of thirteen percent or greater. Note that the prevalence of ADHD appears to be higher in states with relatively large black populations and that have relatively high out-of-school suspensions.

According to published sources, prescribed medications to control or treat ADHD are generally categorized as either stimulants or non-stimulants. Central nervous stimulant (CNS) medications are the preferred chemicals which are believed to improve concentration and energy levels by increasing dopamine and norepinephrine found in the brain. Common CNS medications include brand names such as Adderall and Ritalin. Other drugs prescribed in ADHD cases include non-stimulants and antidepressants which are used alone as well as in conjunction with CNS medications in some cases.

Unfortunately, medications used to treat ADHD in children have unwanted side effects. According to WebMD (March 16, 2016), some of the side effects associated with CNS medications include weak appetites, abdomen discomfort, and insomnia. More serious side effects involve cardiac concerns, upper torso pain, liver ailments and suicide impulses in rare occasions. Anecdotally, some medications appear to induce what is often referred to as a "zombie" like behavioral response in some children. The account below is an example:

> A couple of adult mentors celebrated their mentees' participation in a mentoring program and their academic achievement by treating them to dinner at a local restaurant. The behavior of one of the boys who normally was engaged and verbal, seemed disconnected. He had been getting in trouble at school for tardiness at the first bell in the morning. On this afternoon, he was not making eye contact with the group and appeared to be lethargic or tired. After a while, one of the adult mentors asked him if something was wrong. The boy stated that he had taken his medicine to help keep him focused. The adult mentor stated afterwards that that was one of the saddest days in his life. The boy appeared to be only a shell of his former self. He lacked energy and his natural glow.

This account, however, is one sided or a form of confirmation bias. Only parents/guardians, close family, and observant teachers know the story. The adult mentors only interacted with the boy a couple of hours per week and was unaware of the challenges he was posing to his mother and teachers. The mentor's image of the student was based on his limited interactions with the student in a small group setting. However, it is logical to wonder, given data gleaned from the CDC, if equally effective treatment options were appropriately vetted. Recall that in general, medication appears preferable over behavioral therapy among older students.

ADHD diagnoses can be used inappropriately to manage troubled youth. Given the stereotypes surrounding boys of color, frequent class disruptions could facilitate an ADHD recommended diagnosis. Parents/guardians are encouraged to seek professional consultation and to research all available treatment modalities when faced with an ADHD diagnosis.

Bullying Victimization

During the last two decades, bullying and the effects of bullying have grabbed the attention of parents, students, educators, law enforcement, and policy makers. In general, bullying is defined as the recurring use of words, gestures/behaviors, images, and symbols during face-to-face and/or online interactions to inflict physical and/or emotional harm and pain upon another person(s).

A national survey of students regarding their experiences related to bullies and bullying is administered periodically in collaboration with the Office of Juvenile Justice and Delinquency Prevention (OJJDP). Results of the 2015 survey showed that among 6th – 12th graders, bullying was prevalent in all types of schools. Girls reported higher levels of bullying victimization; however, boys reported higher rates of physical threats or physical altercations. Black students reported the highest rates of bullying victimization, while Asian students were the least victimized. Overall, self-reported victimization rates peak during middle school and gradually decline thereafter.

Bullying victimization can adversely impact academic success in several ways. Some victims take evasive measures to avoid contact with bullies by finding reasons to skip class or school altogether. There are also mental health outcomes related to bully victimization including but not limited to anorexia, bulimia, depression, and alcohol/drug abuse. In addition, some victims are afflicted with psychosomatic symptoms including severe head and neck aches and stomach cramps.

Negative effects of bullying are exacerbated by several factors. First, social media has made it extremely easy and fast to spread hurtful information to hundreds if not thousands of people. Second, victims are often isolated like a deadly virus and feel alienated or alone. Third, bystanders or witnesses along with victims do not have access to a safe, anonymous bullying alert or disclosure system. As a result, bullying goes unreported in a lot of cases. Finally, there is often a lack of readily accessible professional counselors and/or trained volunteer support networks in poor schools and communities.

To recap, it is important to note that bullying victimization rates appear to be highest among black middle school students. However, there is little attention given to the presence of bullies and bully victims on academic achievement. A take-away from survey results is that bullying is yet another challenge that black students must disproportionately overcome in their quest to do well in school.

Dyslexia

Dyslexia, a disorder of the language system where phonological processing takes place, was identified as a public health problem several decades ago. Its prevalence has been estimated to be fifteen percent or 15M.

Researchers have used functional brain imaging technology to detect disruptions in brain function in the left hemispheric, posterior neurological system as those affected read different texts. It is now understood that these brain disruptions cause dyslexia. Prior to this research, however, dyslexia was essentially a misunderstood and misdiagnosed learning disorder that bewildered and baffled teachers, parents, and students.

According to results of empirical studies, potential indicators or symptoms of dyslexia included the following: low comprehension; involuntary movement of letters and words causing loss in reading location; sight word recognition challenges; difficulty in decoding words and phrases; and trouble sounding out words. Students suffering from dyslexia have difficulty reading and comprehending in the traditional manner but otherwise are equally capable of academic success if given appropriate instruction and accommodations.

Today, many public schools have no or inadequate dyslexia screening systems in place. Students, particularly those in poor or isolated schools, are less likely to be diagnosed properly and more likely to be tracked to special education or in-school disciplinary programs. Even in school districts with dyslexia screening programs, lack of funding inhibits hiring certified dyslexia instructional personnel who have been in high demand. Competitive salaries and benefit packages for those "specialized skill sets" must be weighed against cost of core instructional demands.

Autism Spectrum Disorder (ASD)

Autism is the result of abnormalities in the development of the brain. Though it can be detected at an early age, currently there is no cure. The concept of spectrum is used to reflect the range and severity of observed symptoms. Researchers have found that effective emotional and behavioral therapy can help decrease or control some of the disruptive symptoms or associated behavior patterns.

ASD is a diagnosis that has become more prevalent in the last two decades. In 2018, the Centers for Disease Control reported that the prevalence of ASD increased by fifteen percent between 2012 and 2014. Among a national sample of eight-year-olds, the prevalence went from 1 in 68 to 1 in 59. In addition, prevalence remained higher among white students followed by black and Hispanic. The gap between boys and girls closed, but boys were still at least four times more likely to be autistic. Finally, the modal age for ASD detection was four, but research findings indicate that it can be reliably diagnosed at age two.[148]

According to information obtained from the Mayo Clinic and other reputable sources, symptoms of autism include the following: 1) challenges communicating; 2) lack of empathy; 3) unscheduled anger out-bursts; 4)

---

148 (https://www.autismspeaks.org/science-news/cdc-increases-estimate-autisms-prevalence-15-percent-1-59-children)

seemingly uncontrollable repetitive behavior (e.g., rocking, spinning, or clapping hands); and 5) stiff resistance to change in routines.

The increasing prevalence of ASD is a growing challenge for both parents/guardians and school districts. School administrators and teachers often feel ill-equipped to effectively manage the wide range of behavior patterns among students in classrooms. Funding limitations are often blamed for inadequate or no relevant student support services to help increase academic success among more of the affected students.

Official education outcome data have repeatedly shown glaring racial disparities but do not tell the whole story. The prevalence of medical and mental challenges among poor and isolated school students is often unknown. Parents have horror stories of not being able to receive appropriate screenings or having to secure assistance on their own. Among lower income households, securing screenings and appropriate academic support services for their children has been challenging. Surely, a fraction of racial gaps in academic success can be attributed to factors often neglected in reports and public forums.

SECTION XVI: PUBLIC SCHOOL STUDENTS AND ACADEMIC SUCCESS

This section presents the results of the investigation related to the roles students play in generating test scores and academic attainment and impacting overall school or district ratings. Given the preponderance of evidence revealed previously related to the host of challenges confronting African American students, the investigation sought data and information to address the following question:

> "To what extent have black students narrowed educational attainment gaps despite facing challenges seemingly beyond their control?"

CHAPTER 1

Profile of Public School Students

A 2015 report by the National Center for Education Statistics revealed that the population of first through twelfth graders increased noticeably between fall 2002 and fall 2012, increasing from 48.2M to 49.8M. The report projected the enrollment to surge to approximately 60M by 2024. As of 2012, the racial makeup of public-school students was as follows: white (51%); black (16%); Hispanic (24%); Asian/Pacific Islander (5%); mixed race (3%); and American Indian/Alaskan Native (1%). Over half of all public-school students were white, and many of them attended predominantly white schools. With the exodus of whites from cities to suburbs, private and faith-based schools and choice have reinvigorated "separate" education systems based on income and race in many areas. While black students make up only sixteen percent of public-school students, they receive at least ninety percent of related negative media coverage.

The U.S. Census has traditionally partitioned public-school students as follows: pre-school (early childhood-kindergarten); elementary (1st-4th); middle (5th-8th); and high school (9th-12th). A key realization is that academic achievement and attainment follow a developmental model requiring mastery of specific skills and acquisition of knowledge at each stage. In general, students who do not acquire age-appropriate instruction and skills face challenges in subsequent stages or grades.

CHAPTER 2

Students' Modes of Adaptation

Based on official data, it appears that most black public-school students aspire to matriculate. In addition, it is indisputable that students in poor and isolated schools are confronted by socioeconomic issues, school policies, and inadequate student support services that combine to thwart their academic attainment. Drawing from strain theory, students who face these conditions should be expected to respond by adopting individual level modes of adaptation. Possible adaptations are described below.

Conformers

First, conformers include students who have academic and career aspirations and believe that they have the capacity to be successful despite perceived barriers. They utilize academic best practices and dedicate sufficient time and effort to their schoolwork.

Innovators

Second, innovators also have relatively high academic aspirations but often perceive their paths to success to be limited or blocked by external forces beyond their control. They do not have books, broadband connectivity at home, and parents/guardians who are equipped to assist them with their schoolwork. But these students find ways to acquire knowledge and skills to do well in school. Many defy low expectations and the overwhelming odds against them.

Ritualists

Third, ritualists do not have traditional academic aspirations for one reason or another; however, they have relatively good attendance, complete homework assignments, and even graduate. This group of students is motivated by one of two reinforcements. Some have no choice but to go to school and put forth sufficient effort to avoid punishment or negative reinforcements. Another group will put in enough time and effort to become or remain eligible to play sports or participate in other extracurricular activities. Conformers, innovators, and ritualists account for the bulk of students who earn diplomas.

Rebels and Retreatists

The remaining two student adaptations account for a large portion of classroom disruptions, no or incomplete homework, in and out of school suspensions, and dropouts. Rebels often reject or are void of academic aspirations and refuse to adhere to traditional student expectations. This adaptation begins to clearly emerge in middle to junior high school in most cases. Students in this category often have chronic absences and have been held back in at least one grade. They just will not conform or obey school policies and spend a quarter or a third of the school year in both in and out of school suspension or expelled.

Similarly, retreatists/isolationists do not appear to have academic or career aspirations and they tend to be loners in and outside of school. These students may be disproportionately challenged by physical disabilities and medical and/or mental illnesses that make them attractive targets of bullies, and they often lack adequate access to appropriate student support services. Rebels and ritualists account for a majority of students who drop-out or fail to earn diplomas.

Academic Best Practices

Certainly, a portion of gaps in educational attainment must be attributed to the adoption of patterns or practices among black students that decrease their grade point averages. Based on their study of nearly one thousand black college students in 2016 and related literature, Ray and Stevenson confirmed significant relationships between social and behavioral patterns or practices and mean grade point averages.

There is a relatively large body of knowledge related to what are commonly called academic behaviors or best practices. The researchers found that students who took quality notes, sat near the front, participated in study groups, and worked at least twenty hours per week reported higher grade point averages.

School Attendance

An indisputable truth is that students who receive more hours of instruction, on average, do better than those who miss significant instructional time. Over the years, educators have looked at school attendance in at least two ways. The first is average daily attendance (ADA) which looks at the percent of students who are enrolled that show up on each day. In comparison, there is what some called "chronic absences" which is often defined as missing ten percent or more of the total number of days within an academic year. For example, a calendar year consisting of one hundred eighty days would set eighteen days as a measure of chronic absenteeism. Invariably, statistical results show inverse relationships between numbers of days missed and grade point averages. Simply put, as the number of days missed increases, students' grade point averages will most likely decrease.

Among their sample of college students, Ray and Stevenson found that students who missed an average of three or more class sessions in a semester had lower mean grade point averages. For many, stating that class attendance is related to academic achievement is simply "emphasizing the obvious." The takeaway is that parents/guardians should encourage and promote school attendance as part of their strategy to help increase their children's grade point averages. For the most part, school attendance, unless suspensions are involved, cannot be blamed on non-familial decision-makers.

CHAPTER 3

Graduation Rates and Race

Presumably, President Trump's indictment of schools serving predominantly black students was primarily based on comparative graduation rates. Official data regarding educational attainment by race reflect phenomenal perseverance and resiliency among descendants of African slaves. Evidence regarding graduation rates was obtained from a 2016 report by the U.S. Department of Education's National Center for Education Statistics (NCES), which is responsible for the Common Core of Data State Dropout and Graduation Rate Data system. According to the NCES, graduation trends for 9th graders between 1990 and 2013 showed a steady increase, rising from a low of 74% in 1990 to a high of 82% in 2013.

High school graduation rates varied greatly by state and race. Nationwide graduation rates by race were as follows: black (69%); Hispanic (73%); and white (86%).[149]

In addition, the report showed that at the state level, graduation rates ranged from a high of 89% in Iowa to a low of 59% in the District of Columbia. An overwhelming majority of former slave states (e.g., Georgia, Florida, South Carolina, Alabama, Mississippi, and Louisiana) with relatively large black populations recorded graduation rates at or above seventy percent (70%).

To summarize, the vast majority of black students have had to overcome a host of challenges to graduate. The list of challenges included the following: 1) inadequately funded school districts; 2) lack of quality early childhood

---

149 http://www.governing.com/gov-data/education-data/state-high-school-graduation-rates-by-race-ethnicity.html

education; 3) under resourced teachers; 4) lack of sufficient teachers and staff who look like them; 5) lack of adequate student support services; 6) less access to personal computers and broadband connectivity; 7) zero-tolerance disciplinary policies; and 8) low expectations. Despite seemingly insurmountable structural and social challenges, almost 7 out of 10 black students earn diplomas. For a moment, imagine what the black graduation rate would be if unnecessary structural and social barriers were decreased or eliminated.

SECTION XVI: POSTSECONDARY EDUCATION AND RACE

This section contains results of an investigation of laws and practices that, more likely than not, have intentionally or unintentionally helped thwart African Americans' college enrollment and degree attainment rates. The investigation focused on the founding of colleges and universities in the United States, admissions requirements, federal and state appropriations, cost of attendance, and student loan debt. The investigation was designed to assess the extent to which laws and practices might have helped to suppress black degree attainment rates. Again in 2016, Ray and Stevenson illuminated the fact that among blacks, a college degree was believed to be the key to racial equality. In general, degree attainment has been identified as the gateway to higher wage jobs/careers, credit worthiness, homeownership, entrepreneurship, profitable social and professional networks, and the accumulation and transfer of wealth.

According to the U.S. census, about 209M Americans are twenty-five or older, and approximately 67M have earned postsecondary degrees ranging from bachelors to professional degrees or doctorates. Only about two out of ten Americans possess four-year college degrees or higher.

To fully appreciate progress made by blacks in terms of postsecondary degree attainment, rates must be examined over different time frames. Data and information regarding postsecondary degree attainment beginning in the 17th century were researched to help establish a plausible baseline or starting point.

Prior to the end of the Civil War, a vast majority of blacks in both the North and South were not afforded quality secondary educational opportunities. Despite cruel and harsh punishment for attempting to learn, a small fraction was able to read, write, and master some mathematics. Similarly, following the end of the Civil War and during Reconstruction, the vast majority of African Americans were agricultural workers and lived at or below the poverty line. Because children, particularly in the Deep South, served as full-time laborers during planting and harvesting seasons, they literally dropped-out of school on a regular basis during the school year. Many blacks were forced to take on year-round employment after completing the sixth grade and even more following the eighth grade. For centuries, college was not an option for an overwhelming majority of blacks in the U.S.

A brief chronology of colleges and universities founded in the U.S. provided evidence of a rigged higher education system. Early colleges for both whites and blacks were privately funded. Established on September 8, 1636, in Cambridge, Massachusetts, Harvard University is thought to have been the first college established in the colonies. Nearly a century and a half later, a practice of allocating public funds or tax dollars to support state colleges began. The University of Georgia was founded in 1785 and is recognized as the first publicly supported postsecondary institution in the U.S.

Birth of HBCUs

Based on information uncovered regarding the founding of private and public colleges, it appears that Black Colleges and Universities (HBCUs) came online nearly two hundred (200) years after the first private Historically White Colleges and Universities (HWCUs) and about fifty (50) years after state tax dollars were first allocated to fund public colleges. The birth of Historically Black Colleges and Universities can be traced back to Philadelphia or the City of Brotherly Love. White abolitionists and religious leaders were progressive in their views regarding affording blacks' opportunities to earn college degrees. A wealthy Quaker named Richard Humphreys has been credited with establishing the Institute for Colored Youth in 1837. He wanted to help produce black teachers and tradespersons. Initially located in Philadelphia, the school was subsequently moved to Cheyney, Pennsylvania and became known as Cheyney University. In 1854, Lincoln University was also founded in Pennsylvania. Later in 1856, Wilberforce University was founded in Ohio, a mere five years prior to the start of the Civil War. It is important to note that HBCUs were initially privately funded institutions that were governed and managed by non-blacks.

Morrill Acts (1862 and 1890)

Results of the investigation contained evidence showing that public funding for black land grant colleges was delayed for decades, thereby stunting the growth and viability of black farmers. The Land Grant Agricultural and Mechanical College Act of 1862 was passed by Congress to create a land grant college in each state. With a target audience of farmers, these colleges focused primarily on agriculture and mechanic arts. In general, the institutions can usually be identified by the word "State" or "A&M" in their names.

Following the end of the Civil War and passage of two Homestead Acts, the number of black owned farms increased, but they had little to no access to the expertise at white land grant institutions. Nearly three decades later, the Morrill Act of 1890 attempted to remedy the situation by forcing states to fund or support the creation of black land grant colleges. HBCUs that were established in response to the legislation are called "1890" schools.

Following the end of the Civil War, the number of HBCUs surged with the goal of providing separate yet unequal postsecondary institutions for blacks. Wildly successful, HBCUs have produced amazing leaders and talents too numerous to list. Without question, these institutions have accomplished more with less funding.

Funding Disparities

Publicly and privately funded colleges and universities are invariably governed by either appointed or repopulated boards. At the state level, governors appoint board members in line with the "states' rights" ideology. However, in most private colleges, boards repopulate themselves. Private institutions rely almost totally on gifts, endowments, tuition and fees, and dollars received through federal agencies and private corporations for research and development.

In comparison, state or publicly funded colleges have similar funding sources as private colleges; however, they are also aided or supported by state taxes. The level of state funding allocated to colleges and universities has been on the decline for decades, resulting in nearly annual tuition hikes.

Whether private or public, funding levels are determined by a relatively small group of elected officials, corporate leaders, and wealthy alumni or friends. Governors and state assemblies determine how many tax dollars go to fund their colleges and universities, and they undoubtedly have some biases related to each institution in their states. Likewise, corporate leaders and wealthy alumni have biases in terms of where they want to gift or invest their resources. In general, the capacity to "give or cause dollars to be given" to support HBCUs and HWCUs varies by race.

With few exceptions, HBCUs have faced severe funding challenges from both federal and state governments. Their existence is amazingly similar to the isolated public schools mentioned earlier. In most states, funding formulas favor HWCUs. As a result, HBCUs face challenges in offering competitive salaries, start-up research packages, modern facilities, state-of-the-art science, technology and engineering resources, residence halls, and other traditional college amenities.

HBCU alumni have been enormously generous to their institutions, but their median income and net wealth trail significantly behind their counterparts. Moreover, supporters of HBCUs are generally in the minority at federal and state levels (e.g., Congress and state legislatures) where funding for colleges is decided. In the U.S. Congress, they lack the seniority and committee assignments to significantly influence or direct federal agencies to funnel research and other programmatic grants to HBCUs similar to that received by HWCUs. For this reason, as in other subsystems, voting matters.

Both private and public HBCUs have produced an amazing number of black leaders and professionals. During the late 1960s, over sixty (60%) of black college students attended HBCUs. In recent years, statistics show that while accounting for only three percent (3%) of U.S. colleges and universities, HBCUs accounted for approximately twenty percent (20%) of degrees conferred to African Americans.

CHAPTER 1

College Admissions and Standardized Tests

Evidence gleaned from the investigation suggests that blacks might have been subject to college admissions tests that unnecessarily blocked or decreased their entrance and financial capacity to attend some colleges. Heated discourse has lingered related to the utility and importance of standardized tests at the collegiate level. Specifically, debates have focused on potential cultural biases inherent in test developers that favor higher socioeconomic students. As a result, black students have been forced to take tests based largely on the perceptions and experiences of people who did not live in their communities and had different lifestyles and experiences.

History of College Admissions Tests

The Scholastic Aptitude/Assessment Test (SAT) was introduced in 1926 but was not initially intended to be aligned with high school curricula. Allegedly, it was developed to help limit the number of students accepted into colleges. It was the only college readiness test until the American College Testing (ACT) was introduced in 1959. Apparently, following the Brown school desegregation ruling, college applications increased, generating demand for another readiness predictor. Everett Franklin Lindquist, a university of Iowa professor, then developed the ACT which is now accepted by all colleges and universities in the U.S. The key revelation is that both the SAT and ACT were developed to limit the number of students admitted to colleges.

While there is certainly nothing inherently nefarious about the race of test developers, the extent to which their life experiences differ significantly from "test-takers" can generate unanticipated negative consequences. Is it reasonable to believe that scores on standardized tests are influenced by several factors including but not limited to cultural/class biases, lack of early childhood education, lack of access to AP courses, and familiarity with test items?

While college readiness tests such as ACT and SAT do not with certainty predict students' academic achievement and attainment at the postsecondary level, they do provide a measure of students' "readiness" to master college level work. Still, discretion is necessary as a significant number of students who scored relatively high on the ACT were subsequently placed on academic suspension. On the other hand, a sizeable number of black students who did not score twenty-one or higher on the ACT went on to earn college degrees. Critics of these tests have alleged that they do not take into consideration students' persistence, resiliency, and faith.

CHAPTER 2

ACT/SAT Coaching and Practice

There is a thriving business sector created to help students score higher on the ACT/SAT. Registration fees for some prominent ACT prep or tutorial sessions range from about seventy-five dollars to over one thousand dollars. Costs associated with ACT tutorials and coaching limit low- and middle-income students' access to those resources.

ACT/SAT prep courses/workshops are analogous to spring practice in athletics. The "playbook" contains information regarding the structure of the tests and time allocation. For example, the ACT is scheduled for four consecutive hours. Students must be emotionally and physically prepared for a grueling test-taking competition. In addition, each subject area is allotted a specific number of minutes, so time management skills are important. Coaches often encourage paying students to first answer the questions for which correct responses are known and then tackle questions that require additional deliberation. ACT prep or workshops introduce students to similar test taking environments, rules, and examples of the types of questions that appear on the tests. Repeated practice sessions should help increase test scores.

Students can take the test multiple times beginning in the eighth grade. A fee starting around forty dollars is normally associated with the test; however, some schools provide financial assistance to low income students.

It is worth noting that some parents and students are unaware of the availability of ACT post-test diagnostics. This intended or unintended, well-kept secret was disclosed and later confirmed. Informed parents/guardians of students who take the ACT on nationally designated days can opt to pay about twenty dollars to receive a debriefing regarding the items they marked incorrectly and suggestions for avoiding future incorrect responses. An online excerpt stated the following:

> "Certain national test dates and centers give you the opportunity to order a copy of your questions, your answers, the answer key, and scoring instructions—plus the writing prompt, scoring rubric, and scores assigned to the optional writing test." [150]

---

150 http://www.act.org/content/act/en/products-and-services/the-act/scores.html

CHAPTER 3

ACT Mean Scores and Race

A comparison between 2014 and 2015 mean ACT scores revealed virtually no changes. The average composite score was 21.01 with the maximum being thirty-six. Subject areas were English, Reading, Mathematics, and Science with composite scores hovering around 20.3 in all areas other than a score of 21.4 in reading.

Some researchers and education leaders have attributed observed race/class disparities in mean test scores to a lack of access to AP courses, especially in isolated schools. An article published by *College Record* in 2016 reported that 53% of Asian, 24% white, 16% Hispanic, and only 12% of black students take pre-calculus or calculus by the eleventh grade. Surely, lack of quality instruction in key exam subject areas can explain some of the racial gaps in terms of ACT mean scores.

Recent ACT mean scores by race were gleaned from an article that appeared in *Inside Higher Education* in August of 2015. See table 4 below.

Table 4: ACT Composite Scores, 2014 and 2015, by Race and Ethnicity

Race/Ethnicity	**2014**	**2015**
Black	17.0	17.1
Native American	18.0	17.9
White	22.3	22.4
Latino	18.8	18.9
Asian	23.5	23.9
Native Hawaiian/Pacific Islander	18.6	18.8
Two or more races	21.2	21.2

Didn't respond	20.7	20.6

(Source: Inside Higher ED, August 2015)

From 1926 to 2015, black students have closed the gap in standardized test scores. While they lag behind their counterparts, at least a fraction of the deficit must be legitimately attributed to poorly funded public schools and lower familial academic attainment due to decades of racial injustices. Their progress suggests that the removal of structural and social barriers can help increase their scores, thereby closing achievement gaps on life-altering college admissions and funding tests.

CHAPTER 4

College Admissions and Affirmative Action

Invariably, results of studies have shown that at least two to three variables appear to increase probabilities of being admitted to colleges in general and so-called elite colleges. First, legacy or students related to alumni are generally overrepresented in entering classes. Second, students related to endowments or financial contributors are admitted at higher rates among applicants. Finally, recruited athletes receive preferential treatment. Only a small fraction of entering freshmen gain admission based solely on high ACT/SAT scores. A take-away from empirical research is that an overwhelming majority of black students do not benefit from legacy and endowment related points in admissions calculations at HWCUs. Their admissions have been granted based on several factors listed in descending order of importance: athletics; ACT/SAT; and ability to pay tuition and fees.

Affirmative Action and College Admissions

Recall that a little less than sixty years ago, colleges and universities were essentially racially segregated, adhering to Jim Crow and separate but equal doctrines. Even after the passage of civil rights legislations in the mid-1960s, some colleges and universities continued admissions policies that systematically thwarted black enrollment numbers. Surely, legacy and donor/gifting admissions points helped non-black students gain acceptance in better funded and so-called elite colleges.

As mentioned previously, affirmative action was designed to satisfy at least two compelling government interests—to make-up for past discriminatory practices against blacks and to usher in racial parity in the federal workforce. Government agencies developed diversity goals and milestones.

Similarly, some colleges and universities subsequently implemented affirmative action admissions policies to satisfy what they believed to be a compelling need for greater diversity and inclusion among students and faculty. The Supreme Court has made several rulings regarding the constitutionality of college admissions policies that consider race/ethnicity in the screening process. Plaintiffs have argued that to achieve diversity in their student populations, some universities assigned points to race or being a member of an underrepresented group. They argued that the practice gave black students an unfair advantage over some non-blacks who had scored higher on the ACT, prompting plaintiffs to allege reverse discrimination. The Supreme Court had to decide if diversity/inclusion was a compelling interest and whether the methods employed were narrowly tailored.

An overview of affirmative action court cases and rulings related to college admissions was found at https://www.cnn.com/2013/11/12/us/affirmative-action-fast-facts/index.html. In 1978, the high court ruled against the use of quotas, finding them unconstitutional and favoring goals or milestones. On June 23, 2003 in Gratz v. Bollinger, the court struck down the use of points given to minorities during the admissions process to help increase diversity. On December 9, 2015, the court heard arguments in the University of Texas case related to its goals of increasing diversity. In a 4 to 3 vote, the Supreme Court ruled that narrowly tailored affirmative action programs were constitutional. When considering admissions, colleges can weigh a number of factors including class rank, socioeconomic status, community service, and zip codes.

Despite affirmative action programs, official statistics do not show a surge in the percent of black students at HWCUs, especially among scholarship students, excluding athletes. Void of official data, it can be assumed that black "star" students who gained admissions with the help of affirmative action goals earned degrees at rates similar to their counterparts. However, opponents of Affirmative Action cannot put forth a credible case that those black students did not deserve an opportunity to attend those colleges.

ACT/SAT and Fraud

In schools, teachers are responsible for instruction and awarding grades. However, a network of "insiders" is tasked with developing, administering, and scoring the ACT/SAT. In addition, those proctoring the tests are trusted to ensure that all test-takers are treated equally and fair. In mid-March of 2019, the United States attorney for the District of Massachusetts issued indictments based on the results of an exhaustive investigation that has become known as "Operation Varsity Blues." The indictments charged dozens of well-to-do parents of fraud and tax evasion related to a national "pay to be great" scheme designed to fraudulently gain their children admission to selected elite colleges. The system involved bribing coaches, cheating on ACT/SAT, and manipulating athletic performance visuals. The cost for the fraudulent services ranged from a quarter of a million to over $6.5M.

In terms of ACT/SAT test scores, the rigged system involved several schemes. Some students benefitted from being diagnosed with learning disabilities that allowed for special accommodations or "assistance." In other cases, people were paid to take the test for rich students. Finally, some of the people administering the tests were paid to correct answers. No one knows how widespread ACT/SAT fraud is at local levels, but it is reasonable to assume that it is not restricted to those indicted in the Varsity Blues case. Based on this discovery, to what extent could fraudulent ACT/SAT results account for some of the observed race and/or socioeconomic disparities in mean group scores?

CHAPTER 5

ACT/SAT and Student Loan Debt

Unfortunately, ACT composite scores have both short- and long-term economic consequences in terms of personal debt, credit worthiness, and wealth accumulation. Colleges and universities have placed a great deal of confidence in college readiness tests to selectively place students in remedial programs, thereby extending their stay and increasing their college loan debt. Students who score from 21 to 36 are usually eligible for either partial or full ride scholarships. In comparison, students who score less than twenty in most cases are forced to pay for tuition, room and board, books, and miscellaneous expenses, totaling tens of thousands of dollars in loan debt. Still, many black students' aspirations include earning a postsecondary degree by any means necessary.

Based on their overall ACT mean score, it is not surprising that upwards of 86% of black college students obtained loans, meaning that only about fourteen percent earn scholarships/fellowships. Recent official reports showed that the percent of Hispanics and whites who obtained student loans was 65% and 60%, respectively.

An estimated 44M Americans have a total student loan debt in excess of $1.2 trillion. Moreover, a disproportionate fraction of the student loan debt is on the backs of students with an ACT composite score of nineteen or less. Results of an analysis of college graduates average loan debt by race was summarized as follows:

> "Black students also graduated with the highest amount of debt from public colleges in 2012 — $29,344, on average.

> Hispanic students, though, had the highest burden among those who attended private colleges, with an average debt of $36,266. These numbers are likely even higher today. The average college graduate in the class of 2016 left school owing $37,172."[151]

There is virtually no escape from repaying federal student loan debt. Repayments must begin about nine months after leaving college with or without a degree or a job. Among black borrowers, the challenge is compounded by the fact that they must repay student loans or risk having their already lower wages garnished.

Black student loan debt has caught the attention of financial advisors who attempted to weigh the costs and benefits of accruing huge debt among non-scholarship students. Data and information contained in a 2018 CNBC article entitled "For African Americans Student Debt Makes College More of a Risk" prompted some critical thinking. The article drew attention to the fact that, in general, black students have reported greater loan debt and lower prospects of landing higher income jobs. While the article did not discourage degree attainment; it did increase awareness of financial risks related to "unforgiveable" high-interest student loans.

Postsecondary Degrees and Race

According to the National Center for Education Statistics (NCES) Fast Facts, between academic years 2000–01 and 2015–16, there have been shifts in degree attainment by race and sex in the U.S:

> "The total number of postsecondary degrees awarded increased at all degree levels: certificates by 70 percent (from 553,000 to 939,000), associate's degrees by 74 percent (from 579,000 to 1.0 million), bachelor's degrees by 54 percent

151 https://studentloanhero.com/featured/study-student-loans-weigh-heaviest-black-hispanic/

> (from 1.2 million to 1.9 million), master's degrees by 66 percent (from 474,000 to 786,000), and doctor's degrees by 49 percent (from 120,000 to 178,000)."][152] There were minor gains in the percent of black postsecondary certifications and degrees earned compared to both Hispanics and whites. Among blacks, increases were promising at all levels. First, the number of certificates awarded increased by 63 percent, moving from 99,400 to 162,400. Second, the number of associate degrees awarded to blacks saw a 110 percent increase, from 63,900 to 134,000. Finally, at the bachelor's degree level, the number of degrees awarded increased by 75 percent, surging from 111,300 to 194,500.

According to the report, postsecondary degree attainment rates varied by race and gender. Women outpaced their male counterparts. Black women accounted for a whopping sixty-four percent of degrees earned among African Americans. In comparison, women accounted for fifty-six percent (56%) of degree earners among whites. Additional details regarding these shifts can be found at: https://nces.ed.gov/fastfacts/display.asp?id=72.

152 https://nces.ed.gov/fastfacts/display.asp?id=72

NOTES

SECTION XVII: HEALTHCARE SYSTEM AND RACE

President Trump did not address black health and wellness in his rigged system proclamation. Nevertheless, this section was designed to disclose evidence of laws and patterns or practices that have combined to adversely impact both infant mortality and life expectancy among African Americans. Moreover, the investigation sought evidence regarding African Americans' extreme health resiliency in the face of unequal access to quality healthcare and other life-shortening environmental and social conditions.

History of Healthcare

Public health is a relatively young concept in the U.S. For centuries, relief, not cures of illnesses or diseases, was the goal of family members and self-trained health providers. From a historical perspective, imagine the quality of healthcare provided to slaves. Surely, many slaves were forced to self-medicate in a foreign land with unfamiliar vegetation, herbs, and spices.

In the colonies, selected men were afforded the opportunity to practice medicine. Most went through informal or formal apprenticeships prior to medical schools being established. It is reasonable to assume that most of the early healthcare providers gained on-the-job experience on battlefields during fights with Native Americans and subsequently during the War of Independence.

The Founding Fathers also failed to address public health in the Constitution because healthcare was a privilege not a constitutional right. Those who had knowledge and/or money received better healthcare than illiterates and the poor. As a result, advancements in caring for and curing some illnesses and diseases were only gradually disseminated to slaves and their descendants.

Slaves were extremely valuable, so owners driven by profit margins provided some healthcare. While doing so, some blacks engaged in unofficial medical apprenticeships. Because they routinely took on the role of mid-wives, who often delivered babies, and collected and applied herbal concoctions to relieve pain and cure the sick, black women served as early healthcare providers.

In terms of formal training, the first medical schools were founded at the College of Pennsylvania in 1765 and at Harvard during the mid-1780s. In a related development, Pennsylvania Hospital was the first public medical facility that opened in 1751. Reportedly, private hospitals were present as early as 1736.

Prior to and even following the end of the Civil War, African slaves and their descendants were systematically denied medical training and access to early hospitals. In fact, historians have stated that some blacks had to go abroad to receive medical training prior to the Civil War. Dr. James McCune Smith was identified as the first black to earn an MD, practice medicine, and operate a pharmacy in the U.S. He earned his MD in Scotland and practiced medicine between the 1840s and 1865. Historians further credit Rebecca Davis Lee Crumpler for becoming the first black woman to earn an MD in the U.S. from a school for women in Boston, Massachusetts in 1864.

Following the Civil War, medical schools that admitted blacks and confirmed their degrees were minimal, thereby creating a paucity of black doctors. Imagine newly freed slaves and their descendants being forced to visit uninviting and racially segregated doctors' offices, emergency rooms, and hospitals to seek medical assistance. Unfortunately, doctors and other healthcare providers fall somewhere along the prejudice-discrimination spectrum (i.e., mostly fair, conditionally fair, or mostly unfair) despite taking and believing in their Hippocratic Oath. Surely, the overwhelming majority of medical professionals do their absolute best to help and not harm patients regardless of their race, sex, age, religion, or country of origin.

Slowly, black medical schools were established following the Civil War. Howard University's School of Medicine was founded in 1868, and Meharry Medical College located in Nashville, Tennessee was established in 1876, approximately eleven years following the end of the Civil War. Those institutions were established to perpetuate separate and unequal healthcare systems.

CHAPTER 1

Infant Mortality and Life Expectancy

In terms of health outcomes and race, the investigation focused on two indicators, infant mortality and life expectancy. For the purpose of this investigation, infant mortality refers to the death of children under one year old and is generally reported in terms of the number per one hundred thousand children in that age cohort. In comparison, life expectancy is generally understood to refer to the average age at which persons sharing similar characteristics (i.e., race/ethnicity and sex) typically die. Of course, there are exceptions to the milestone markers. The following paragraphs contain briefs related to factors that have been linked to infant mortality rates and life expectancy in the U.S.

Environment and Health

For centuries, power and politics have influenced and perpetuated what is now coined environmental racism. In 2019, Harriet A. Washington released a painful and illuminating book entitled *A Terrible Thing to Waste: Environmental Racism and Its Assault on the American Mind.* The research included reviews of public policies that have disproportionately exposed blacks to harmful toxins. Evidence cited by Dr. Washington was extensive and compelling.

In general, local, state, and federal regulatory boards and agencies have been comprised of political appointees that mirror the race of gerrymandered elected leaders, so in many cases the poor and blacks have been underrepresented or excluded altogether from decisions pertaining to the placements of residential developments and potential hazardous industries.

Past institutional discrimination in terms of residential segregation provided the foundation for environmental racism. Communities and neighborhoods were racially separate and "unequal." Today, planning and zoning boards determine the character and make-up of local geographical areas with input from homeowners and developers. The latter develops subdivisions with specific buyers' purchasing power or credit limits in mind which often limit the percent of poor and blacks who can afford to buy in those areas. On the other hand, low to moderate income housing and multi-family housing and/or apartment complexes generally are affordable, thereby more accessible to lower income residents.

Social activists have been calling for environmental justice, meaning equality in terms of living conditions. Through elementary observational studies, residents and classes can map and characterize a host of factors that exist in different neighborhoods and communities. Some potential items to include on the environmental inventory include sidewalks, curbs and gutters, streetlights, proper drainage during heavy rain, repugnant odors, dilapidated houses, old and abandoned industrial structures, quality of recreational opportunities, and sufficient "green" space. Unfortunately, casual observations will not uncover the more hazardous environmental offenses. A plethora of documented and published accounts reveal how decision-makers have allowed blacks to be disproportionately exposed to lead paint, contaminated water, toxic dumps, poor air quality, and chemical runoffs that undoubtedly have increased infant mortality and decreased life expectancy. For example, in 2003, an estimated $700M award was given to about 20,000 residents of Anniston, Alabama. Solutia, Inc. and the Monsanto Corporation were defendants in the PCB contamination case that had lingered in state courts for decades. The sad fact is that no amount of money can buy back the harmful effects of PCB contamination on the lives of both parents and their children. Dr. Washington's book addresses additional cases; likewise, the U.S. Environmental Protection Agency (EPA) lists civil cases and settlements at https://cfpub.epa.gov/enforcement/cases/.

Food Deserts

Food and nutrition are two interrelated factors that contribute to health and wellness. Food consumption or diet has differed by race for centuries. Recall that for a long time, African slaves were not allowed to own livestock. According to published accounts, they were often given leftover meat, including intestines. Of course, meat was preserved in salt, and lard, or the fat from animals, was used for frying. Fat meat was also used to season vegetables while processed sugar was used in baking and canning fruit. According to medical professionals, overindulgence or consumption of saturated fat, table salt, and processed sugar contributes to several conditions including high blood pressure and diabetes that are found disproportionately among African Americans.

Today, access to nutritious food items still appears limited or blocked in some communities. In fact, some poor and communities of color have been called "food deserts" because there are no grocery stores or vegetable markets nearby. In those communities, grocery shopping requires prior planning and logistics because transportation to and from grocery stores is challenging for many low-income residents. Upon their entrance into most grocery stores, blacks find products displayed on the outer isles far more nutritious yet more costly than those often found in the center of stores. To make "ends meet," many poor and blacks are forced to load up on the less expensive but lower nutritional processed foods that have been found to be related to the on-set and/or aggravation of some chronic diseases.

Criminal Victimization

Accessible recreational amenities alone are not sufficient because some low-income areas are plagued by violent crimes that limit some outdoor experiences. Violent crime victimization rates appear higher in lower SES neighborhoods in which blacks are overrepresented. It is hypothesized that intrarracial (black-on-black) homicides can help explain some of the gap in life expectancy. According to an online search of official Bureau of Justice

Statistics (BJS) and Federal Bureau of Investigation (FBI) tables, homicide victimization data for 2005 showed that the black rate was over six times that of their white counterparts. Moreover, over nine out of ten blacks were murdered by another black during the same time frame. An indisputable fact is that black-on-black violent crimes contribute to decreased life expectancy, especially among black men.

Unsafe Work Environments

Some work environments have also been found detrimental to overall health outcomes among African Americans. They have been overrepresented in employment sectors void of unions and employment health and safety regulations. During the Richard Nixon administration, the Safety Bill of Rights Act or the Occupational Safety and Health Administration (OSHA) was enacted in 1971. The purpose of the legislation was to help decrease job-related injuries, diseases, and deaths. Employers were asked to adopt and implement industry-specific safety "best practices" to prevent accidents and illnesses. Companies have been fined for OSHA violations.

It is believed that many OSHA violations go unreported by low-wage workers because they fear retaliation from their employers. Imagine being injured on the job and then being terminated after seeking medical assistance and/or temporary unemployment. Keep in mind that blacks have been disproportionately employed in agriculture, service sector, and what has come to be known as the "gig economy." Based on official data, OSHA has not been active in those sectors.

CHAPTER 2

Medical Research and Race

Some African Americans still do not trust physicians and avoid them like a plague. Narratives regarding medical personnel engaging in unsafe practices involving the poor and blacks are widespread. Before family planning centers were established, sterilization was used to prevent some women from becoming pregnant. That practice cast a shadow on subsequent family planning efforts to supply contraceptives to help prevent unwanted pregnancies and the spread of sexually transmitted diseases. Unfortunately, because community health resources have a checkered past among blacks, they are often perceived as tools to eliminate or avoid the alleged existential threat generated by the projected "browning" of America phenomenon.

Human Research Subjects

Revelations regarding the involuntary and inhumane treatment of black men in experiments paved the way for legislation to protect human research subjects and has potentially served to save hundreds if not thousands of lives. Prior to the establishment of safety protocols related to human subjects, unknowing black men were used to track and assess the health outcomes related to untreated cases of syphilis. According to official documents, the disease was intentionally allowed to incubate inside of black men between 1932 and 1972. In that experiment black men went untreated even though a cure in the form of penicillin was available beginning in 1947. Why would health professionals allow those black men to go untreated for at least forty (40) years, while unknowingly infecting untold numbers of innocent victims?

Merton's thesis regarding personality types characterized by the intersection of prejudices and discrimination seems applicable in this situation.

National Research Act of 1974

Unethical human research has been documented repeatedly with one significant case or incident that usually forces reforms. Breaking news stories about the forty-year-long U.S. Public Health Service Syphilis Study at Tuskegee led to thunderous public calls for the enactment of laws to protect human subjects. The National Research Act of 1974 created the National Commission for Protection of Human Subjects of Biomedical and Behavioral Research. Subsequently, the commission issued the Belmont Report that contained ethical guidelines and rules governing research involving human subjects:

> "The Office of Human Research Protections oversees Title 45, Part 46 of the Code for Federal Regulations, which pertains to human-subjects research. That office indirectly oversees human-subjects research through local institutional review boards (IRB)." [153]

Unfortunately, African Americans have been coerced and tricked into serving as unwilling human research subjects and have suffered untold ailments and deaths. The passage of the National Research Act of 1974 reflects the government's awareness and need to police research involving human subjects.

153 https://www.ncbi.nlm.nih.gov/pubmed/18811995

CHAPTER 3

Access to Healthcare

Infant mortality and life expectancy are related to persons having access to quality and affordable healthcare. It is indisputable that certain segments of the U.S. population have greater access to healthcare than others. Access to quality health care is primarily a function of employment benefits, socioeconomic status, age, and zip codes.

History of Medicare and Medicaid

According to the Centers for Medicare and Medicaid Services' website, in July of 1965 President Lyndon B. Johnson signed a bill creating both Medicare and Medicaid. [154]

Medicare had two components, hospital and general medical insurance coverage. Benefits and coverage have been expanded to include those sixty-five and older, the disabled, persons suffering from certain chronic illnesses, and prescription drugs.

In comparison, state legislatures have greater discretion when awarding Medicaid benefits. Initially, Medicaid was restricted to only those persons receiving cash welfare payments. Current eligibility can be met by low income families, persons with disabilities, pregnant women, and persons requiring long-term medical care. It is important to note that there are significant variations in Medicaid benefits amongst states. In earlier RSIs, blacks invariably were disadvantaged in states with relatively large black populations. Additional

154 https://www.cms.gov/About-CMS/Agency-Information/History/

research is warranted related to racial disparities in terms of Medicaid coverage and benefits.

Affordable Care Act (ACA)

Affordable healthcare was deemed a compelling government interest during the Obama administration. In response, Congress passed the Affordable Care Act (ACA) that was signed into law on March 23, 2010. The purpose of the Act was to expand healthcare to uninsured Americans including those with pre-existing conditions who had previously been excluded by insurance companies; moreover, it was intended to make health insurance more affordable. The federal government gave attractive subsidies to states that were willing to expand their Medicaid programs to cover more unemployed and lower to moderate income households. Unfortunately, many Republican governors and legislatures refused the funds, thereby denying millions of Americans greater access to affordable healthcare.

In the private sector, some unscrupulous employers implemented policies to decrease the number of primarily low-income employees who had previously been covered by their group insurance. In some cases, hours were reduced to less than thirty per week. Consequently, many blacks suffered decreases in take-home pay and denial of health insurance. Their plight was exacerbated in states that declined ACA funding.

The ACA was initially viable as young adults were required to purchase insurance to help offset the inclusion or coverage of more of the poor and those with pre-conditions. In addition, insurance coverage was made mandatory, and violators were assessed fines. However, some Republican-led states filed lawsuits arguing that the mandate to have insurance was unconstitutional, and the Supreme Court ruled in their favor. The court's decision instantly decreased the number of younger and healthier individuals in the pool, leaving the older, poorer, and higher risk. More importantly, the court's decision and related outcomes provided insurance companies plausible justification for increasing premiums, deductibles, and co-pays.

Prescription Drugs and Health

A major concern related to accessible and affordable healthcare is the availability of affordable medicines. Pharmaceutical companies continue to record astonishing profits while many poor and blacks cannot afford to purchase prescribed medications. News stories and documentaries have showcased African Americans who are forced to make life-threatening decisions each month between food, light bills, rent, or their life sustaining medications. In the world's model democracy, citizens are forced to pay ridiculously higher prices for the same medication than citizens of other democracies around the world. Surely, decision-makers can negotiate more affordable drug costs for all Americans to help decrease health gaps between blacks and other races in the U.S.

Options available to Americans to obtain prescribed medicines often place blacks at a disadvantage. They include the following: 1) retirement benefits; 2) private insurance; 3) Medicare plans with a drug coverage option, and 4) public assistance (e.g., Medicaid or State pharmaceutical assistance programs). Unfortunately, blacks have been less likely to retire with health benefits. The cost of private insurance including co-pays, deductibles, and monthly premiums are outside the budgets of the poor and a large fraction of the middle class. Finally, public assistance eligibility standards disqualify some needy individuals and families.

Results of some studies have found regional differences related to public assistance for prescription drugs. Allegedly, assistance for medication was relatively lower in the Southeast where, coincidentally, many blacks reside. In comparison, more liberal public drug plans for Medicare recipients were cited in New Jersey, New York, and Pennsylvania, or the Northeast.

Results of empirical research have revealed disparities in the use of prescription drugs among Americans with chronic illnesses that require sustained and regular medication. Unfortunately, blacks have been found more likely to go without their prescribed medications. This underutilization of prescribed medications for chronic diseases often results in debilitating health outcomes which was confirmed by research in the article "Racial and Ethnic Disparities in Prescription Coverage and Medication Use." The researchers observed that:

> "...elderly black beneficiaries are three to four times more likely than white beneficiaries to undergo amputations of lower limbs or implantations of shunts for renal dialysis due to uncontrolled diabetes." (See: Gornick, 1999, 2000; Gornick et al., 1996).[155]

In terms of affordable healthcare, results of empirical studies have repeatedly found that blacks utilize health services at a significantly lower rate than their counterparts and they undergo more severe treatments as a result. Surely, access to preventive health screenings, effective and timely medical treatment, and access to prescribed medications for all regardless of race, sex, income, age, or country of origin will go a long way towards healthcare equality in the U.S.

Upward Mobility and Health

Interestingly, some factors that seem to prolong white lives appear to decrease life expectancy among blacks. For decades it has been hypothesized that upwardly mobile blacks face a unique social dilemma. They are often marginalized in that they are not fully accepted by whites or less upwardly mobile blacks. That condition frequently leads to stress, hypertension, depression, and/or alcohol/drug use/abuse.

In 2017, Collen et al. authored a ground-breaking article entitled "Racial Disparities in Health among Non-poor African Americans and Hispanics: The Role of Acute and Chronic Discrimination." Published in the *Journal of Social Science & Medicine,* results of the study showed that the health of blacks who were upwardly mobile lagged behind that of their non-black counterparts.

---

155 Geiger, 2000; Mayberry, Mili, and Ofili, 2000

The authors reasoned that upwardly mobile blacks find themselves in the "minority" whether at school, on the job, or in boardrooms. This leads them experiencing more instances of racism and discrimination than other blacks which results in greater stress/strain. Unfortunately, among some upwardly mobile blacks, striving for and achieving some aspects of the American Dream can be hazardous to their health.

CHAPTER 4

Health Outcomes and Race

Despite the host of factors that have adversely impacted health outcomes among blacks, official data show unbelievable progress in terms of quality of health indicators, infant mortality and life expectancy.

Infant Mortality

In 2017, the Economic Policy Institute (EPI) published results of statistical comparisons related to a host of quality of life indicators by race/ethnicity. According to the report, over a fifty-year time frame (i.e., 1967 to 2017), the infant mortality rate for blacks had improved, decreasing from 34.9/100k (1968) to 11.4/100k (2017); however, the lower rate was still over twice that of whites. Decreases in black infant mortality rates must be attributed to a host of factors including greater access to prenatal care, access to healthier foods, and improved living conditions.

Life Expectancy and Race

Historical records from the 17th century related to life expectancy in the colonies focused almost exclusively on Europeans with little or no attention given to African slaves. Invariably, life expectancy estimates found for settlers hovered between thirty-five and forty years. Imagine what it was for African slaves.

The Centers for Disease Control's National Center for Health Statistics (NCHS) is the foremost repository for quality of health data. Information regarding health indicators by race/ethnicity can be found in the report entitled "United States Life Tables 2017." According to the report, overall life expectancy in the U.S. has been declining since about 2015. Suicides and drug overdoses were identified as two of the leading causes, and the prevalence appeared higher in the Midwest, Northeast and mid-Atlantic regions.

In 2018, the average life expectancy in the U.S. was 78.7 years. Curiously, life expectancy appears to vary by at least sex and race/ethnicity. On average women live about ten years longer than men. Current projections estimate that on average the milestone is 86.1 years for women compared to 76.3 years for men. [156] [157]

Similar gaps in life expectancy were found by race/ethnicity. Policy analysts and researchers generally agree on the following average life expectancy: Hispanics (81.4); whites (78.8); and blacks (74.8). Considering the overwhelming historical health disparities, it is nothing short of a miracle for the black life expectancy to lag behind its white counterpart by only three to four years. It is reasonable to predict, however, that life expectancy disparities will gradually disappear with greater racial justice and equality.

---

156 https://www.kff.org/other/state-indicator/life-expectancy-by-re/?currentTimeframe=0&sortModel=%7B%22colId%22:%22Location%22,%22sort%22:%22asc%22%7D

157 https://www.cdc.gov/nchs/fastats/life-expectancy.htm

SECTION XVIII: SPORTS/ ENTERTAINMENT SYSTEM

Given the mostly positive optics and narratives related to African Americans' roles and participation in amateur and professional sports, the suggestion that President Trump's rigged system theory was applicable to sports/entertainment would be laughable among most Americans. But, the fact that racial prejudice and discrimination has been repeatedly verified in other social and economic sectors, it is highly unlikely that blacks have been given a "pass" in sports/entertainment. A rigged system investigation was launched to identify and assess the consequences of laws, public policies, and/or discriminatory patterns or practices that have limited or blocked blacks from occupying specific roles or positions (e.g., quarterback, catcher, athletic directors, coaches/managers, executives, and majority owners).

Based on historical accounts, slaves were often organized to entertain their owners in an array of sporting-like competitions such as fighting, wrestling, and track and field. Some accounts indicate that slaves were forced to race horses in front of relatively large crowds. Blacks were not allowed to compete against whites. On rare occasions when they did compete against whites, most were smart enough to lose or they would have been subjected to cruel and unusual punishments.

Between 1865 and the early 20th century, blacks broke into professional sports primarily in individual competitions because of Jim Crow norms that disallowed interracial team sports. An online *Newsday* article contained a list of the first black champions in selected sports including the following: 1) John Arthur Johnson during the height of Jim Crow became the first black world heavy-weight boxing champion in 1908; 2) Jessie Owens was a multiple gold medalist in the 1936 Olympics; and 3) Arthur Ashe was a pioneer in professional tennis in the early 1960s.

Sports and the American Dream

Merton's and Agnew's general strain theories would assumed that a lot of black youth have material aspirations consistent with ideas related to the American Dream. However, many of them have perceived their chances of being treated fairly in educational institutions, employment sectors, and by the government to be slim to none. Their collective, perceived lack of racial equality and injustices led to sports/entertainment being perceived as the pathway of least resistance to both fame and fortunes. That perspective is consistent with the 100 Black Men of America's proclamation: "Black boys will be what they see."

Mass Media and Team Sports

Mass communication enterprises have played an effective role in promoting certain sports and athletes. Programming or coverage of team sports is primarily a function of projected viewership and ratings. Corporations pay a premium price for advertising time during specific shows and athletic competitions. Among team sports, football, basketball, and baseball seasons generate a large fraction of advertising income for the networks. Optics and narratives related to those sports and athletes have created and perpetuated the myth that blacks are overrepresented in all of team sports. Those optics, however, give a lot of black youth hope.

Delinquency Prevention and Sports

For a long time, sports have been utilized to occupy black boys' free time and idle minds. Team sports have been marketed as the optimal environment for promoting and encouraging discipline, teamwork, leadership, sportsmanship, and integrity. As a result, youth sports leagues emerged simulating aspects of professional sports which include coaches, uniforms, playing fields, referees, and even cheerleaders. Those programs have help divert hundreds of thousands of black boys away from the juvenile justice system. They have also had the unanticipated effect of glorifying sports at the expense of 21st century job skills and academic success.

Many youth sports leagues are now the training camps for school districts. Children are closely monitored, tracked, and assessed in terms of their athleticism. Those showing promise are tracked into school sanctioned sports earlier and earlier. School districts promote their athletic facilities and athletes like prominent colleges and universities. Anecdotal accounts allege that a few parents have moved to a new district because of its competitive athletic programs instead of more rigorous curriculum.

CHAPTER 1

High School to College Pipeline

Based on data regarding the high school to college sports pipeline, it is conceivable that some Americans would argue that a massive fraud has and continues to be perpetrated. Whether intentional or unintentional, optics and narratives related to the racial composition of major team sports have created unrealistic expectations among BYMOC regarding the number of available open slots at collegiate and professional levels each year. Most youth have focused solely on the relatively small number of athletes who played college and/or professional sports without considering the tens of thousands who unsuccessfully competed for those slots.

Data obtained from the National Collegiate Athletic Association (NCAA) website on March 22, 2016 showed that there was a great deal of participation in sports beginning in K-12. It was estimated that in 2015, approximately 8M youth participated in public school sports. However, less than 500K were projected to move to the collegiate level, and only a small fraction of those to ultimately play professionally. Yet an overwhelming percent of young black boys and an increasing percentage of black girls dream of playing collegiate and professional sports.

The sad fact is that while many black student-athletes and their parents/guardians have been serious and committed to pursuing collegiate and professional opportunities, many appeared unaware of the tremendous odds against them. Most student athletes do not fully understand that the deck is stacked against them.

In addition to just the sheer number of eligible players and limited scholarships, a host of other contributing factors severely decrease the number of athletes who successfully transition from high school to college sports. For example, to be eligible to play football, basketball, and/or baseball for a Division I (D1) school as a freshman, high school seniors must have earned at least an eighteen ACT composite score. Those failing to earn an 18 must enroll in a community college where they frequently "leak out" of the college to pro pipeline.

There is something interesting about the role ACT scores have played in terms of the awarding of scholarships at D1 colleges. Black student athletes with an ACT mean score of 18 or greater have been awarded coveted "full-ride" scholarships. In comparison, non-athletes who scored 18 or higher have been forced to pay the full cost of attending the same schools. The message appears to be that the ACT is a more reliable predictor of college readiness for non-athletes than athletes who will likely spend less time engaged in academic behaviors. Imagine that.

A lot of star high school athletes who earned an 18 or greater ACT composite score have encountered other unforeseen challenges in their pursuit of D1 scholarships. Some unanticipated barriers included lack of media coverage, size of their high schools, level of competition, number of scholarships available, team needs, and their high school coaches' contacts at the collegiate level.

CHAPTER 2

College Sports

As a system, collegiate sports have rules and regulations that are managed by the National Collegiate Athletic Association (NCAA). Among observers, the NCAA is akin to the criminal justice system. At the institutional level, it is responsible for a wide range of policies and procedures including the following: rules; enforcement of rules; investigation of alleged violations; rendering verdicts; and issuance of sanctions or sentences.

The NCAA is also responsible for the overall welfare of student athletes. It determines eligibility criteria, financial support levels, official training schedules, and sanctions for rule violations. Readers are encouraged to examine the racial/ethnic composition of the NCAA governing body and executive team.

Contrary to broadcast optics and narratives, African Americans are overrepresented in a couple of team sports but are not the majority of collegiate athletes. In 2014-2015, the racial composition of collegiate student athletes was as follows: black (27,071); white (36,881); American Indians/Alaskan Natives (320); Asian (363); Hispanic/Latino (2,660); Native Hawaiian/Pacific Islanders (652); and mixed (2,538) for a total of 72,788.

Collegiate Sports and Big Money

At the collegiate level, participation in sports is the equivalent of a job. However, no employment guidelines or minimum wage requirements exist. Student athletes are "at will" employees, meaning that they can be discharged from a team without cause. As a group, black student athletes generate a disproportionate amount of enthusiasm, public recognition, and income for many of colleges.

A 2018 *Forbes* article entitled "College Football Most Valuable Teams" ranked colleges in terms of their average revenue generated between 2014 and 2017. Results of their analysis revealed that some of the top money makers brought in more than one hundred million dollars annually. Data were gleaned from required revenue filings to both the NCAA and the U.S. Department of Education.[158] Texas A&M, University of Florida, and University of Texas generated the top three revenue streams from ticket sales, royalty and merchandise licenses, conference revenue sharing, and alumni donations.

At the ticket gate, Texas A&M fans paid a whopping $41M and ranked third in that category. Conference revenue sharing also infused millions into collegiate sports. Southeastern Conference member teams received $41M compared to $34M for each in the Big 12. University of Texas led the way in royalty and license income at $31M leaving their counterparts in the distance by about fifty percent. Alumni donations or gifts to athletic programs were stunningly generous. Texas A&M athletic department received $260M in gifts nearly doubling all their counterparts for the time period in question. Over $119M was given to football alone. The University of Florida was second at $138m followed by UT at $123M.

158 (https://www.forbes.com/sites/chrissmith/2018/09/11/college-footballs-most-valuable-teams/#3bdfe2126c64).

CHAPTER 3

College Coaches and Race

While sports have been a platform that showcase racially integrated teams on which black and white players give their all for one another on and off playing fields, mysteries surround the relatively low percentage of black head coaches at the collegiate and professional levels. Is it counter intuitive to find that African Americans were severely underrepresented among the head coaches of team sports in which they hold many of the performance records?

The racial make-up of head coaches is not a common topic for discussion or research. Without a doubt, effective coaching requires additional skill sets to those required to be successful at a single position on a team. Skills obtained in liberal arts are highly valued and essential to be successful coaches. Most are excellent communicators and possess effective empathic sensory analytical skills. A majority earned postsecondary degrees and were given opportunities to become assistant coaches by head coaches or athletic directors who looked like them. One must at least wonder if Merton's revised prejudice/discriminatory personality types have influenced the number of black head coaches hired.

In general, high school, college, and professional coaches are seen and treated as powerful leaders, superb role models, teachers, and team builders. Traditionally, credit for winning teams has been awarded to head coaches. They are evaluated based on their mastery of integrating the personalities and skill sets of a vast array of players to focus on a common collective outcome, winning. The value and influence of head coaches have been reflected in multi-year and multi-million dollar contracts at both collegiate and professional levels. Some coaches have even gone on to earn millions as television personalities.

According to data reviewed on the official NCAA website in 2016, a lack of diversity among coaches in the three major sports was observed. In 2014-15, the racial composition of football coaches at HWCUs was as follows: white (575); black (32); American Indians/Alaskan Native (2); Asian (2); Hispanic (3); Native Hawaiian/Pacific Islanders (3); and mixed (5). Clearly, a potentially implicit or explicit message or perception is that smart, black professionals and/or standout black former athletes have not been judged capable of serving as head coaches and winning.

In terms of basketball, the optics regarding the race of coaches were not dissimilar to those of football. In 2014-15, a total of 1,044 head basketball coaches was recorded. The racial breakdown of non-HBCU head basketball coaches was as follows: white (876); black (140); American Indians/Alaskan Native (3); Asian (1); Hispanic (13); Native Hawaiian/Pacific Islanders (3); and Mixed (5).

Data related to baseball showed that in 2014-15, a total of 918 head baseball coaches was recorded. By race, the numbers were as follows: white (877); black (5); Asian (4); Hispanic (21); Native Hawaiian/Pacific Islanders (2); and mixed (6).

When Historically Black Colleges and Universities (HBCUs) were included in the analysis, a slightly more favorable picture emerged. However, it is important to note that HBCU coaches often receive significantly lower salaries and team budgets than their counterparts. Data were gleaned from NCAA documents pertaining to the racial breakdown of the three major sports in 2014-2015. In football there were 672 head coaches and by race the breakdown was as follows: white (579); black (77); and mixed (5). Among the 1,102 basketball head coaches, the breakdown was white (882), black (192), and Hispanic (13). Finally, out of 958 head baseball coaches, the racial breakdown was as follows: white (892); black (28), and Hispanic (23).

Based on the number and tenure of black head coaches across the three major sports, many black student athletes do not see coaching as an attainable job/career. Moreover, among blacks who have been given head coaching positions, one losing season in a two to three year "rebuilding" campaign can be career-ending. In comparison, they have witnessed their counterparts with similar or identical "win-loss" records being given additional opportunities to serve as head coaches. Throughout history, blacks have been managed by non-blacks on slave ships, plantations, battlefields, in public works, and even in jail/prisons, so statistics regarding the racial composition of head coaches at the collegiate level are disappointing but not surprising.

According to the *Forbes* article regarding income in collegiate sports, between 2014-2015 and 2016-17, the top twenty-three public colleges on the list combined to spend an average of approximately $240M on coaches. On the other hand, they expended about $90M per year for student aid.[159]

For decades, some fans and student athletes have alleged that blacks had been excluded from playing certain positions. Undoubtedly, racial stereotypes have helped to limit the number of black quarterbacks and centers in football, point guards or floor generals in basketball, and pitchers and catchers in baseball. Players who by design control the ball in team sports have traditionally been described as smart, natural leaders, and effective decision-makers. Those descriptors were in stark contrast to the optics and narratives related to black athletes in a lot of cases. During the past two decades, tremendous progress has been made in terms of leadership roles held by black athletes in team sports, especially in football and basketball.

---

159 (https://www.forbes.com/sites/chrissmith/2018/09/11/college-footballs-most-valuable-teams/#3bdfe2126c64).

CHAPTER 4

Financial Aid and Academic Achievement

For decades, student athletes were denied cash for normal extracurricular college expenses. As a result, student athletes and their advocates have fought for the NCAA to close the gap between the cost of attendance and official scholarship support. Some student athletes who come from poverty or low-income families received scholarships to cover room and board, books, and school related fees. Unfortunately, they had little or no money to purchase clothes, go on dates, and/or socialize with friends. The lack of discretionary funds limited their capacity to have experiences similar to other students. Beginning in 2015, the NCAA approved cash payments to student athletes to help cover those expected costs.[160] Still, the aid given to student athletes pales mightily to the total amount of revenue their performances or work generates for colleges. Even more gripping is the reality that on any given day, student athletes can and do face "career-ending" injuries without disability insurance and a pension.

Academic Achievement

In the not so distant past, it was alleged that colleges were exploiting student athletes by allowing them to play but not progress toward earning their degrees. Accounts of college personnel completing homework and taking tests for star athletes surfaced. Moreover, a small fraction of star collegiate athletes revealed that they participated in sports at each level and performed well but were

---

160 (https://money.cnn.com/2015/09/04/news/companies/extra-cash-college-athletes/index.html).

unable to read proficiently at the third-grade level. Most of the academically unprepared athletes found professional sports life and retirement extremely challenging; however, a small fraction was able to eventually overcome their deficiencies. Fortunately, in recent years, the NCAA implemented more stringent accountability measures to ensure that student athletes declare majors and make steady progress in both number of credit hours earned and grade point averages. Remarkably, it is not unusual at some colleges for student athletes collectively and/or by sport to earn higher grade point averages than the general student population. The point here is that despite negative optics and narratives regarding student-athletes, an increasing fraction of those who had professional career aspirations fulfilled or exceeded academic requirements.

CHAPTER 5

Professional Sports and Race

Professional sports have been identified as an industry or employment sector in which African Americans have been overrepresented, especially in terms of the workforce. However, when patterns related to coaching staffs, team executives, and majority ownership were investigated, stunning racial disparities were uncovered. Richard Lapchick's 2014 article entitled "Three Leagues, 92 Teams, and One Principal Black Owner" was the impetus for initiating an exploratory rigged system investigation surrounding selected professional sports.[161]

According to the article, Professor Lapchick and his team analyzed variables or measures from the 2013 season of National Football League (NFL), National Basketball Association (NBA), and Major League Baseball (MLB). His research found shocking racial differentials in terms of players, coaches, management, and owners spanning a total of ninety-two teams. In addition to Lapchick's publication, annually, he leads a research team that assesses progress in terms of diversity in sports. The reports have been published by The Institute for Diversity and Ethics in Sports (TIDES) at the University of Central Florida and prominently featured by ESPN. Their 2018 report card served as the primary reference source for assessing diversity/inclusion in the remainder of this section.

As in all businesses, the "buck" stops with the owners. Among professional sports, owners possess decision-making powers in terms of hiring and firing players, coaches, and management teams; salary caps; salaries; dress codes/

161 https://fivethirtyeight.com/features/diversity-in-the-nba-the-nfl-and-mlb/

uniforms; adoptions of rules and penalties; on and off the field conduct of players; schedules; number of games; league expansion; and ownership of franchises.

For decades, *Forbes* has estimated and publish values of professional sports teams. The primary finding was that NFL, NBA, and MLB franchises ranged in value from hundreds of millions to over a billion dollars. The number of teams listed in the top 50 in 2018 by league was NFL (29 of 32); NBA (8 of 30), and MLB (6 of 30).[162]

To protect franchise values, earnings, and to theoretically achieve parity regarding strength of teams, negotiated salary caps have been adopted to some extent in the three major sports. Salary caps are only placed on the amount paid to players on teams. There are no restrictions on how much each player earns per year as long as the team salary cap is not exceeded. In 1994, the NFL salary cap was set at about $35M and has been reported to be just a little over $200M in 2020. In comparison, recent salary cap estimates for the NBA and MLB were $115M and $206M, respectively. It is worth noting that the NBA and MLB do not have a hard and fast salary cap but have set a threshold payroll mark and receive a luxury tax from teams that exceed the suggested payroll total.

Annual salaries of players vary widely. Data retrieved from online sources often included both average and median salaries. However, average salaries, as reported earlier, can be misleading because of a few extremely high or low salaries. A recent report showed that quarterbacks in the NFL had an average salary of about $5.5M, but the median salary was about $1.1M. Recall, the median salary is the mid-point income at which half (50%) of all players in a sport or position earn more or less than that dollar amount.

Before examining the culture of the three major professional sports, it is important for aspiring student athletes to be empowered to assess their

162 https://www.forbes.com/sites/kurtbadenhausen/2018/07/18/full-list-the-worlds-50-most-valuable-sports-teams-of-2018/#32013046b0ef

probability of being eligible to be drafted by a professional team. The NCAA has published sport participation data that are readily accessible for each sport. Sources have suggested a formula for estimating the number of draft eligible collegiate athletes by sport annually. Stakeholders should obtain the number of players in a sport in a specific year and divide that number by 4.5 which represents the average number of years to graduate. The resulting number would be an estimate of the size of the eligible draft pool in that cohort or year. Roughly a little less than twenty-five percent (25%) or 1 out of 4 student athletes are eligible for a draft in a given year. Yet, the real challenge is that there are usually only a few draft slots available.

Football, NFL, and Race

Historians have concluded that football as it is played today is actually a hybrid of the sports of rugby and soccer. The first game was played between Rutgers University and Princeton in 1869. The game and rules evolved primarily among what are called Ivy-league schools during the Reconstruction and the Jim Crow eras.

Today, in most states, football is the big daddy of all sports. On average high school, football teams will have between 40 and 80 players on their rosters. According to the 2013-14 High School Athletics Participation Survey, in 2014 there were roughly 1.1M high school football players in the U.S. compared to 72.1K collegiate players. The cold fact is if high school athletes were aware and understood their odds of playing in college, many would suffer a dampening in their outlook for reaching the pros.

At the collegiate level, blacks were slowly recruited and allowed to play. In many cases, one or only a few blacks played on college teams, but their electrifying performances increased demand for more of them. In 1961, Ernie Davis, who followed Hall of Famer Jim Brown as running back for Syracuse University, became the first African American to win the Heisman but was surely not the first to deserve it.

The Heisman is the most coveted award in college football. Winners invariably get drafted high and receive million dollar contracts and potential endorsement income. Sources indicate that about 870 media representatives from six regions of the country vote for Heisman nominees. Little is known about the make-up of those decision-makers, but without a doubt some can be accurately profiled on the prejudice-discrimination spectrum as mostly fair, conditionally fair, or mostly unfair. Today, all living Heisman winners can vote.

Early NFL teams appeared to have had quotas in terms of black players. A review of related newspaper articles revealed that when the NFL was started in the 1920s a handful of black athletes were allowed to play. However, between 1932 and 1946, discriminatory, informal practices eliminated black players from team rosters. Following the end of WWII, Kenny Washington, a former UCLA standout was signed by the Los Angeles Rams at the age of twenty-eight in 1946. His signing, however, was not void of controversy as it took public outcry through local newspapers to integrate the team. [163]

For decades, football has defied norms regarding black-white relationships in the U.S. Consider the following account:

> Back in the late 70's, I performed in a high school play with a mixed or integrated cast. A black male was assigned a thought provoking line. He was unable to make one of the performances, so I was asked to say his line. It was as follows: "Football is my favorite sport, because it is the only sport in which a (masked) black man can (violently) hit a white man and fifty thousand whites stand up and cheer."

Among college football players, the odds are extremely small of being drafted, regardless of one's talent. In 2013-2014, of the roughly 71K pool of players,

---

163 https://www.washingtonpost.com/lifestyle/kidspost/kenny-washington-paved-way-for-black-players-in-nfl/2014/02/19/063ad55e-98c2-11e3-80ac-63a8ba7f7942_story.html?noredirect=on&utm_term=.23a1e6ee0092

only 15.8K were defined as draft eligible, or 15 out of every one hundred players. However, there is usually only about 256 open slots to be filled each year in the NFL. In sum, less than two percent of collegiate players who are deemed draft eligible go pro through the draft. Of course, these statistics do not include opportunities in other professional leagues including Canadian and arena football.

The NFL has the most stringent draft guidelines for high school graduates who opt out of attending college for one reason or another. They must wait three years after their graduation and be at least twenty-one.

Recent salary data for the NFL showed the average salary at $2.7M and the median was a relatively low of $860,000.[164]

Lapchick's 2018-2019 NFL diversity report card was not a source of hope for aspiring black coaches, executives, and/or prospective owners. In 2019, seventy percent or over 2 out of 3 NFL players were black. On the other hand, blacks were under-represented at both team and league levels in terms of management and executive positions. How could that be true? In 2005 the NFL implemented the most aggressive and intentional diversity enhancement system in the history of professional sports. According to Lapchick:

> "The NFL's Rooney Rule, named after the legendary Pittsburgh Steelers owner Dan Rooney, was 'designed to provide increased consideration for people of color in head coaching positions' by requiring teams to interview at least one person of color for a head coaching vacancy. In 2009, the policy was expanded to include senior football operations positions and, in 2018, it was improved to require a team to interview at least one person of color from outside

164 https://www.cnbc.com/2019/02/01/heres-what-the-average-nfl-players-makes-in-a-season.html

> its organization or from a list of recommended candidates managed by the NFL's Career Development Advisory Panel."[165]

Despite the Rooney Rule, the evaluation showed little improvement in terms of the number or percent of diverse team coaches, managers, and owners.

It was reported that between 1963 and 2019 or about fifty-six years, only eighteen different African American and four other people of color served as head coaches in the NFL. Similarly, according to Lapchick, at the beginning of the 2018 season there were eight head coaches of color, but by the end of the season there were only three. Records showed that four were terminated and one resigned.

Comparisons between NFL league and team diversity in terms of office personnel were investigated. Results of the 2018 report card showed that at the league level "28.3 percent of the 1,006 employees were people of color, and at the team level only 25.8 percent of the 8,679 full-time employees were people of color." Upon closer examination of the numbers of executives, a clearer picture emerged. For example, the percent of people of color that held vice president positions at the league and team levels was 22% and 11.7%, respectively. In terms of majority ownership, to date, no person of color has been a majority owner of an NFL team.

Some observers have pointed to the lack of diversity among decision-makers in the NFL as at least a partial explanation for cultural clashes between management and players. For about three years, some NFL players have protested the shootings of unarmed black men by police and other racial injustices by kneeling during the National Anthem prior to kickoff.

According to numerous published sources, the league has instituted a policy that limits players' freedom of expression rights. The policy requires players

---

165 https://www.espn.com/nfl/story/_/id/25825224/nfl-work-do-make-their-workplace-truly-diverse

to either stand or remain in the locker room during the anthem, and those violating the policy will face fines or even termination.

The NFL's new policy regarding players' protests appears to clearly impinge upon their First Amendment "freedom of expression" right. The optics and context of the policy in light of the racial make-up of "owners" and their "employees" paint a disturbing picture. Employers' harboring a distinct personality type (i.e., mostly fair, conditionally fair, or mostly unfair) primarily have the authority to restrict their black employees from engaging in non-violent protests.

Health and Wellness

Throughout history, the poor and blacks have been overrepresented in dangerous and labor-intensive employment sectors. Their labor has generated huge profits for their owners and/or employers, but they often suffered short and long-term injuries and illnesses while being denied medical insurance, unemployment benefits, and pensions.

Lucrative NFL franchises were slow to negotiate with the players' union for post-employment benefits. While helping to generate upwards of $7B annually, NFL players and veterans who suffered career and life ending injuries only recently negotiated for a defined pension plan and affordable healthcare.

Unfortunately, results of medical research have shed light on a silent but lethal disease that disproportionately impacts football players. Brain injuries from repeated concussions from high speed helmet to helmet explosions have been found as the leading cause of Chronic Traumatic Encephalopathy (CTE), thereby putting blacks at higher risk.

A segment on HBO's Real Sports that aired in February 2019 examined trends in youth participation in football. Employing freedom of information Act (FOIA) rights, data obtained revealed that the percent of poor students is increasing, while the percent of middle- and upper-income players is decreasing. Interviews with both student athletes and parents/guardians found that despite dangers related to CTE and other injuries, football is still seen as one of the most accessible pathways to achieving aspects of the elusive American Dream among a lot of black youth.

Basketball, NBA, and Race

The game of basketball is thought to have been invented and demonstrated in about 1891. Online sources indicated that blacks became engaged in organized basketball around 1904, and teams were referred to as the "Black Fives." This history associated with African Americans' participation in basketball was outlined by the Black Fives Foundation whose "mission is to research, preserve, showcase, teach and honor the pre-NBA history of African Americans in basketball." [166]

During this period, all black leagues were common and African Americans participated in the "Colored Basketball World Champions." However, little is known about statistics and records set by individuals and teams that played in that league. About four years after Kenny Washington was signed to play professional football and only a year after Jackie Robinson's breakthrough in baseball, the National Basketball Association (NBA) opened its courts and signed a few black athletes. According to sources, in 1950 Charles Henry "Chuck" Cooper, Nat "Sweetwater" Clifton and Earl Lloyd were hired by NBA teams. In fact, Chuck Cooper was the first African American drafted by an NBA team and was the first pick in the second round.

The odds of BYMOC playing collegiate or professional basketball are as daunting as in football. Data revealed that over 541K high school students played basketball in the 2013-14 school year. During this period, at the men's collegiate level, there were 18,697 players: black (8,429); white (7,687); American Indian/Alaskan Native (57); Asian (104); Hispanic (528); Hawaiian/Pacific Islanders (32); and mixed (632). Surprisingly, blacks had only a narrow advantage over the number of white college basketball players.

---

166 https://www.blackfives.org/

The journey from college to professional basketball sees many casualties. Approximately 4,071 or 22% of college basketball players were eligible for the 2013 NBA draft. It should be noted, however, that there were only 60 draft slots and only 47 (1.2%) of eligible student athletes were drafted. This fact should be a cause for pause and full due diligence on the part of black boys and their parents/guardians.

In the last decade or so, the NBA increased draft eligibility standards for high school graduates. Unlike in previous decades, high school graduates must wait at least one year and be nineteen or older before becoming eligible for the draft. The NBA based this rule change on a desire for young players to mature and further develop their skills before entering the professional ranks. Prior to the rule change, several high profiled high school graduates were drafted including Kobe Bryant, LeBron James, and Travis Outlaw.

NBA players outpaced their counterparts in terms of salaries in recent years. According to a 2019 Basketball Reference.com story, the average NBA salary was a whopping $7.7M and the median was about $3.1M.

The 2018 National Basketball Association Racial and Gender Report Card (RGRC) showed little change or improvements over the 2017 evaluation. Still, the NBA outpaced the other two major sports in terms of diversity and inclusion related to professional staff and management. Based on official league and team personnel statistics, the 2018 Lapchick-led evaluation awarded the NBA an A-plus for racial hiring practices and a B for gender hiring, with an overall grade of A.

As noted earlier, blacks make up about thirteen percent (13%) of the U.S. population. In comparison, the percent of black NBA players during the 2018-2019 season was about 80% or 8 out of 10 players.

While leading the pack, the hiring and retention of black head coaches in the NBA remained a challenge. Only about thirty-three percent (33%) of NBA coaches was black in 2018-2019. The historical trend was stated as follows:

> "The NBA started on June 6, 1946. That was seventy three years ago. Believe it or not there have also been seventy three Black head coaches. That is one per year. This year the number remains at nine at the beginning of 2019-20 season."[167]

According to the Lapchick report card, the percent of people of color in different NBA management and/or executive positions was as follows: "team vice president (25.4%), team management (31.2%), team professional staff (39.5 percent), assistant coaches (45.7 percent), CEO/president (9.8%), general manager (20%), and professional staff at the NBA League Office (36.4 percent)." Most notably, the representation of people of color in general manager positions doubled the mark set in 2017, bolstering its leadership in this area among all-men professional sports.[168]

Interestingly, while scoring relatively high in terms of overall diversity/inclusion, the number of NBA presidents of operations and general managers has never exceeded three to four in any one season. The approximate ratio of black to white NBA front office executives was roughly 3:10 despite overall winning records.

The history of black ownership in the NBA is a fairly recent phenomenon. Online searches revealed some astonishing data related to majority and minority equity positions in NBA teams. According to several sources, former co-founder of Black Entertainment Television (BET), Robert Johnson, became the first black majority owner of an NBA franchise in 2004. He acquired the Charlotte Bobcats (a.k.a. the Charlotte Hornets). In 2010, NBA legend Michael Jordan became majority owner and reportedly controls over ninety five percent (95%) of the equity in the franchise that has been valued in excess of one billion dollars. As of June 2019, there had been only two

---

167 https://basnnewsroom.com/2019/11/10/nba-black-head-coaches-a-2019-20-perspective/

168 https://www.espn.com/nba/story/_/id/23911578/gender-race-report-card-confirms-nba-continued-leadership

other non-white majority owners, India's Vivek Ranadive (Sacramento Kings) and Moroccan-born Marc Lasry (Milwaukee Bucks).

Baseball, MLB, and Race

Historical data and evidence relating to discriminatory practices surrounding professional baseball has been researched and archived in a source entitled "Negro Baseball Leagues (1920-1950)." [169] The history of baseball in the U.S. is both joyful and painful. Prior to and after the Civil War, baseball was played and enjoyed by both racially segregated and integrated teams. But, in about 1868, the National Baseball Players' Association voted to make mixed teams ineligible for league play at the amateur level. A few years later, professional baseball was born, and black players played on integrated teams until the late 1890s when they were slowly pushed out of professional baseball. In 1920, independent black teams formed what was called the Negro Baseball League which flourished in northern cities between the 1930s and 1950s. Black urbanites earned relatively good income from war industries, and baseball became the entertainment of choice for many of them. The league had its own World Series and All-Star celebrations. However, salaries and travel accommodations were woefully non-competitive with the white league; moreover, Negro League statistics took a back seat to the MLB.

Nearly a year after Kenny Washington broke the race barrier in the NFL again, professional sports took center-stage when Jackie Robinson integrated Major League Baseball (MLB). His signing and playing is still one of the most celebrated and heralded breakthroughs or advancements in race relations. He appeared on the diamond with the Brooklyn Dodgers on April 15, 1947 at the age of 28 becoming a role model for tens of thousands of young boys, especially BYMOC. His presence, accomplishments, and public recognition made the once impossible, possible in their eyes.

---

169 https://www.blackpast.org/african-american-history/negro-baseball-leagues-1920-1950/

Robinson's signing was bitter-sweet. Breaking the imposed color-line and opening the flood gates for other all-star black players resulted in an unintended consequence. The loss of "star-power" and access to improved integrated baseball parks took needed revenue from the Negro League causing it to fold.

Within black communities, it appears that baseball has lost some of its appeal since the mid to late 1970s. Compared to football and basketball, several factors may have combined to make baseball less attractive in black neighborhoods. First, baseball requires more equipment including bats, shoes, gloves, and specialized practice equipment. Second, it needs more open green space to practice. Third, prominent baseball stars today hail from other countries including the Dominican Republic, Caribbean, Japan, and Mexico. Fourth, poor youth are excluded from summer and travel leagues due to exorbitant fees or funds required to participate. Finally, many colleges do not give full scholarships to baseball players. That practice has turned a lot of black athletes away from baseball. Interestingly, there has not been an outcry to give full scholarships to more collegiate baseball players and/or charges of alleged "discrimination" against them.

According to the Lapchick report card, in 2017, the black male NCAA Division I pipeline for baseball, football, and basketball was 3.7%, 44.2%, and 53%, respectively.

In a concerted effort to increase participation levels in baseball and softball among BYMOC and girls, the MLB designed and launched its Reviving Baseball in Inner Cities (RBI) initiative. Amazingly successful, the RBI in recent years has impacted hundreds of thousands of underrepresented American youth. Recently, it was reported that the RBI was composed of 300 sites in about 200 cities worldwide. The success of the initiative can be judged by the fact that 2018 marked the third consecutive year in which an alumnus of the program was selected among the top five picks in the MLB draft.

In 2013-2014, there were approximately 7,429 draft eligible athletes, yet only 1,216 MLB slots were available. Roughly 638 (8.6%) of college players were drafted. To round out the draft, a stunning 382 high school players were chosen.

Major League Baseball has the most liberal draft rule for high school players. To be eligible, students must only graduate and not attend a postsecondary institution. If they enroll in a four-year college, their eligibility begins in their junior year. Ironically, while many black student athletes aspire to play professional sports, their participation has been declining in baseball which provides the least restrictive path from high school to a professional career.

According to Lapchick, in 1991 roughly eighteen percent of MLB players were African Americans. Unfortunately, during the past twenty-seven years, nearly an eleven percentage point decline yielded only 7.7% in 2018. At the close of the 2018 season, the racial breakdown of MLB players was as follows: white (58%); Latino (32%); black (8%); and other (2%).

Routinely, baseball is called America's favorite past-time sport, despite its lower broadcast ratings. Traditionally, far more MLB games have been played during normal work hours than the NFL and NBA. As a result, only certain segments of the population (e.g., executives, self-employed, salaried employees with leave time, and the wealthy) have had the luxury of attending many of those games.

In 2018, the salaries of MLB players were sandwiched between those of the NBA and NFL. The average and median salary was 4.4M and $1.4M, respectively.

The MLB also lagged behind its counterparts in terms of diversity and inclusion related to non-player personnel. In 2018, the MLB received a "B" for racial diversity progress and a "C" in terms of growth for the hiring and promotion of women.[170]

The lack of black managers or skippers in the MLB remained a source of frustration among Hall of Famers, players, and some fans. Able and successful black coaches appeared to have been overlooked when filling coaching vacancies. Jackie Robinson was inducted into the baseball Hall of Fame in 1962, and during his acceptance speech, he advocated for black managers and skippers. Reflecting on Robinson's plea nearly sixty years ago, a sportswriter stated the following:

> "It's likely Robinson would be disgusted by how little has changed and how this problem has uniquely affected African-Americans. Sixteen black men have ascended to manager since he spoke out, filling 27 jobs — 10 interim and 17 full-time. Over that period, 224 men were hired to fill 470 openings (many jobs came open several times."[171]

To its credit, the MLB outpaced the other two major sports by far in terms of diversity among its coaches. In 2018, a whopping forty six percent of coaches was of color. An observation worth noting is that the MLB had the lowest percent of non-white players.

Diversity at team and league levels related to management or executives' positions differed significantly in 2018. At the team level, only two (2) people of color served as general managers. In comparison, MLB's front-office demographics in terms of racial and gender diversity have been improving. According to Lapchick, in 2018, ["the percentage of people of color in the league office increased by 5.7 percentage points to 33.8 percent and the percentage of women increased by 2.5 percentage points to 31.8 percent."]

---

170 https://www.espn.com/mlb/story/_/id/23132253/major-league-baseball-gets-average-marks-hiring-practices

171 https://theundefeated.com/features/the-state-of-the-black-manager-in-major-league-baseball-would-disgust-jackie-robinson/

However, when regarding majority ownership, the MLB and the NFL have posted identical records. In the history of the MLB, there has not been a black majority owner of a single franchise.

Evidence contained in this section indicated the presence of discriminatory patterns or practices in the sports industry that have thwarted the range of opportunities afforded blacks. Despite individual and institutional discrimination, black athletes in the three major sports have exhibited extraordinary perseverance and phenomenal resiliency. They have had to overcome negative optics and narratives, racial stereotypes, increasing academic standards, long and exhausting training, short and long-term injuries, limitations related to positions and roles played, and relatively low compensation in a lot of cases. Hope can be found in the fact that some black athletes serve as role models for youngsters around the world.

NOTES

AFTERWORD

The investigation and the resulting body of knowledge contained in this book took more time and energy than expected. It taught me some invaluable lessons related to the importance of patience, empathy, learning to read and moreover the power of reading to learn. The latter gave me the capacity to retrospectively take mental snapshots of the "black experience." My primary focus was on trials and triumphs experienced by blacks between 1619 and 2019. Unlike the bulk of previous investigations that focused on one or two structural determinants of racial inequality, it was critically important for me to clearly identify and assess the combined impact of an array of laws and social policies within various subsystems.

Surprisingly, this attempt to investigate the merits of President Trump's rigged system theory related to the plight of blacks in the U.S. was the source of severe emotional mood swings between depression and extreme pride. At times it was depressing to uncover evidence that certain laws and policies had intentionally or unintentionally limited or blocked many blacks from fairly competing for resources to achieve aspects of the American Dream.

On the other hand, a sense of extreme astonishment and pride was generated while reading an array of documents that described the progress or advancements blacks have made despite seemingly insurmountable barriers. They reacted to challenges in different ways. Evidence contained here suggest that blacks have adopted different modes of adaptation (i.e., conformers, innovators, ritualists, rebels, or retreatists) to help them cope and manage the stress/strain generated by severe racial discriminatory systems at local, state, and federal levels. Without question, their advancements have been realized by their faith, grace, and cohorts of decision-makers who could have been categorized as mostly fair, conditionally fair, or mostly unfair. Their persistence and resiliency were fueled by a collective desire to achieve aspects of the elusive American Dream through promised fair and untethered competition.

Given the abundance of evidence suggesting that blacks are extraordinarily persistent and phenomenally resilient, America's neglect of underutilized and stored African American human capital is nothing short of mind-boggling and symptomatic of premeditated ignorance. Imagine how much more economically self-sufficient and assured this country would be if thirteen million more of its citizens were "made whole" and fully afforded equal rights and privileges as promised in the U.S. Constitution.

Woke Challenge

Armed with data and information contained in this book, I respectfully challenge readers regardless of their race, sex, age, income, religion, and/or country of origin to pretend to be either the entire jury or judge in the "Rigged System" civil case and render verdicts related to the following questions: 1) Based on the totality of evidence presented, "is it more likely than not that President Trump's rigged system indictment of the U.S. government has merit and was corroborated by objective evidence; and 2) Did the evidence corroborate the claim that African Americans have exhibited phenomenal persistence, resiliency, and patriotism in the face of indisputable discriminatory laws, public policies, and patterns/practices.

Recommended Group Activity

After playing the role of jury or judge in the rigged system civil case, hopefully readers will be empowered to effectively engage in public discourse regarding race in the U.S. In small group settings, readers are encouraged to discuss and seek consensus related to the following:

List the most compelling examples of "rigged systems" found in the book;

Assume that a court found the U.S. government liable for past intended or unintended discriminatory laws and/or public policies. Should blacks be awarded punitive damages?;

Can African Americans be "made whole" or sufficiently compensated for limited or blocked access to freedom, justice, educational opportunities, equal pay; free federal land, credit/loans, public assistance, and health and wellness resources?; and

If yes, how can they be "made whole" or fully compensated in each of those areas?

ABOUT THE AUTHOR

Dr. Melvin C. Ray is a thought-leader, author, entrepreneur, and supporter of youth development initiatives. Upon his retirement in 2014, he was awarded emeritus status as Associate Vice President for Economic Development and Associate Professor of Sociology at Mississippi State University. Being both blessed and prepared, he was a trail blazer during his nearly thirty-year tenure serving with distinction in the following roles: Associate Professor of Sociology/Criminology; academic coordinator, research fellow, Associate Vice President for Research, interim Vice President for Research, Special Assistant to three consecutive chancellors, and Associate Vice President for Economic Development. Dr. Ray has conducted numerous quantitative and qualitative studies and published over two dozen refereed articles and book chapters. In 2016, he co-authored the book entitled *Why College Degrees Still Matter: Success Strategies.* The ground-breaking study was based on results generated from an online survey of nearly one thousand African American college students. In terms of service above self, Dr. Ray has served in leadership roles for many consequential initiatives including: The Local Learning Community Foundation, Boys & Girls Clubs of the Golden Triangle, Starkville-Oktibbeha My Brother's Keeper Community Challenge, Men Mentoring Boys Institute, and BullyStoppers: A Call to Action. Dr. Ray graduated from Dumas High School in Dumas, Arkansas, University of Arkansas at Pine Bluff (B.S), and Iowa State University (Ph.D.). Dr. Ray is an active member of the historic Syrene Missionary Baptist Church which is nestled away among corn and cotton fields in the Arkansas Delta. He and his wife Valerie L. Ray are proud parents and grandparents.